Leading the
Self-Managing School

Education Policy Perspectives

Leading the Self-Managing School

Brian J. Caldwell

and

Jim M. Spinks

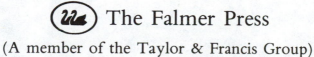 The Falmer Press

(A member of the Taylor & Francis Group)
London • Washington, D.C.

UK   The Falmer Press, 4 John Street, London WC1N 2ET
USA   The Falmer Press, Taylor & Francis Inc., 1900 Frost Road, Suite 101, Bristol, PA 19007

First published 1992

A catalogue record for this book is available from the British Library

Library of Congress Cataloging in Publication Data are available on request

ISBN 1 85000 656 3 cased
ISBN 1 85000 657 1 paperback

Cover design by Caroline Archer

Typeset in 9.5/11 pt Bembo
by Graphicraft Typesetters Ltd., Hong Kong

Printed in Great Britain by Burgess Science Press, Basingstoke on paper which has a specified pH value on final paper manufacture of not less than 7.5 and is therefore 'acid free'.

Contents

Contents

Preface

In our preface to *The Self-Managing School*, published in 1988, we suggested that the title might be greeted with incredulity or scepticism by readers associated with publicly funded schools which have been directed and supported for decades in a complex arrangement of roles and responsibilities involving authorities at the national, state and local levels. We expressed the view that, while schools must continue to work within a framework of policies and priorities set at the system level, they could otherwise be largely self-managing. In the first chapter of that book we described initiatives in self-management in Australia, Britain, Canada and the United States. We offered a case for these developments, drawing on perspectives in political economy, organisation theory, school effectiveness and teacher professionalism. The remaining chapters contained descriptions and illustrations of a model for self-management derived from an Australian study of effective schools which had proved helpful in supporting change in several Australian states, notably Victoria.

There have been dramatic changes in the management of education since 1988. Those foreshadowed in England and Wales came to pass in the 1988 Education Act where self-management is described as the Local Management of Schools (LMS). Implementation is now well under way, with further changes foreshadowed with the recent release by the Department of Education and Science of *The Parents' Charter*. Similar far-reaching changes have now been made in New Zealand. The most centralised of state education systems in Australia in New South Wales is being transformed, with a leaner central arrangement directing and supporting schools which are moving toward self-management. In the United States self-management, or school-based management as it is called in that country, is emerging as a major element in a series of related reforms in a comprehensive restructuring of education. In these countries and others, the central authority, wherever located, retains a powerful but more focused role, determining broad goals, setting priorities and building frameworks for accountability. At the same time, appearing paradoxical at times, major responsibilities are being shifted to the school level. There is thus simultaneous centralisation and decentralisation.

Some commentators describe these changes as the most far-reaching of the twentieth century, possibly since the establishment in the late nineteenth century of large government or public school systems. Others, writing and speaking more generally, see changes in education in the same context as changes in the delivery of other public services. Everywhere, it seems, large central bureaucracies are collapsing in favour of a shift to self-management. Whatever the scope of change, it is evident that the development of a capacity for self-management is now a requirement in schools in many nations around the world.

As authors, we are fortunate to have been directly involved in change in a number of countries, largely through extended consultancies in which we were invited to introduce practitioners to the model described and illustrated in *The Self-Managing School* and to advise senior officers at the system level on elements in the framework within which schools will be self-managing. We have both been involved in these ways in Australia, Britain and New Zealand. Jim Spinks' work has been mainly in the form of consultancy, visiting Britain on three occasions from 1988 to 1990 for a total of nearly twelve months of training programs for officers, governors, principals and teachers in more than one-third of the local education authorities. He also worked with about ten thousand parents, principals and teachers in an extended consultancy throughout New Zealand in 1989. Brian Caldwell undertook a study of emerging patterns in the management of education for OECD and completed several consultancies at the system and school levels in Australia and New Zealand. We have studied at first hand some key developments in other countries, notably Canada and the United States. In 1991 Jim Spinks was appointed Superintendent (Self-Management) in Tasmania, a position unique in Australia. He had the responsibility of working with others at the system and school level to guide schools in that state further down the path to self-management. He is now Principal of Sheffield District High School in Tasmania where he is continuing the developmental work at the school level.

We have, throughout this time, monitored the way in which practitioners have utilised the model for self-management. As a result, we are now able to make a number of refinements and these are described and illustrated in *Leading the Self-Managing School*.

It may be stating the obvious, but it became evident that the model for self-management was as useful for private or non-government schools as it was for public or government schools. We defined self-management in the context of the latter, and our illustrations and most of our consultancy work were in that setting, but we have learned of many of the former which have utilised the model, especially as far as approaches to policy-making, budgeting and evaluation are concerned.

It seems that schools, like other public and private enterprises, must cope with continuing change. Expectations that curriculum and organisational structures might be stabilised are unlikely to be fulfilled. Schools will thus require a capacity to manage continuing change throughout the 1990s. We give particular attention in the refined model to ways in which this capacity can be developed through processes variously described as school development, school self-renewal, school improvement or school-level strategic planning. The framework at the system level within which this capacity can be exercised is also established.

More importantly, however, our recent work has enabled us to discern in a clearer way than before the requirements for leadership in a system and in a school where self-management has been encouraged. *Leading the Self-Managing School* gives special attention to these requirements, with a model for leadership within which the model for self-management can proceed. Illustrations are provided for all levels of the system.

We wish to express our appreciation to those people who have made arrangements for our work in different countries and who continue to inspire our efforts in a variety of ways. David Hill and Brian Oakley-Smith, Directors of Cambridge Education Associates, invited Jim Spinks to join them in their consultancy work on the Local Management of Schools in England and Wales. Tony Stanley, Principal of Evans Bay Intermediate School in New Zealand, recognised at an early stage the relevance of our model for self-management to developments in New Zealand and subsequently worked with others to arrange our involvement in that country. Bob Smilanich, Associate Superintendent of Edmonton Public School District, Alberta, Canada, has kept us informed of developments in a system which has, in so many ways, pioneered and sustained self-management in North America. Edmonton's Superintendent, Dr Michael Strembitsky, the pioneering leader of self-management in that system, has also briefed us on likely directions. Margaret Vickers laid the foundation for Brian Caldwell's international studies when she was with the Centre for Educational Research and Innovation at OECD. Hedley Beare, Professor of Education at the University of Melbourne, helped us gain an understanding of administrative restructuring, while Jerry Starratt, Professor of Educational Administration at Fordham University, New York, has illuminated our thinking on leadership and has challenged us to change the language. Our employers at the University of Tasmania, the University of Melbourne and the Department of Education and the Arts in Tasmania allowed us the time to travel widely since 1984. Ian McKay, Senior Research Fellow at the University of Tasmania, assisted with the design of figures in the text.

We dedicate this book to the leaders of our schools, especially those who have taken the initiative to shape their own destiny, in partnership with their colleagues and members of their communities. We share their vision that the outcome will be sustained satisfaction and a major contribution to the quality of learning and teaching.

Part A

A New Context and an Updated Model for Self-Management

1 The New Realities in Education

The scope and pace of change in education at the start of the 1990s are nothing short of breathtaking.

In Britain, England and Wales now have, for the first time ever, a national curriculum framework and provision for nation-wide tests at the primary and secondary levels. All secondary schools and most primary schools have total control of their budgets, with schools having the power to opt out of control by their local education authorities on the majority vote of parents. Plans for the further empowerment of parents are apparent in the release of *The Parent's Charter*.[1]

Many Australian states which underwent radical decentralisation in the 1970s and 1980s are now building stronger frameworks of direction and support, while others, notably New South Wales, Queensland and Tasmania, are just starting on major programs of reform which include shifts toward school self-management. At the same time, the elements of a national curriculum framework are starting to emerge and a national initiative to restructure the teaching profession is underway.

A national system of education in New Zealand has been, literally, turned upside down (or should it be downside up?) with the dramatic empowerment of boards of trustees at the school level in what was already a relatively decentralised system. Remaining to provide a framework is a small central authority which includes a powerful review and audit function.

In the United States the so-called 'second wave' of reform is sweeping over the nation, with virtually every aspect of schools and systems which direct and support schools under critical examination. The key word is 'restructuring' and it is being applied to curriculum, pedagogy, administrative structures, governance, teacher training and retraining, and to the teaching profession itself.

The pioneering system of self-management in Canada, the Edmonton Public School District in Alberta, continues to evolve, with a vision of empowerment at the student level now emerging.

There is evidence of similar far-reaching change in virtually every nation in the Western world with signs of major change now clear in Eastern Europe and the Commonwealth of Independent States.

It is no wonder that many commentators believe these changes to be the most far-reaching of the century, indeed, since the late nineteenth century when large public or government school systems were established. Moreover, these changes have been continuous since the early 1980s, with all evidence pointing to their acceleration. Many participants and observers find the changes contradictory in nature and are disconcerted by an apparent lack of stability in any arrangement, either organisational or pedagogical, and a perceived lack of integration among the many changes which appear to be proceeding in unplanned piecemeal fashion. It seems that change, including turbulence, is a permanent condition in education.

In 1981 Peter Drucker wrote a book about managing in turbulent times.[2] He described the conditions which would be encountered by private and public organisations throughout the decade. In 1989 he wrote again about 'the new realities',[3] describing with extraordinary foresight the events to occur later in the year in Eastern Europe and projecting the steady decline of large, centralised bureaucracies in the public sector and the emergence of the organisation we would describe as self-managing. Drucker was writing in general terms, but it is clear that he would include the management of education in his analysis.

Self-Management Defined

This book is concerned with leaders and leadership in self-managing schools. Our primary interest is schools in government or public school systems, or schools in systems of non-government schools, although the approaches to self-management we describe are just as relevant within schools which are in most respects independent of government or systemic controls. Indeed, we are aware of private or non-government schools which have utilised the model we described and illustrated in *The Self-Managing School*,[4] especially those aspects concerned with policy-making, budgeting and evaluation.

Within the sphere of our primary interest, a self-managing school is a school in a system of education where there has been significant and consistent decentralisation to the school level of authority to make decisions related to the allocation of resources. This decentralisation is administrative rather than political, with decisions at the school level being made within a framework of local, state or national policies and guidelines. The school remains accountable to a central authority for the manner in which resources are allocated.

Resources are defined broadly to include knowledge (decentralisation of decisions related to curriculum, including decisions related to the goals or ends of schooling); technology (decentralisation of decisions related to the means of learning and teaching); power (decentralisation of authority to make decisions); materiel (decentralisation of decisions related to the use of facilities, supplies and equipment); people (decentralisation of decisions related to human resources, including professional development in matters related to learning and teaching, and the support of learning and teaching); time (decentralisation of decisions related to the allocation of time); and finance (decentralisation of decisions related to the allocation of money).

We draw attention to the breadth of this concept of self-management in that it goes beyond the relatively narrow focus on finance which was evident in the 1970s and 1980s in developments known as school-based budgeting (Canada and the United States) or the local financial management of schools (Britain). We note also the distinction between the concept of self-management and other terms which have been used such as self-government and self-determination, these implying the lack of a centrally determined framework for the management of schools. While some scenarios suggest that such schools will emerge over the next decade, we believe self-management is the more accurate descriptor for what is happening in systems of government and non-government schools.

The Scope of Change

It is helpful to establish the scope of the changes we described at the outset, especially in relation to broader changes which are occurring around the world in different fields of endeavour. This will provide the context for our exploration of leadership in the self-managing school. Our appraisal of the scope of change is consistent with Drucker's warning that 'the greatest and most dangerous turbulence . . . results from the collision between the delusions of the decision makers, whether in governments, in the top managements of businesses, or in union leadership, and the realities.'[5] What follows is a summary of our understanding of these realities. But we share Drucker's optimism when he argued, further, that 'a time for turbulence is also one of great opportunity for those who can understand, accept, and exploit the new realities. It is above all a time of opportunity for leadership.'[6]

The concept of megatrend

John Naisbitt coined the term 'megatrends' to describe broad social, economic, political and technological changes which influence in very powerful ways the direction of change in different fields of endeavour.[7] A school may experience a decline in enrolment because of short-term changes in the local environment such as falling birth-rates or a decrease in employment opportunities in local industry. A short time later a different pattern may emerge when local conditions change. It may not be possible to discern a consistent long-term trend. However, such a school is affected by factors which are shaping society as a whole and which have consistent and long-term impact. The microchip is an example. It is change of this order that Naisbitt described as a megatrend.

Naisbitt's 1982 book, *Megatrends*, foreshadowed a number of trends which he believed would occur in the 1980s: (i) from an industrial society toward an information society, (ii) from forced technology toward a 'high tech/high touch' people-oriented use of advanced technology, (iii) from reliance on a national economy toward involvement in a world economy, (iv) from preoccupation with the short term toward consideration for the long term, (v) from centralisation toward decentralisation, (vi) from institutional help toward self-help, (vii) from representative democracy toward participatory democracy, (viii) from communication and control in hierarchies toward networking, (ix) from a concentration of interest and effort in the 'north' (developed countries) toward concern for the 'south' (less developed countries), and (x) from consideration of 'either/or' toward a 'multiple option' range of choices.

While the outcomes have been uneven, it is fair to say that most have occurred in the manner foreshadowed by Naisbitt. Their effects in education are evident, especially in regard to trends to an information society, decentralisation, self-help, participatory democracy, networking and multiple options.

Megatrends in the 1990s

Naisbitt was joined by Patricia Aburdene in the 1990 publication, *Megatrends 2000*.[8] Again, ten megatrends were identified, with many being a continuation of or development from those set out in the earlier book: (i) a booming global economy, (ii) a renaissance in the arts, (iii) the emergence of free-market socialism, (iv) global lifestyles and cultural nationalism, (v) the privatisation of the welfare state, (vi) the rise of the Pacific Rim, (vii) the decade of women in leadership, (viii) the age of biology, (ix) a religious revival, and (x) the triumph of the individual.

It is likely that most will influence or be associated with developments in education in the 1990s, with implications for the management of education in each instance.

We should note here our reservations about the reduction of complex developments and their encapsulation in simplifications which amount to slogans. On the other hand, we also note that the broad brush writing of Naisbitt and Aburdene is consistent with that of others such as Peter Drucker. We proceed, however, in the spirit of Naisbitt and Aburdene who suggested that 'You need not agree with or accept every element of this world view . . . The important thing is to craft your own world view. . . .'[9]

Megatrends in education

Some trends in education have been underway for a sufficient time and have sufficient depth and strength that they constitute megatrends in education. They appear to be associated with and largely a consequence of the megatrends described by Naisbitt and Aburdene, thus justifying the use of the word in a special field. Each shapes developments in particular areas within the broader field of education. Each is stated in the future tense, although current strength is evident in most instances.

1 There will be a powerful but sharply focused role for central authorities, especially in respect to formulating goals, setting priorities, and building frameworks for accountability.
2 National and global considerations will become increasingly important, especially in respect to curriculum and an education system that is responsive to national needs within a global economy.
3 Within centrally determined frameworks, government schools will become largely self-managing, and distinctions between government and non-government schools will narrow.
4 There will be unparalleled concern for the provision of a quality education for each individual.
5 There will be a dispersion of the educative function, with telecommunications and computer technology ensuring that much learning which currently occurs in schools or institutions at post-compulsory levels will occur at home and in the workplace.
6 The basics in education will be expanded to include problem-solving, creativity and a capacity for life-long learning and re-learning
7 There will be an expanded role for the arts and spirituality, defined broadly in each instance; there will be a high level of 'connectedness' in curriculum.
8 Women will claim their place among the ranks of leaders in education, including those at the most senior levels.
9 The parent and community role in education will be claimed or reclaimed.

10   There will be unparalleled concern for service by those who are required or have the opportunity to support the work of schools.

Appraising the scope of change

Among structural changes alone, what has occurred thus far is historic. In Britain, for example, there is no precedent for each of the major elements in the 1988 legislation: never before has there been a national curriculum nor have there been nation-wide tests at primary and secondary levels. While schools have always had some authority in respect to resource allocation, never before have they had total control over their budgets. Schools have never had the authority to opt out of control by their local education authority.

The scope of change in Australia is best summarised by Hedley Beare, Professor of Education at the University of Melbourne and one of the nation's most respected commentators:

The overwhelming impression left by the most recent round of reconstructions is that there has been a profound reconceptualisation of the organisation of Australian education, in schools no less than systematically. Bluntly, there has been a paradigm shift.[10]

R.J.S. Macpherson was a participant-observer in the preparation of the Picot Report, which led to the reform of education in New Zealand, and has subsequently written of these experiences and those of a similar nature in the state of New South Wales in Australia,[11] where he assisted in the review of administration conducted by Brian Scott. He characterised events in New Zealand as a 'political intervention into education on a scale never before seen. . . .'[12] William Lowe Boyd, another scholar who has written widely on developments in the United States and in other countries, notably Australia, has observed that 'since 1983, American public schools have been experiencing the most sustained and far-reaching reform effort in modern times.'[13]

Accounting for Megatrends in Education

It is worthwhile to examine the evidence for these megatrends in education and to discern factors which underpin them. What is clear in the following brief account is that they are interrelated and shaped in large measure by broader trends of the kind described by Naisbitt and Aburdene, and others. A number of implications for schools emerge from this account and these will be explored throughout the book in the manner summarised at the end of Chapter 1.

Concern for quality and strategic capability in education

In each of the countries described at the beginning of the chapter it is apparent that central authorities, whether at national or state levels, have adopted a powerful but sharply focused role. It is essentially one of determining goals, setting priorities and building frameworks for accountability. In the case of England and Wales these represent stronger powers than ever before assumed at the national level. In Australia the Commonwealth government has, for the first time, worked with the states to lay the foundations for a national curriculum framework. Indeed, most of the important policies in education now reflect a national perspective, achieved through cooperative arrangements of commonwealth and states, despite the fact that constitutional powers for education in Australia rest with the states. In the United States the national role has been minimal, although former Secretary for Education, William Bennett, used the 'bully pulpit'[14] to help catalyse the extraordinary changes in that country since 1983. The so-called 'first wave' of reform was marked by a mountain of reports and state legislation on curriculum and testing, with the specification of minimum competency standards for students and, in some instances, for teachers. Noteworthy in New Zealand is the formation of a powerful review and audit agency at the national level to monitor the manner in which schools address national goals and priorities.

A major factor underlying this centralising trend is concern about quality. The widespread concern about quality in education is clear from recent OECD reports, including one devoted exclusively to the issue which stated that 'concern for the quality of education in schools is today among the highest priorities in all OECD countries. It will remain so for the foreseeable future.'[15] The report acknowledged different meanings of the term and differences in approach when efforts are made to effect improvement. It concluded that definitions of quality 'are crucially determined by educational aims'[16] and that 'how the curriculum is defined, planned, implemented and evaluated ultimately determines the quality of education that is provided',[17] hence, in our view, the centralising trend we have defined above.

There is, however, a broader concern for quality that is having an impact on patterns of management in education. This is the concern for general quality in life which is now determined in large measure by the capacity of a nation to perform well in a global economy, a condition included by Naisbitt and Aburdene in their list of megatrends. There is a sense in many nations, including those considered in this chapter, that they may 'fall behind' and that, to become more competitive, they must ensure a highly responsive economy which calls, in turn, for a highly responsive system of education that equips citizens with required knowledge, skills and attitudes. This relationship between education and economic needs has, of course, always been there. Education has always made a significant contribution to economic well-being. The recent rhetoric of governments has simply brought the relationship into sharper focus, with a stridency and urgency that many educators find discomforting. Nevertheless, it is currently a reality which accounts in part for the stronger role governments are taking in many areas of policy in education.

It is important to note that the trend to self-management is not directly connected to concern for economic well-being. Guthrie made this clear in his recent review of developments around the world:

> Not all emerging education system similarities are aimed at enhancing national economic development. For example, higher and lower education policies regarding 'choice' and 'privatisation' and the devolution of lower education management to school sites are generally intended more to enhance the productivity and efficiency of schooling systems themselves than to enable education to aid a nation's economy.[18]

Apart from gaining an understanding of the scope of the issue and the underlying reasons, there are implications for leaders in education of concern for quality. For those at the national, state or system levels, it means the development of a capacity to set goals, establish priorities and build frameworks for accountability. These capacities have not always been well-developed in the past when education was relatively stable and such direct connections between education and the economy were not stated so clearly or were subject to such rapid change. Officers at the system level were then able to perform a range of functions within bureaucratic structures which was, in many respects, highly appropriate in an age of stability. Management in a climate of continuing change demands a large measure of 'focused flexibility'. Leaders at the school level will require the capacity to manage within a centrally determined framework, something which to a degree has always been the case except that more recent developments involve adaptation to a changing set of priorities and a more demanding set of accountability requirements.

Schools in the 1990s will require a high-level capacity for strategic planning; that is, to see 'the larger picture' and, on a continuing basis, set and re-set priorities in a simple school development plan which will provide the framework for the annual operational plan. The model for management set out in *The Self-Managing School* gave particular attention to the annual operating plan within a framework of policies and priorities. We acknowledged the importance of strategic planning and priority-setting, but the context for schools in the 1990s makes this capacity a more powerful imperative. For this reason, we give particular attention in *Leading the Self-Managing School* to techniques for school-level strategic planning and the preparation of a school development plan. We take this up in Chapter 5.

Every interpretation of the sources cited thus far points to the necessity of taking account of national and global considerations in the management of education at all levels. Perhaps the most important strategic capability is concerned with curriculum, which must be highly responsive to the needs of the nation. This has always been so but, whereas these needs in the past tended to be relatively stable from year to year, there may now be considerable change from one year to the next. The notion of a national curriculum which has a high level of specification will not satisfy this requirement. What is required is a curriculum framework within which these changes can occur. It is interesting that what has started as an exercise in national curriculum has invariably ended with the publication of a broad framework. That was the outcome in England and Wales and is the likely end of a process in Australia which has seen, first, a statement on national goals and, second, an effort to 'map' the curriculum across the different states and territories. One state, Victoria, has established its own curriculum framework with a level of specification which seems ideal for a national effort.

On a personal level, the curriculum must afford the individual an opportunity to acquire the knowledge, skills and attitudes to participate productively and satisfyingly in a world of work which will see continuous change. Recognition of this is now so wide that another of our megatrends in education seems almost self-evident, namely, that the basics in education will be expanded to include problem-solving, creativity and a capacity for life-long learning and re-learning.

Another important strategic capability is concerned with learning and teaching. At one level this calls for a range of approaches at the school level to match the curriculum, and this may mean change in situations where, for example, problem-solving and creativity have not been emphasised in the past. At another level, however, is the need to utilise the wealth of learning opportunities which have been created by advances in telecommunication and computers. Computers can now be utilised across the curriculum, including the arts, and learning of a kind which was once laborious or difficult can now occur with ease in any location. Students will have access to information sources around the world. With the increasing use of lap-top computers, this information can be acquired quickly and unobtrusively without jeopardy to patterns of human interaction which we hold to be so important in the educative process. We summarise the reality and potential of these developments in our view that there will be a dispersion of the educative function, with telecommunications and computer technology ensuring that much learning which currently occurs in schools or institutions at the post-compulsory level will occur at home and in the workplace.

Equity, choice, resource allocation and the emergence of a de facto educational voucher

Strategic capability in respect to curriculum and learning will be shaped by a core value which is influencing public policy in most fields on a global scale, namely, equity. In educational terms, this means that every child, regardless of circumstance, will receive an education which will enable the full development of capability. This value has, of course, underpinned much of the rhetoric of public education for one hundred years or more, but there is increasingly an insistence that this rhetoric be brought to realisation. The particular outcomes, or indicators of outcomes, which have been specified in public policy pronouncements have varied from nation to nation, but these include an increase in retention rates of students, at least to the end of secondary school, implying a reduction in failure rates at key stages of secondary schooling. The particular processes of policy implementation have included approaches to resource allocation, since an implication of the foregoing is that schools shall be provided with the resources to enable them to meet the individual learning needs of every student. This suggests a form of decentralised school-based budgeting in contrast to centralised, relatively uniform approaches to allocating resources to schools which, in the past, were assumed to be equitable.

We offered analysis along these lines in *The Self-Managing School* but have since been participant-observers in several countries where efforts have been made to introduce related approaches to resource allocation, especially in Britain through the Local Management of Schools (formerly known by a title which emphasised its focus on resources: Local Financial Management), New Zealand, and in Australia, especially in New South Wales and Tasmania. We have monitored developments in Edmonton, Alberta where school-based decision-making, formerly known as school-based budgeting, has been in place for more than a decade. It has taken time in each place to determine the criteria for allocating resources to schools, and some of the difficulties are described in Chapter 8 where leadership at the system level is described in some detail. It is essentially a process of determining what it costs to provide different educational experiences to students with different educational needs and then devising a schedule of grants to schools which are combined to form a school's total allocation.

One perspective on this process is of interest. The total resource allocation to a school is, in effect, determined by the number of students who attend the school, the educational needs of those students, and the kind of educational programs they will undertake. Expressed simply in stark financial terms, 'the money follows the student.' The process is accomplishing in important ways what the so-called 'voucher schemes' were intended to achieve. These have never been implemented in the manner proposed by Friedman and others: in their original form they were conceived as sums of public money given to parents who would then pay for the education of their children according to their choice of school. Similar schemes calling for tuition tax credits have often been formulated but have not been implemented, although a variant was adopted in Minnesota.

The issue of equity was often raised in opposition to these proposals, which invariably involved a uniform amount of money in the voucher or for tax credit. How could the different educational needs of students be satisfied, given that different costs would be involved? How could parents exercise choice given their different bases of knowledge and interest in education? What is emerging, however, is a situation where, to use an image offered by Thomas,[19] the student is, in effect, the voucher, but where equity objections have been satisfied through differentials in grants to schools in school-based budgets which take account of the educational needs of students. The educational voucher may become a reality but not in the form originally envisaged by its proponents.

The foregoing accounts for our identification of a megatrend along the lines that there will be unparalleled concern for the provision of a quality education for each individual, with an implication that the educational voucher will appear in the 1990s, although not in the form originally conceived and advocated, thus providing schools with a new focus for marketing and a restructured source of public funding.

Connectedness and continuity

Thus far we have accounted for several megatrends which concern curriculum and learning. We see evidence of another, namely, that there will be an expanded role for the arts and spirituality, defined broadly in each instance; there will be a high level of 'connectedness' and 'continuity' in curriculum. A number of interrelated influences are at work here. At one level there is the need to ensure that matters which have always been regarded as important in education should be sustained. In addition to the so-called basics, these include learning in the arts, defined broadly to include literature, music, drama, art and so on. An historical perspective is also important. Essentially this means that schools will continue to be, as D'Arcy has described them,[20] 'centres for communicating civilisation', thus achieving the 'continuity' noted earlier. This may be one manifestation in the school of Naisbitt and Aburdene's megatrend for the 1990s which described a renaissance in the arts. On another level, however, the pace of change and a number of global issues are giving rise to a new interest in spirituality, again defined broadly. Naisbitt and Aburdene included this as a megatrend in the 1990s, but there is a school-level counterpart. In an eloquent paper, written as a talk with his grandchildren, Hedley Beare draws on Thomas Berry in offering this view of schooling:

But most of all, I want your schooling to be a liberating experience, opening your eyes to the awesome harmonies inherent in the
cosmos. The universe is a 'communion and a community', Thomas
Berry tells us, linked by 'an unbreakable bond of relatedness'. To
use his words, I want your schooling to introduce you to the
'creative energy' of the universe, and to teach you to identify with
'the earth as a self-emerging, self-sustaining, self-educating, self-
governing, self-healing, and self-fulfilling community of all living
and nonliving beings of the planet'. It's a tall order, and it will
require some quite special teachers and principals.[21]

Beare is giving expression here to a number of curriculum developments
which are embodied in the notion of 'connectedness' in the different and
constantly changing elements in the educational experiences of our students.

Self-management and the collapse of bureaucracies in education

There is considerable evidence, sampled at the beginning of this chapter,
that self-management in education is now on a scale that warrants its
classification as a megatrend. Expressed as a continuing development, this
means that government schools, within centrally determined frameworks,
will become largely self-managing, and that distinctions between government and non-government schools will narrow. We offered the arguments in favour of self-management in our earlier book, with these drawing
broadly from the fields of political economy, organisation theory, school
effectiveness and professionalism. Some of these arguments have been
presented as the various reforms have been introduced around the world.
    Recently, however, the case has been put rather more bluntly on the
grounds that it is simply more efficient and effective in the late twentieth
century to restructure systems of education so that central bureaucracies
are relatively small and schools are empowered to manage their own affairs within a centrally determined framework of direction and support.
Two arguments have usually been offered, one is concerned with responsiveness, the other with priorities for resource allocation in times of
economic restraint or budgetary crisis.
    An example of a powerful argument on grounds of responsiveness is
that offered by Brian Scott following his review of the Education Department in the government school system in the Australian state of New
South Wales, one of the largest education systems in the world. The
following are excerpts which focus on the lack of responsiveness:

Many problems in school education in this State today are directly
attributable to the fact that systems have rigidified. The Department has not recognised the full extent of the challenge of accelerating change in today's society. Nor has it been sensitive to the

fact that in the modern world we now live in, school education —
its curriculum, its teaching and learning processes, and its delivery
systems — should be in a continual state of adaptation.

The message . . . is clear enough. While many of the same questions
need to be asked about content, structure and delivery of school
education as in the past, the assumption that has guided the development of the New South Wales State school system for more
than 100 years — namely, that the quality of school education is
best achieved through a centralised system — is no longer valid
for a modern, technologically-advanced state. The inflexibility of
the Department's structures and procedures has made it unresponsive to the real educative needs of students and teachers.[22]

Among other reasons, the analysis drawn from organisation theory
we offered in *The Self-Managing School* accounts for this lack of responsiveness.[23] A centralised, bureaucratic form of management is appropriate
where the tasks to be performed are relatively uniform in nature and stable
over time, with few exceptional cases among the range of tasks. These
were the conditions which prevailed over much of a century or more in
large government school systems. The greater the commitment to and
understanding of the range of individual learning needs and approaches
to learning and teaching, and the more frequently there is change in the
specification of these needs and approaches, the less appropriate the centralised, bureaucratic form. These are the conditions which prevail in the
1990s. There remains, of course, a range of tasks which can be routinised,
hence some functions are appropriately centralised and managed by bureaucratic means. In general, however, many government or public school
systems around the world have retained relatively centralised and bureaucratic structures for much longer than was appropriate, given the needs
of an education system in the last decade or so of the twentieth century.
In most instances the system itself has proved incapable of making the
necessary structural change and it has taken commissioned reviews such as
those conducted by Scott in New South Wales and Picot in New Zealand
to be the catalyst for action.

Another factor accounting for the shift toward school self-management
has been the re-setting of priorities for government expenditure, especially
in times of financial restraint or budgetary crisis. In a general sense, governments the world over have found it increasingly difficult to resource public
enterprises. Costly technological advances and high public expectations,
the latter now more powerfully articulated than ever before through highly
skilled lobbying efforts, make it difficult for governments to satisfy the
demands of all. Consider, for example, the very high cost of maintaining
a public health service, especially one which can now provide a much
higher quality of medical attention through an impressive array of elective

surgery. Consider also the high cost of increasingly sophisticated approaches to law enforcement, defence, transportation and education. To provide all of these services at the same time that the public is demanding reductions in levels of taxation makes the task of government even more difficult. In places like Australia and New Zealand, with high levels of foreign indebtedness and unsatisfactory terms of trade, the problem is acute. It becomes almost unmanageable in some instances, notably in Victoria, Australia, where the 1990 recession was more severe than elsewhere in the country and the government was faced with huge losses arising from the collapse of public enterprises like the State Bank. Another Australian state, Tasmania, was experiencing similar difficulties. The response around the world, but especially in these states, was to make more severe cuts in educational expenditure at the central level than at the school level. Essentially, then, when faced with the need to set priorities under conditions of constraint such as those described here, governments are opting to support schools at the expense of the centre. As would be expected, there has been strong pressure along these lines from organisations representing the interests of teachers.

It is not yet clear how far this dismantling of centralised bureaucratic structures will go. In England and Wales the local education authority (LEA) as a level in the educational structure may be under threat given the very strong public reaction to the so-called poll tax which led to its abandonment. A significant portion of local revenue is directed to the support of schools through the LEA. While school-based budgeting is an important aspect of the Local Management of Schools, a significant range of services at relatively high cost is still provided by the local authority. The government wishes to limit expenditure on central services at the LEA level to a maximum of 15 per cent of total expenditure on schools. The possibility of removing the education component of local government has been raised, with funds for schools to come directly from Westminster, implying the elimination altogether of local support from schools except to the extent that schools work together to fund such support from their school-based budgets. Indeed, schools or clusters of schools may become key providers of educational support services.

Taking all of these developments and possibilities into account, the movement toward self-management appears to be a megatrend, with differences between government and non-government schools narrowing to the extent that centralised structures for the direction and support of government schools, at least at the local and state levels, are under threat.

The service ethic

An important function at the central and regional levels of school systems has been the provision of support to schools in the areas of curriculum, teaching, management and student services. It has generally been considered more efficient and effective to locate these services at central and regional locations, given that resources and needs are insufficient to place them in individual schools. For some services a high level of specialised expertise is required and relatively small numbers of people available.

The extent and need for these services have been challenged as systems have moved to self-management. Two factors have been evident. One is associated with the economic plight described in the last section: when priorities have been re-ordered or reductions in expenditure made, a curtailment of central and regional services has been a more acceptable course for governments to take than cut-backs at the school level. This has forced governments to examine the nature and extent of central and regional support services to determine those which meet the greatest needs. In effect, these service units have been called on to justify their existence. In some instances, notably in New Zealand and more recently in Victoria, proposals for change have initially been sweeping, and campaigns in the defence of services have been mounted. In the final resolution of these matters, some services proposed for cut-back or elimination have been restored, especially those which concern the provision of support for students with special learning needs.

Another factor has been the response of schools once they have acquired a capacity for self-management. Where school-based budgets allow schools to select the source of special assistance, experience has shown that they will frequently acquire support from sources other than that previously provided at the central or regional levels. The experience in the Edmonton Public School District is interesting and is recounted in more detail in Chapter 8. In brief, a trial in fourteen schools of school-level discretion to choose the source of support and meet the costs from school-based budgets resulted, in the first year of the trial, in a markedly different pattern of support than existed previously, with some schools utilising services from the private sector, or from other schools, or by adding to their own capabilities to address their needs through additional staff or extended professional development. A shift back to utilisation of central services was evident in subsequent years.

The effect of both factors is to focus attention on the quality of service provided to schools. Where the existence of the service was once more or less taken for granted, there is now evidence of more careful design and delivery, often manifested in the formulation of mission statements, strategic plans, needs assessments, careful costing of services, negotiation of relatively explicit 'contracts' between centre or region and schools, and appraisal of the quality of service following its delivery. In several states in Australia services were arranged in what became known as school support centres, essentially 'one stop shop' facilities for a wide range of support. In Victoria, after achieving some measure of stability over three years, the level of service and the number of centres were greatly reduced in the 1990 state budget, resulting in a new round of critical reviews as to the worth of the service provided.

What we are describing here may be viewed as manifestations in the field of education of a megatrend identified by Naisbitt (from institutional help toward self-help) and another identified by Naisbitt and Aburdene (the privatisation of the welfare state) but, in general, it may be more appropriately viewed as an example of the curtailment of centralised services through bureaucratic structures arising from the need for efficiencies in the public sector.

These developments are evident in other fields of public service to the extent that it is now appropriate to refer to a new ethic or culture of service in the public service. We take this up in more detail in Chapter 8 in the context of system transformation.

Empowerment

The final theme that is evident in these megatrends is that of empowerment. We use the term in the sense that certain groups of people in the school community now have the opportunity to influence the course of events in the life of the school to a greater extent than in the past. There are several sources of power in a school, including authority and expertise. For the first of these, a person or group of people acquires power because of the authority they have been granted. Throughout most of the history of large government or public school systems, this kind of power has been exercised by professional educators at the centre of school systems and in schools. Governments have had the constitutional authority throughout this period and are now tending to exercise it to a greater extent than in the past, this being one aspect of the trend described as 'the politicising of education'. In many countries, parents and other members of the school community have had authority to make certain kinds of decisions at the school level, but in most Western countries this authority has been increased to cover a broader range of decisions. These developments have been especially noteworthy in Australia where most states now require or are encouraging the formation of school councils or school boards with powers to set policies, approve budgets and evaluate the programs of the school. Teachers and, in some instances, students have also been empowered in this manner.

Another source of power is expertise. An individual or group can influence the course of events by virtue of the expertise they can bring to bear. There is now broad acceptance of the need for teachers to engage in ongoing professional development, thus acquiring a broader range of knowledge and skill in the areas of curriculum and teaching. There are also programs for parents, especially to help them acquire the knowledge and skill to contribute fruitfully in the decision-making processes, but also, to a lesser extent, to support teachers in matters related to learning and teaching. Thus a wider range of people in the community of the school have the opportunity to influence the course of events through the acquisition of knowledge and skill.

In general, these developments are a movement away from hierarchical controls on schools and their programs, although some hierarchical structures for the exercise of power remain through the centralised arrangements we have included in the list of megatrends in education. To some extent this is an educational manifestation of an item in Naisbitt's first list of megatrends, namely, a trend from communication and control in hierarchies toward networking on the basis of a dispersion of authority and the acquisition by more people of knowledge and skills which enable them to contribute to networking arrangements.

One megatrend that is not now evident in education is that described by Naisbitt and Aburdene as 'the decade of women in leadership'. We note the fact that women currently hold for the first time the most senior positions in education in New Zealand (Maris O'Rourke) and in Western Australia (Margaret Nadebaum), but there seems to be no movement of the kind that can be described as a megatrend, despite the assertion by Naisbitt and Aburdene that organisational needs as far as leadership are concerned are more favourable for women than in the past, when hierarchical command structures tended to favour the roles into which men had been socialised. We have included it in our list of megatrends because we believe that the societal trend noted by Naisbitt and Aburdene will be experienced in education later in the decade when there will be a wider appreciation of the requirements for leadership in new organisational arrangements. We take this up in more detail in Chapter 3 where we explore advances in knowledge about leadership and requirements for leadership in the self-managing school.

Focus on Leadership in Self-Management

A capacity for leadership emerges as the central requirement for schools and systems of schools as events unfold in the 1990s. Using the distinction suggested by James McGregor Burns,[24] this leadership must be more transformational than transactional, with the former implying a capacity to engage others in a commitment to change, while the latter is more concerned with maintaining the status quo by exchanging an assurance of a secure place of work for a commitment to get the job done. Consider the nature of the changes implied by these megatrends in education:

- restructured arrangements at the centre of the system, with a narrower range of functions, a commitment to service and a culture of accountability;

- schools with more authority and responsibility than in the past, more responsive to their communities, yet accountable centrally;
- teachers drawing on a wider repertoire of approaches to learning and teaching to meet the educational needs of all students in their communities, in an environment where the educative function is dispersed through computers and telecommunications;
- new ways of thinking about the curriculum: broader and richer but achieving a connectedness which runs counter to notions of compartmentalisation;
- all in a larger environment of continual change and uncertainty.

The need for outstanding and widely dispersed leadership at all levels is palpable. While we gave some attention to leadership in *The Self-Managing School*, especially that which empowered others, our primary concern was to describe and illustrate a management process which had been identified in research on effective schools and which held promise for guiding efforts to decentralise decision-making to the school level. In *Leading the Self-Managing School* our primary concern is leadership under the conditions we have described throughout this chapter. This leadership may be described as more transformational than transactional, more visionary than managerial, and more artistic than scientific.

The Scope of the Book: Sources of Knowledge and the Need for Ongoing Research on School Self-Management

Purpose

The primary purpose of this book is to refine the model for self-management and to provide guidelines for the exercise of leadership at the school level and at the system level in a system of self-managing schools. The starting point is acceptance of the new realities in education as outlined in Chapter 1. In effect, we are responding to the question: 'How should leadership be exercised for school self-management, given that self-management is a reality or an expectation in the countries under consideration?'

Sources of knowledge

Our sources of knowledge in addressing this purpose include our reflection on experience in working with schools and school systems where adoption or adaptation of the model for self-management outlined in our first book has been encouraged; accounts of implementation of self-management in schools and school systems other than those in which we were directly involved; and contemporary writing about leadership.

Research on self-management

While the model for self-management contained in our first book was derived from research in highly effective schools in two states in Australia (in the manner summarised in Chapter 2), we are mindful of the continuing need for research on self-management and of the contentious nature of much of the existing research literature, especially that of an advocacy nature such as that of Chubb and Moe in the United States.[25] In the Australian study, highly effective schools were identified and approaches to the allocation of resources were studied. The study was conducted in a context of a trend to school self-management. A model was derived which, it was hoped, might guide the efforts of others who sought to make their schools more effective in such a context. The assumption here was that, by developing some of the characteristics of an effective school, a school might itself become more effective. Our account of the processes of self-management was intended to show how this might be brought about.

The research literature which claims a direct cause-and-effect relationship between school self-management and learning outcomes for students is sparse. We have been impressed, for example, by the research of Matthew Miles and his colleagues in urban high schools in the United States which found that substantial improvement at the school level is associated in a causal manner with a relatively high degree of school autonomy, especially in respect to the way in which resources, including staff, are allocated.[26] But much of the research and associated advocacy writing is based on the same assumption noted above, including that by Chubb and Moe, Goodlad, Johnson and Sizer.[27] The limitations of this and related approaches are noted by Malen, Ogawa and Kranz in their review of research on school-based management.[28]

The Chubb and Moe study

The findings and limitations of the Chubb and Moe study of public and private high schools in the United States are worthy of note. In that research:

> we found that, all things being equal, schools with greater control over school policies and personnel — or schools subject to less control over these matters — are more effectively organised than schools that have less organisational autonomy. We also found that autonomy from control is the most important determinant of the effectiveness of school organisation . . . [and] that all things being equal, public schools are substantially less likely to be granted autonomy from authoritative external control . . . than are private schools; and, as important, schools in urban systems —

where the problems of school performance are most grave and where the efforts to solve them have been the most bureaucratic — are much less likely, all else being equal, to enjoy autonomy.[29]

The solution, for Chubb and Moe, is to free schools from regulation by government and school boards.

A powerful critique of this position was offered by Glass and Matthews who note that 'these sweeping recommendations are based on statistical results in which the model accounts for only 5 per cent of the variance in the dependent variable of student achievement.'[30] They question whether this warrants 'the creation of an entirely new system of public education for the nation' and point to the merits of centralised arrangements:

Clumsy though they may be, the rules and regulations often stand as a safeguard against callous and unfair treatment of children, particularly those who suffer handicaps or are ethnic minorities. Have we reached an enlightened state in this country where those safeguards can be dispensed with for the sake of teachers' and administrators' autonomy? Some will doubt it.[31]

In our view this critique points to the merit of school self-management which allows for a high degree of school autonomy within a centrally determined framework of goals, policies, priorities and standards. Such a framework should address, among other things, the concerns for equity which are the subject of the rules and regulations about which Glass and Matthews were writing. As we show in Chapter 8, the best practices in school self-management currently address issues of equity in the important matter of allocating resources to schools.

In the final analysis, however, we believe that the case for school self-management rests on a much broader base than gains in student learning which may accrue, even if these are as small as suggested in the Chubb and Moe study. Indeed, those who would halt or delay the adoption of school self-management or school-based management until the evidence is in on a powerful and direct causal effect on student performance are, to a large extent, failing to take account of the wider range of reasons for these approaches to school management as well as the realities of the broader international context outlined in Chapter 1. We believe, nonetheless, that ongoing research on school self-management is critically important. There are certainly great opportunities for this as design and implementation proceeds around the world.

Organisation of Chapters

We have organised the book in three sections. Part A is entitled 'A New Context and a Refined Model for Self-Management'. In Chapter 1 we have used the concept of megatrend to describe developments in Australia, Britain, Canada, New Zealand and the United States. While there is evidence that governments are assuming a more powerful and focused role in key matters, it is clear that schools are moving toward self-management in restructured school systems. Leadership is central to achieving success under these conditions. We explained that the book is intended as a guide to good practice in schools and school systems where decisions had already been made to proceed, but acknowledged the need for ongoing research on school self-management. In Chapter 2 we review the model for self-management as set out in *The Self-Managing School*. We propose refinements on the basis of our experience in several countries and the more complex and challenging requirements for school management in the 1990s. We note some criticisms of the earlier model and conclude the chapter by referring to the strengths and limitations of models as a guide to practice. In Chapter 3 we review the major features of what is now known about leadership and offer generalisations for the guidance of leaders in self-managing schools. This chapter serves as a framework or point of departure for what follows in succeeding chapters which are concerned mainly with strategies for leadership in the self-managing school.

Part B is entitled 'Leadership in the Self-Managing School'. Our intention in Chapters 4 to 7 is to describe and illustrate approaches to leadership in those aspects of the refined model which seem especially important in the 1990s. Chapter 4 is concerned with cultural leadership and the role of the leader in creating and sustaining a culture of excellence in a self-managing school. Chapter 5 deals with strategic leadership and provides a model for strategic planning, essentially a structure and a process wherein strategic leadership can be exercised. We offer guidelines and illustrations on how school leaders can work with others in the school community to prepare and utilise a simple school development plan. Chapter 6 is concerned with educational leadership and the particular ways in which teachers, parents and others can play their part in achieving excellence. The focus is on learning and teaching and outcomes for students. Professional development is a primary consideration. Chapter 7 takes up the issue of responsiveness and deals explicitly with the demand for accountability which characterises the delivery of public services in the 1990s. We outline ways in which a school can be accountable to its local community and to society at large, without compromising the values which drive the refined model for self-management.

Part C is entitled 'Transforming Our Schools'. In Chapters 8 and 9 we consider the means by which schools and school systems can be transformed to achieve self-management. Chapter 8 focuses on school systems and the role of leaders at the centre. We acknowledge the perils of restructuring, and suggest ways in which resources can be allocated more equitably among schools, the roles of teachers' unions can be changed, a culture of service can be nurtured, and a more caring approach to system restructuring may be taken. We conclude in Chapter 9 with a vision of the self-managing school as the century draws to a close. We sketch some scenarios for what might transpire throughout the decade and conclude on an optimistic note, reflecting our belief that leadership of the transforming kind is required, and is available or can be developed.

2   Updating the Model

The model we set out in *The Self-Managing School* has been the starting point for our work in schools and school systems in Australia, Britain and New Zealand and has attracted interest in other places. Our own involvement in many projects and ongoing developmental work at Rosebery District High School in Tasmania, which furnished the model in its original form, have resulted in refinements and new insights as to how schools can develop their own approaches to self-management and how they may be supported in their efforts.

The purpose of this chapter is to provide a brief review of the model, and the research and developmental effort which underpinned our work and that of others who were involved in various implementation projects. We then describe the refinements we have made to the model, noting the particular contributions that others have made to our thinking, especially in New Zealand where we have found the notion of a school charter to be helpful in integrating a self-managing school's philosophy, mission, vision and goals within a centrally determined framework of policies, priorities and standards for accountability. Attention is then given to our use of the word 'model' as far as its descriptive and prescriptive nature is concerned, thus offering a guide to those who wish to make use of the refined version. We do this after reviewing three critiques of the original model.

Initial Research in the Effective Resource Allocation in Schools Project: 1983

Rationale and general approach

The initial research in the Effective Resource Allocation in Schools Project (ERASP) was described by Caldwell and Spinks, Caldwell, Misko, and Smith and was summarised in *The Self-Managing School*.[1] The value of

ERASP was suggested by developments in Tasmania, Australia, where schools have had, since the mid-1970s, a relatively high degree of responsibility for allocating resources compared to their counterparts in mainland Australia. The White Paper on Tasmanian Schools and Colleges in the 1980s had recommended an extension of this responsibility toward the end of the decade.[2] The introduction by the Government of Tasmania in early 1982 of a form of program budgeting had implications for the way resources were allocated within and among schools. In anticipation of further change, the Education Department of Tasmania and the Centre for Education at the University of Tasmania sought the support of the Commonwealth Schools Commission in a project for the professional development of school administrators. Awareness of similar developments in other places suggested its value as a Project of National Significance. Support was received in the amount of $35,000, with the project commencing on 1 December 1982 and concluding on 31 December 1985, with reports of all stages published in 1986. A Steering Committee of five people was established, these being nominees of the Director-General of Education in Tasmania, the Director of Catholic Education in Tasmania, the Commonwealth Schools Commission, the Australian Council for Educational Administration and the Institute of Educational Administration. Director of ERASP was Brian Caldwell. Josie Misko, then Research Fellow in Educational Administration at the University of Tasmania, served as Project Officer.

The project was carried out in three stages: (i) a nation-wide survey to determine the manner in which resources were allocated to schools, (ii) case studies in two states — Tasmania and South Australia — of schools where resources were seen to be allocated effectively, and (iii) the design, writing and testing of an integrated comprehensive program for the development of skills in school-based resource allocation.

In similar fashion to Peters and Waterman's *In Search of Excellence: Lessons from America's Best Run Companies*, a decision was made from the outset to base books and other materials in ERASP on practice in highly effective schools.[3] The strategy was to identify schools which were highly effective in a general sense and in the manner in which resources were allocated, with schools identified in both categories being chosen for detailed study. Two issues had to be resolved in implementing this strategy for research and development: first, which criteria would be used to identify schools, and second, what the process of identification would be.

A comprehensive review of literature associated with the effective schools movement was undertaken to provide a list of characteristics of highly effective schools. The limitations of this movement and associated research were acknowledged. Literature related to the allocation of resources was also examined to identify characteristics of a high degree of effectiveness in this area.

Limitations of time and other resources did not permit an empirical study based on the above characteristics. A decision was made to use a modification of the so-called 'reputational approach', with the people best suited to judge the reputations of schools considered to be regional super-intendents, regional directors, directors of primary and secondary education for government schools, senior officers for systemic schools and Common-wealth Schools Commission personnel for non-government schools. In addition, it was decided to employ two different sets of judges: one set to nominate schools on the basis of their general effectiveness and the other to nominate schools on the basis of their effectiveness in resource allocation. Those schools selected by both sets were included in the case study phase of research.

The process of identification is illustrated here for government schools. Those providing nominations were asked to read the relevant set of characteristics and then nominate schools on the basis of their knowledge. They were also asked to consider schools which had shown marked im-provement in areas in which they had been deficient and to take account of the location and socio-economic environment of schools. Each person provided up to three nominations in categories which reflected differences in terms of level of schooling, size, socio-economic setting and location. Schools which were nominated by both sets of judges were considered further, and those receiving the highest number of nominations were se-lected for study, with these comprising seventeen government and sixteen non-government schools in Tasmania and South Australia.

The case studies

Once schools had been identified, researchers visited schools and collected information through interviews with principals, teachers, parents and, in some instances, students. Interviews were semi-structured, with questions related to the budgeting process, knowledge and skill required for effective budgeting and problems encountered. Respondents were asked to identify attributes of principals which made them effective in budgeting and principals were invited to provide advice to principals new to the process of budgeting. Respondents in non-government schools were also invited to complete a comprehensive questionnaire. Case studies of varying length were then written and validated by principals as far as factual accuracy was concerned.

Findings for government schools

A detailed account of the findings was provided by Misko.[4] The approach to resource allocation at Rosebery District High School in Tasmania was selected for special consideration in the preparation of a training program because (i) the school had received more nominations than any other in the Tasmanian component of studies in government schools; (ii) the process for resource allocation met in varying degrees all of the criteria for effectiveness, including an emerging, systematic approach to program evaluation which was generally absent in other schools; (iii) the school council had, by agreement with the principal, assumed a policy-making role within a framework of state requirements; and (iv) a pioneering approach to school-level program budgeting had evolved (government interest in program budgeting had been a factor in the decision to conduct ERASP).

Professional development program

The final phase of ERASP was to design, write and test an integrated comprehensive program for the development of skills in school-based resource allocation. A preliminary analysis of key skills enabled project staff to make a selection for consideration in such a program: an integrated approach to school management linking policy-making, planning, budgeting and evaluating in a continuous cycle; management of change; management of conflict, including negotiation and building of consensus; and selecting appropriate roles for staff and the community.

A four-day workshop was conducted in January 1984 based on the aforementioned skills. A program budgeting focus was adopted, given interest which prevailed at the time. Nine modules were prepared. Resource people consisted of the Project Director, Project Officer, the principal and two senior staff from Rosebery District High School, leaders from two other schools and an officer from the South Australian Education Department. Thirty-four people from Tasmania, Victoria and the ACT participated in the program and gave high ratings in their post-workshop evaluation.[5]

Development, Dissemination and Utilisation: 1984–86

The opportunity for immediate dissemination came with an invitation from the Department of Management and Budget in Victoria to conduct training programs for principals and others in a trial and pilot of school-level program budgeting. Brian Caldwell as Director of ERASP and Jim Spinks, Principal of Rosebery District High School, worked under the auspices of ERASP in this phase of the project. Materials were refined and incorporated in a comprehensive training package. Details of this work follow a description of the model for resource allocation which became the centrepiece of the package.

Figure 2.1. The Original Model for Self-Management

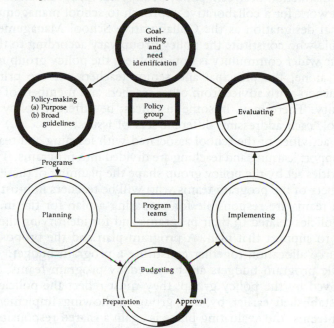

Note: This is described in *The Self-Managing School* as 'The Collaborative School Management Cycle'; B. Caldwell and J. Spinks (1988) *The Self-Managing School*, Lewes, Falmer Press, p. 22.

The initial model for self-management

The model was essentially that found at Rosebery District High School in the research phase of ERASP. As illustrated in Figure 2.1, the model has six phases: goal-setting and need identification; policy-making, with policies consisting of purposes and broad guidelines; planning of programs; preparation and approval of program budgets; implementing and evaluating.

The cycle is similar to others which may be found in general texts on management and administration. The special contribution which it makes is based on three characteristics: (i) the clear and unambiguous specification of those phases which are the concern of the group responsible for policy-making in the school ('policy group') and of other phases which are the concern of groups responsible for implementing policy ('program teams'), (ii) a definition of policy which goes beyond a statement of general aims or purposes but is not so detailed as to specify action — it provides a brief statement of purpose and a set of broad guidelines, and (iii) it organises planning activities around programs which correspond to the normal patterns of work in the school.

The distinction between 'policy group' and 'program teams' provides the framework for a collaborative approach to school management, hence its original designation as the Collaborative School Management Cycle. The people who constitute the policy group vary according to the setting. Where the wider community is not involved, the policy group may be the principal alone, the principal and senior teachers, or the principal and senior teachers with advice from other teachers and members of the school community. There may, in some instances, be different policy groups in the school, each addressing different sets of issues.

The activities of the school associated with learning and teaching and which support learning and teaching are divided into programs. The policies and priorities set by the policy group shape the planning of these programs by members of the program teams who will be teachers in most instances. Program teams are responsible for preparing a plan for the implementation of policies related to their programs and for identifying the resources required to support that plan. A program plan and the proposed pattern for resource allocation together constitute a program budget.

While program budgets are prepared by program teams, they must be approved by the policy group; they must reflect the policies and priorities established earlier by that group. Following implementation by program teams, the evaluating phase is again a shared responsibility, with program teams gathering information for program evaluation and the policy group gathering further information as appropriate to make judgments on the effectiveness of policies and programs.

In general, then, referring again to Figure 2.1, the policy group has responsibility for those phases which are emphasized in black — largely those above the diagonal line — while program teams work within a framework of policy to take responsibility for the remaining phases — largely those below the diagonal line. It is important to note that while a clear distinction is made between the responsibilities of the policy group and program teams, there will, in fact, be a high degree of overlap as far as personnel are concerned and a continuing, high level of formal and informal communication. The principal and some teachers will, for example, be members of the policy group and program teams where the policy group is a school council or board of governors which includes representatives of teachers. The policy group may frequently depend on the principal and program team for the development of policy options. Illustrations and guidelines for each phase of the model are contained in *The Self-Managing School*.

Adoption in Victoria

Caldwell and Spinks conducted seminars from 1984 to 1986 for more than 5000 principals, parents, teachers and students from about 1100 of 2200 schools, with senior officers in the regions of the state conducting others. A subsequent study found that 71 per cent of schools had made a decision to proceed, with the majority of schools making progress on one or more phases.[6] During this three-year consultancy it became apparent that the Collaborative School Management Cycle provided a helpful framework for other initiatives in Victoria, especially for schools in the School Improvement Plan and for the implementation of government policy on school councils. In the final year of this consultancy the various materials were refined and published as a book by the Education Department of Tasmania,[7] with a multi-media implementation kit also prepared as a guide to adoption.

Further Research: International Comparative Studies 1986–88

An international comparative study of emerging patterns in management in education was undertaken by Caldwell in 1986–88, with information collected in visits to Britain, Canada and the United States. It became apparent that the materials and other insights which resulted from ERASP matched needs for professional development in a number of countries. The common thread in all of these developments was the shift of power to make certain kinds of decisions from a central authority to a school. In each instance the school continued to work within a framework of legislation, policies and priorities determined by the central authority. These decisions were mainly concerned with the allocation of resources, in the narrow financial sense in all instances, but often in the broader sense in the areas of curriculum, personnel and facilities. In general, the intention was to foster a measure of self-management in the school within a centrally determined framework.

The concept of 'self-management'

The concept of 'self-management' proved helpful in describing the capacities required at the school level in these countries. A self-managing school was defined as one for which there has been significant and consistent decentralisation to the school level of authority and responsibility to make decisions related to the allocation of resources, with resources defined broadly to include matters related to curriculum, personnel, finance and facilities, in a system of education having centrally determined goals, priorities and frameworks for accountability. The concept of self-management is thus more constrained than concepts like self-government or self-determination; the intention is not the privatisation of public education.

Development, Dissemination and Utilisation: 1988–91

Materials and publications from ERASP were revised in 1987 and 1988 to take account of emerging patterns and the concept of 'self-management'. The earlier book was revised and published as *The Self-Managing School*. A chapter containing an international comparison of trends was added and new perspectives on leadership and school culture were incorporated. Apart from minor changes in terminology to suit the international setting, the descriptions, illustrations and guidelines for the Collaborative School Management Cycle remained unchanged.

National and international interest in the model has increased significantly since the publication of *The Self-Managing School*. In Australia, there have been consultancies in the Australian Capital Territory, New South Wales, Northern Territory, Queensland and Western Australia where a range of initiatives in self-management had been taken. We have been directly involved in change in Britain and New Zealand, largely through extended consultancies in which we were invited to introduce practitioners to the model for self-management and to advise senior officers at the system level on elements in the framework within which schools will be self-managing.

Jim Spinks' work has been mainly in the form of consultancy, visiting Britain on three occasions from 1988 to 1990 for a total of nearly twelve months of training programs for officers, governors, principals and teachers in more than one-third of the local education authorities. He also worked with about ten thousand parents, principals and teachers in an extended consultancy throughout New Zealand in 1989. Brian Caldwell undertook a study of emerging patterns in the management of education for OECD and completed several consultancies at the system and school levels in Australia and New Zealand. We both studied at first hand some key developments in other countries, notably Canada and the United States. We have, throughout this time, monitored the way in which practitioners have utilised the model for self-management. Jim Spinks remained principal at Rosebery throughout this eight-year research, development and dissemination effort, except in 1991 when he became Superintendent (School Self-Management) in the Department of Education and the Arts in Tasmania during which time he assisted in the development of a central framework for school self-management and conducted training programs for principals, parents and others around the state. Refinements in the model, as published and advocated in professional development programs and related work, reflect changes in approaches to management which have occurred at Rosebery as well as what has been learned from the national and international consultancy effort. Spinks became Principal of Sheffield District High School in 1992.

Figure 2.2.   *The Refined Model for Self-Management*

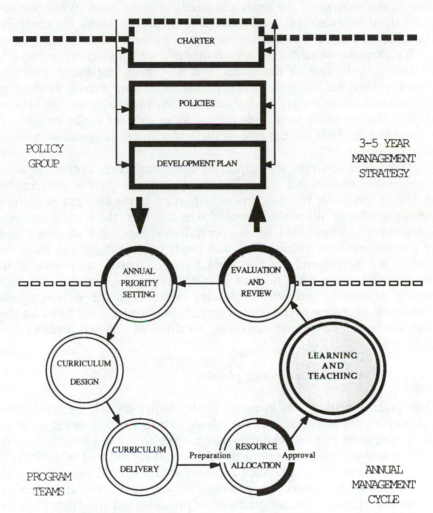

The Refined Model

The model has been refined in a number of ways as illustrated in Figure 2.2. There are several noteworthy features: a broadening of the context for policy-making, planning and evaluation to take account of a school's culture, mission and the centrally determined framework; a more explicit acknowledgment of the importance of strategic planning and the incorporation of related guidelines; and a change in terminology and approach to highlight the centrality of curriculum and learning in approaches to self-management.

Broadening and specifying the context for self-management

The earlier version suggested that policy-making and planning should occur in the context of the goals and needs of the school. While we acknowledged its existence, we believe it is helpful to show the centrally determined framework as an element in the model.

We also acknowledged the importance of a school's culture, especially in relation to the role of the leader, but have been impressed with the increasing body of evidence which points to its importance in shaping what occurs in ordinary day-to-day activities. As a consequence, we believe that it is also necessary to include culture as an element in the model and to provide guidelines for the role of the leader in creating and sustaining a strong culture.

Two other concepts are helpful in completing the context for self-management: mission and vision. We highlighted the latter in referring to the role of the leader but feel it is as important as the concept of culture in shaping what occurs in the school. Taken together, the context for self-management is determined by the centrally determined framework and the culture, mission, vision, goals and needs of the school and its community. We have found the notion of a school charter, as pioneered in New Zealand, to be a helpful way of integrating these concepts. We will develop this notion and offer a glossary of terms in the section which follows this overview of the refined model. In Chapter 4 we focus on the leader's role in creating and sustaining a culture of self-management.

The importance of strategic planning

While priority setting was included in the earlier model, we have now made explicit the importance of the school having a management strategy and development plan. A school development plan is not a long-term plan in the sense that a relatively immutable document is produced which covers the next three to five years. Such approaches are of little value given the pace of change (if, indeed, they were ever of value). We are referring instead to a relatively concise statement of priorities and strategies to guide annual operational planning which is constantly reviewed to take account of strengths, weaknesses, opportunities and threats which continuously arise in the school's external and internal environment. Strategic planning is a means to help the school manage effectively in an era of continuous and often turbulent change.

In Chapter 5 we adapt the work of Bryson in offering a model for strategic planning in the self-managing school.[8] The role of the leader is described in some detail, with illustrations from several settings. Guidelines for action are provided.

Taken together, referring to Figure 2.2, the central framework, charter, policies and development plan provide a three to five year management strategy for the school. In other words, a preferred future in terms of educational outcomes is identified and a rationale for desired change is established. Furthermore, a pathway to the preferred future is outlined in terms of activities to be carried out and time frame to be observed. The three to five year management strategy provides the basis for the annual management cycle which readers will recognise as the essence of the original model for school self-management as illustrated in Figure 2.1.

The management strategy, particularly the central framework and charter, also provides the basis for accountability. In essence, the charter articulates the intentions of the school as far as educational outcomes for students are concerned, thus suggesting criteria for evaluation and monitoring and facilitating accountability to both the government or central authority on the one hand and the local community on the other.

The relationship between the three to five year management strategy and the annual management cycle, and its implications in respect to accountability, are highlighted in Figure 2.2 by the broad arrows. That above the circle labelled 'evaluation and review' indicates that information arising from this process may be utilised in a review of the charter, policies and the development plan. It will also be utilised in reports to the central authority and local community as requirements for accountability are addressed. The issue of accountability is taken up in Chapter 7 in the context of what we describe as responsive leadership. The broad arrow above the circle labelled 'annual priority setting' indicates that these arise from the central framework, charter, policies or the development plan.

Sharpening the focus on curriculum and learning

The refined model as illustrated in Figure 2.2 makes clear that the focus of self-management is on curriculum and learning. Phases in the cycle labelled as planning, implementing and evaluating in the original model are now labelled curriculum design, curriculum delivery, learning and teaching, and evaluation and review.

These refinements are more than cosmetic. Practice in the self-managing school reflects the trends outlined in Chapter 1, especially those concerned with 'an unparalleled concern for a quality education for each individual', 'the basics in education . . . include problem-solving, creativity and a capacity for life-long learning', and 'an expanded role for the arts and spirituality . . . [and] . . . a high level of "connectedness" in curriculum.' Essentially these trends mean that schools must design and deliver a broad curriculum to meet the needs of all of its students and achieve some measure of coherence and connectedness in a time of continuous change. They mean that the most important management activities are concerned with curriculum and learning and the support of curriculum and learning.

While patterns vary among countries with which we are familiar, it is clear that trends to self-management are accompanied by a heightened concern for these phases of the model. Perhaps the most comprehensive response has been in the United States where school-based management is seen as an aspect of the so-called restructuring movement, with efforts to improve curriculum and learning and to make reforms to the profession of teaching being a highlight.[9] We take up these matters in Chapter 6 in the context of educational leadership.

There is general concern too about the evaluation phase of the model. We found very few schools engaging in systematic approaches to program evaluation, despite the rhetoric of accountability and the practice of or planning for state or national testing programs in some countries. These aspects of the centrally determined framework are now at centre stage so, in the refined model, we take up the manner in which school-based program evaluation can be integrated with requirements for system level accountability. Addressing the twin concepts of responsiveness and accountability is our major concern in Chapter 7.

The School Charter: A Unifying Concept in Self-Management

The simultaneous shifts toward centralisation of some decisions (centrally determined goals, policies, priorities and frameworks for accountability) and decentralisation for others (school self-management, especially in matters related to the allocation of resources and the empowerment of the school community) often result in confusion among those who are attempting to exercise leadership at different levels of schools and school systems. How can apparently contradictory requirements be reconciled? Within each level of the school system there is a bewildering array of expectations as far as statements of mission and vision are concerned. Are these any more than management jargon, initially having a religious or spiritual connotation, borrowed by business and now to be slavishly followed in the educational setting? How are these helpful in matters related to learning? What should be made of the recent interest in the culture of the school? Will the call to nurture the culture of the school be yet another distraction for educational leaders?

We believe that all of these developments have the potential to make a contribution to the quality of education in a self-managing school but agree that there is considerable confusion, caused in part by the jargon which has been borrowed so freely from other settings. There is a need for clarification of concepts and integration of processes, with these incorporated in the refined model for self-management in a way which makes good educational sense.

We address these requirements in this section of the chapter, choosing as our integrating device the notion of the school charter as it was pioneered and developed in New Zealand in the reforms which followed the adoption by government of the major recommendations in the Picot Report.

Clarifying the concepts

The first task is to clarify the somewhat bewildering array of concepts which provide the framework or organisational context for self-management. What follows are some definitions which we have found helpful, acknowledging that others have offered alternative meanings in some instances. We note, for example, that words like 'mission' and 'vision', and 'goals' and 'objectives', are often used interchangeably. Our definitions suggest a kind of hierarchy in the sense that the overarching concept is mission, which is given expression from time to time in a vision for the school which, in turn, may incorporate various goals and objectives. Frameworks for action are provided by policies which are then implemented through plans and procedures, and so on. It may be helpful to see these concepts in hierarchical form but there are strong interrelationships. Assumptions, values and beliefs about education and schooling pervade all.

The *mission* of the school is its purpose for existence in a particular community. A statement of mission usually includes major beliefs about the particular kind of schooling to be offered and the broad goals which will give shape to its program. It will preferably contain some words which establish its context, noting particular characteristics and educational needs of the community in which it is located. Mission statements come in various forms but in our view are best expressed concisely, in less than one hundred words, so that they can be reproduced easily to provide a focus of attention in important documents and at times and places which will gain the interest of all in the school community.

A *vision* is a mental picture of a preferred future for the school. Taken in its literal sense, those who hold a vision for the school are carrying around in their minds, and are able to give expression to, an image of the way they would like the school to be at some time in the future. This image will be relatively explicit, with mind and word pictures of what students will be engaged in, what their accomplishments will be, what resources have been acquired, how those resources will be deployed, what processes of learning and decision-making will occur, how particular needs and problems currently experienced will be addressed. A vision will be consistent with the mission of the school and, given its relatively explicit nature, will frequently incorporate some objectives to be attained. While the mission of a school may remain unchanged from year to year, visions may be reformulated as particular objectives are achieved or new opportunities (or threats) arise. Visions are often expressed in written form and in this respect seem indistinguishable from statements of mission. In that it is intended to be unifying and inspiring, a vision for a school may be expressed best in oral or artistic form.

Underpinning the mission, vision and other concepts described below is the *philosophy* of the school. The philosophy of the school is the set of assumptions, values and beliefs about such matters as the nature and purpose of education and schooling, including approaches to learning and teaching and the ways in which members of the school community shall relate to one another and make decisions.

A *goal* or *aim* is a statement of broad direction, general purpose or intent; it is general and timeless and is not concerned with a particular outcome at a particular time. Goals may be established for the school as a whole or for particular aspects of the school program. Goals may give some sense of direction to the broad statements of belief about schooling which are contained in the philosophy of the school. They also provide a means of specifying the mission or vision for the school and may be incorporated in statements thereof.

An *objective* is a statement of outcome, often expressed in measurable terms, which is to be achieved in a particular period of time. It may be appropriate to specify one or more objectives in a statement of vision for the school.

A *need* exists when 'what is' falls short of 'what should be' as far as inputs, processes and outcomes are concerned.

A *policy* is a set of guidelines which provides a framework for action in achieving some purpose on a substantive issue. The guidelines specify in general terms the kind of action which will or may be taken as far as the issue is concerned: they imply an intention and pattern for taking action, providing a framework, often with some basis for discretion, within which the principal, staff and others in the school community can discharge their responsibilities with clear direction. Policy statements will invariably reflect the beliefs and values held about schooling and may provide a framework for addressing goals and achieving objectives.

A *program* is an area of learning and teaching, or an area which supports learning and teaching, corresponding to the normal pattern of work in a school. Programs will invariably reflect the mission, vision, philosophy, policies and priorities.

The *priorities* of the school are orders of importance, need or urgency which are established from time to time among goals, programs and policies.

A *rule* or *regulation* is a statement which directs action, usually specifying who is responsible for implementing a policy or program. A *procedure* is a further specification of who does what, how and in what sequence, in the implementation process. Some rules and procedures may be mandatory, that is, they specify what action shall occur; others may be discretionary, specifying what action may occur.

A *plan* is a specification of what will be done, when it will be done, how it will be done and who will do it. Policies are usually addressed by preparing plans for their implementation. Plans will usually incorporate procedures. There are different kinds of plans in a school, including development plans, curriculum plans, program plans, learning plans, instructional plans and financial plans (budgets).

A *development plan*, often described as an improvement plan or a strategic plan or a corporate plan, is a specification in general terms of priorities to be addressed, and of strategies to be employed in addressing those priorities, as the school seeks to achieve multiple objectives over a number of years. A development plan, along with the charter and policies of the school, is an outcome of three to five year strategic management as illustrated in the refined model for self-management in Figure 2.2. The development plan calls for the exercise of strategic leadership in a process of strategic planning in the manner described and illustrated in Chapter 5.

A *budget* is the financial translation of an educational plan, usually containing estimates of expenditure and forecasts of revenue.

Evaluation is the gathering of information for the purpose of making a judgment and then making that judgment. In addition to evaluation for the purpose of making judgments about the progress and achievement of students, evaluation in a self-managing school is concerned with gathering information to make judgments about the extent to which visions have been realised, progress toward goals has been made, needs have been satisfied, priorities have been met, policies have been implemented, and resources have been allocated with efficiency and effectiveness.

Over time the ways in which things are done in a particular school fall into a pattern and the school's culture starts to emerge. Expressed simply, the *culture* of the school is 'the way things are done around here'.[10] Culture has intangible manifestations: the assumptions, values and beliefs which constitute the philosophy of the school. The tangible manifestations of culture may be found in the various words (oral and written), behaviours and materiel. The various concepts we have defined thus far are among the tangible manifestations of a school's culture but the most important are behaviours as reflected in rituals, ceremonies, approaches to learning and teaching, indeed, in the ordinary day-to-day activities which make up the life of the school. Culture develops over time and is a more pervasive and enduring phenomenon than school climate which can be relatively transient in nature. How a culture may be created and sustained is considered in Chapter 4 where particular attention is given to the cultural aspects of a leader's role in a self-managing school.

The school charter

We have indicated our belief that a school charter, along the lines pioneered in New Zealand, is a helpful device for integrating concepts such as those listed above, especially at a time when trends of a centralising and de-centralising nature may appear confusing and contradictory.

A *school charter* is a document to which both government and school policy group (council, board) have given their assent, containing a summary of the centrally determined framework of priorities and standards; an outline of the means by which the school will address this framework; an account of the school's mission, vision, priorities, needs and programs, together with an overview of the strategies which will be followed in addressing them; reference to key decision-making processes and approaches to program evaluation; all reflecting the culture of the school and an intended pattern of action in the medium to longer term. Once approved, the charter becomes the basis for allocating resources and monitoring outcomes.

School charters are most relevant to government schools or systems of non-government schools. To some extent they are also relevant to non-systemic non-government schools in receipt of government grants and to schools which, in other ways, are accountable to a central authority. A well-established, truly independent school may not need a charter along the lines we have described here: its articles of incorporation and whatever documents have proved helpful in the management of the school in the past may be all that is required.

It is difficult to formulate a concise set of guidelines for the preparation of a school charter since such a document is itself an amalgam of different documents or excerpts thereof. The following may be helpful for schools and school systems which would like to adopt the approach.

1   **The school charter should be about five pages in length**. Consistent with guidelines we have offered in *The Self-Managing School* (no policy should exceed one page, no program plan and budget should exceed two pages, no report of a program evaluation should exceed two pages), we suggest a document which is relatively easy to write and easy to read, expressed in language which is readily understood by all in the school community. Detailed specifications are not required. Concise statements can be organised under headings such as mission, vision, goals, needs, priorities of government, priorities of the school, strategies for addressing priorities, approaches to decision-making, and approaches to program evaluation, including indicators related to specified objectives.

2   **Guidelines for policy-making may be followed in the formulation of the school charter**. If all components of the charter have already been determined, are located in different documents and are non-contentious, then the policy group for the school may designate one person or a small group to draft the charter, circulate it for critical reaction, make refinements on the basis of response, and then present the final draft to the policy group for consideration and approval. Where key documents or aspects of key documents are contentious, then the policy group should establish one or more working parties to gather information and prepare options along the lines contained in the model for policy-making set out

in Chapter 6 of *The Self-Managing School*. Different options may be discussed by the policy group with a view to building consensus and subsequent adoption.

3 In systems of government and non-government schools where centrally determined frameworks must be addressed in the school charter, there should be ongoing consultation with system officers to ensure that the framework is addressed in appropriate fashion. The intention here is to ensure that the school charter, once adopted by the school's policy group, will be readily ratified by the central authority. For this aspect of the process, as well as in the internal processes at the school level, the criteria for involvement are defined by the key questions: 'who has an interest?' and 'who has a stake in the outcome?'

4   Once assent is given by the central authority and the school policy group, the charter should be printed in attractive, easy-to-read form and made available to all staff and members of the policy group, and to others in the community upon request. Like the policies and plans of the school, the school charter is intended to be a dynamic and useful document. In a system of schools it may be the basis for allocating resources to the school and the first point of reference in an external review. Within the school the charter should also be a widely used reference during the different phases of the model for self-management as illustrated in Figure 2.2.

5   Procedures should be established for the review of the school charter. In a system of schools it is likely that the term of a school charter will be specified; for example, there may be provision for review every three years. This term may coincide with the cycle for external review where these occur. In general, however, it is suggested that the school charter should be a relatively stable document, unlike the develop plan which should be the subject of regular review and refinement along the lines set out in Chapter 5.

Appraising the Model for Self-Management

So far this chapter has presented the broad outline of the refined model for self-management. In summary, it contains two broad activities: three to five year strategic management and annual management. The first is accommodated in three kinds of documents: (i) the school charter, which takes account of the centrally determined framework, mission, vision, goals, needs and priorities, although it may address other matters such as key policies, strategies and plans for evaluation; (ii) policies; and (iii) the development plan. The second contains the six phases of the refined annual management cycle: (i) annual priority setting, selecting matters for attention in the year ahead from among the policies and development plan for the school; (ii) curriculum design; (iii) planning for curriculum delivery;

(vi) the preparation and approval of plans for resource allocation, (v) the implementation of learning and teaching programs; and (vi) evaluation and review. We have endeavoured to provide an even sharper focus on curriculum and learning. As in the original model, there are clearly defined roles for the policy group and program teams, with processes which call for a high degree of involvement according to interest and stake in the outcome of decisions. Guidelines for policy-making, planning and evaluation were contained in *The Self-Managing School* along with a guide to the management of conflict in the self-managing school. We provide guidelines for the refinements to the model in the remaining chapters of this book, giving particular attention to creating and sustaining a culture of self-management in Chapter 4, strategic leadership in Chapter 5, educational leadership in Chapter 6 and responsive leadership, including accountability, in Chapter 7.

We have worked in a variety of settings in several countries since 1984, first with the original model and now with the refined version. We have learned something of its robustness. We have read with interest the critical commentaries which have appeared in reviews and in more substantive treatments in books and journals. What follows is a summary of these self-appraisals and critiques, together with some reflections on the nature of models drawn from the theoretical literature.

What we have learned about the model

We invariably encountered a favourable reaction to the model in the workshop setting when participants were in the early stages of system-wide adoption of approaches to self-management. The model seemed to integrate and organise a number of activities which were already in train. The guidelines were helpful in suggesting approaches to activities which were foreshadowed for the months to follow. Participants gained confidence that self-management was feasible and that the different partners in the enterprise — principals, teachers, parents, students and others in the school community — could play their part. Distinctions between policy group and program teams proved helpful. All seemed reassured with the time-line for adoption, which we set in the range of three to five years.

When we met with many participants in follow-up workshops or during site visits, we noted that an extraordinary array of variations to the model had been developed. We have seen scores of diagrams which differ in locally important ways from the illustrations which appear in Figures 2.1 and 2.2. Furthermore, there seemed to be no best point of entry to the model. Some schools initially made changes to their budgeting processes while others began a systematic approach to the formulation of policy. Some were not ready to start until some form of program evaluation had been undertaken. In general, we observed the process of 'mutual adaptation' which is typical of adoption of an innovation:[11] practices at the school level were changed with the assistance of a local adaptation of the model as originally presented in workshops or through reading in *The Self-Managing School*.

We soon felt the need to refine the model to help schools cope with the accelerating rate of system-initiated changes. We were aware of only a few schools which regarded adaptation of the model as a major or burdensome change in its own right. Most seemed to be using it as an aid to coping with continuing changes of the kind outlined in Chapter 1. This accounts for the addition of three to five year strategic management. We also noted some confusion about the use of terms like 'mission' and 'vision' as well as with the apparently contradictory trends of a centralising and decentralising nature. We were impressed with the notion of the school charter along the lines outlined in the previous section of this chapter and, accordingly, incorporated it in the refined model. At the most fundamental level, however, we appreciated what so many have observed, that the restructuring of schools and school systems and the adoption of broad frameworks for self-management will, of themselves, have little effect unless the focus of effort is on the classroom and on approaches to curriculum and learning. This has been one of the major developments at Rosebery District High School in Tasmania, which has furnished the prototype of the model, and we note the special attention being given to these matters in reforms elsewhere, especially in the United States.

The critiques of others

Setting aside what has been written in reviews, we have been interested in substantive critiques which have appeared in journals or books. A number of these refer to the model in connection with efforts to restructure schools through approaches such as the local management of schools or school-based management. For example, in their recent book on school finance in the United States, Swanson and King describe and illustrate approaches to school-based management (SBM) and report that 'Of all the models for implementing SBM, we are most impressed with one developed in Australia.'[12] They provide a relatively detailed explanation of the model.

In this section of the chapter we refer to three critiques which take issue with various features of the model. The first appeared in Colin Marsh's book on school improvement where he included the model among several which might guide the efforts of practitioners.[13] He classifies the model as having a primarily technological orientation as opposed to political or cultural. While recommending the model, he notes what he perceives to be shortcomings, including an undue separation of policy groups and program teams, a lack of detailed attention to the role of parents, its apparent reliance on a strong principal which may have both positive and negative consequences as far as staff initiative is concerned, its overemphasis on the financial aspects of planning, its demanding nature, and its apparent dismissal of 'the spontaneities, wide-ranging discussions, outbursts and arguments that so often occur in schools'.[14]

We believe these to be constructive comments, identifying areas for vigilance in the implementation or adaptation of the model rather than constituting shortcomings in the model itself. We offer two observations. First, we were conscious in our first book that we should address the needs of principals and others in school systems which had no provision for school councils and other systematic approaches to securing the involvement of parents. We gave less attention than we would wish to the role of parents. As described in Chapter 1, the number of school systems without a framework for parental involvement is now negligible and the evidence for the positive impact of parental involvement is mounting. Second, we have been pleased to note that adoption of the model for self-management seems to have been accomplished with the empowerment of staff. While strong, charismatic principals have been evident in many instances, we have also sensed that many with a less visible approach to their role have been energised by a systematic approach to management which empowers others.

Brown expressed two concerns about the model in his study of decentralisation and school-based management.[15] One was related to the origin of the model itself, appearing to be based largely on practice in one school in Tasmania and on the experience of the authors in consultancy work as they assisted schools and school systems in the implementation of the model. While the various elements of the model were demonstrated more comprehensively at Rosebery District High School than in any other school at the time, we draw attention to the research in the Effective Resource Allocation in Schools Project, summarised earlier in the chapter, which furnished evidence in effective schools of systematic approaches to management of the kind contained in the model. Rosebery supplied illustrations of the model for the developmental efforts in different places. As we have noted elsewhere, we have seen countless variations of the way in which the model has shaped management practice in different schools. In our current book we have made refinements to the model based on the context of the 1990s and on what we have learned from more extensive work in different countries. We provide few illustrations from Rosebery, preferring to generalise wherever possible. A second concern expressed by Brown, noted also by Glatter in a review of the earlier book,[16] was the effort we made to delineate the benefits of the model. We recorded what had been the experience at Rosebery and in other schools where we were able to observe what had occurred. We attempted to address some of the problems and concerns which had been expressed by those who were adopting or adapting the model, having recorded these in systematic fashion throughout our consultancy in Victoria. Our further work has led to refinements of the kind set out in this chapter. In general, however, we draw attention to the fact that the essence of the model is really a fairly straightforward if not standard management cycle which can be implemented in countless ways. Brown's comments and those of Corson below raise the important issue of the nature of models and we return to this at the end of the chapter.

Corson offered a powerful critique of the policy-making phase of the model, questioning why we selected three in proposing the number of policy options a working party dealing with a contentious policy issue might explore, noting that policy-makers might overlook more suitable options, and pointing out that our criteria for selecting a preferred option (desirability, workability and acceptability) have not been operationalised in the school setting.[17] He concludes that this phase of the model offers no advance over a commonsense approach.

As with the critique of Marsh, we see Corson directing our attention to the shortcomings of an unnecessarily rigid use of the model. We proposed at least three options, rather than the fixed number of three, but would expect that working parties will identify as many as seem necessary to reflect the interests, preferences and expertise of those from whom information is gathered. We have found in our workshops and from accounts of practice that those involved may sift through dozens of possibilities, quickly and orally in some instances, before settling on whatever number of options are presented to the policy group. The procedures we recommend for the regular evaluation of policy should enable 'errors' to be rectified. The criteria of desirability, workability and acceptability must, of course, be operationalised, and the particular matters to be taken into account and their relative weighting will vary from issue to issue and setting to setting, calling for a degree of judgment and sensitivity which makes the model more than a technological shell.

These critiques focus attention on the limitations of the model for self-management. To place these in perspective we turn finally in this chapter to some of the theoretical literature on models.

Reflections in the light of the theoretical literature

Dye defined a model as 'a simplified representation of some aspect of the real world' and proposed six criteria for appraising the utility of a model: capacity to order and simplify, identification of significant features, congruence with reality, communicative power, explanation of a total process, and a basis of enquiry and research.[18] It seems that the model for self-management generally satisfies these criteria.

Interestingly, although derived from case studies of practice in schools nominated as effective and then refined in the light of observation, experience and new contextual factors, the model was usually received by the practitioner as theory. The task as perceived by the practitioner was to make this theory practical.

Sergiovanni and Starratt drew attention to the limitations of models and the role of model-builders:

> The real 'culprits' . . . may not be the theorists and researchers but the educational synthesisers and model-builders. The synthesisers and model-builders are less concerned with creating new knowledge, focusing instead on integrating and developing knowledge into broader forms and arrays which can be more directly applied to practice.[19]

In a critical comment on models for supervision, Sergiovanni and Starratt asserted that 'when proposed and marketed as truth and prescribed . . . as a one best way to achieve, they are likely to be ill-fitting to the realities of practice.' They proposed that models be viewed as ways to think about practice, providing 'frames for understanding the problems professionals face'. Models, they believe, 'are not true with respect to telling the professional what to do but are useful for informing the professional's judgement, guiding the decision-making process, and making professional practice more rational.'[20]

Sergiovanni and Starratt summarise what we believe the refined model for self-management should be as far as its contribution to practice is concerned. Their view coincides with our own observations about the way in which the model has been utilised and accommodates the helpful comments of those who have written about it.

The stage is now set for a more detailed exploration of the refined model in Chapters 3 to 7, commencing with an examination of what we now know about leadership. We undertake this exploration in the hope that we will indeed make the contribution described above, that is, that we may inform judgment, guide decision-making and make professional practice in self-management more rational.

3   What We Now Know about Leadership

It is clear that special kinds of leaders and leadership are required for school self-management, both at the system level and at the school level. For example, there is no place for an autocratic leader who is unwilling to empower others; in a self-managing school, leadership pervades the school community. Leadership is exercised within the policy group where there may be a number of working parties, within program teams, and within organisations of teachers, parents and students. This widely dispersed leadership is, of course, in addition to that exercised in the course of day-to-day activities in the classroom and around the school.

There have been major advances in knowledge about leadership during the last ten years which, in very important respects, confirm key elements in the model for self-management, including those concerned with empowerment and dispersed leadership. There is now a rich body of knowledge to guide professional practice and it is the purpose of this chapter to highlight some of the major concepts, perspectives, generalisations and theories which are relevant to leadership in a self-managing school and, at the central level, where the intention is to create and sustain a system of self-managing schools. The chapter includes six key guidelines which reflect what we now know about leadership in the self-managing school from recent research and from our direct observation and experience. Brief illustrations are provided throughout; more are provided in chapters which follow. We conclude the chapter with an examination of what we consider to be the 'core' role for leaders in self-managing schools, namely, the exercise of educational leadership.

Leaders and Leadership in the Self-Managing School

Two key questions should be addressed at the outset. Who is a leader? What does such a person do to exercise that which we call leadership?

Definitions abound in the literature but, as Duke observed, 'Leadership seems to be a gestalt phenomenon; greater than the sum of its parts.'[1] Dubin's definition of leadership dealt only with 'the exercise of authority and the making of decisions';[2] Fiedler was concerned with the leader as 'the individual in the group given the task of directing and coordinating task-relevant group activities';[3] Stogdill referred to 'the process of influencing the activities of an organised group toward goal setting and goal accomplishment';[4] Pondy described 'the ability to make activity meaningful . . . not to change behaviour but to give others a sense of understanding of what they are doing'.[5] Each contributes to the gestalt but is limited in its own right, as indicated by some of the key phrases: exercise of authority (Dubin), task of directing (Fiedler), influencing the activities (Stogdill), make activity meaningful (Pondy). We take the view that each reflects a facet of what different people called leaders do in different settings under different circumstances.

This view of leadership as a gestalt phenomenon seems appropriate as far as leadership for self-management is concerned since it is consistent with the notion of leadership which is widely dispersed in the school community. Some leaders are indeed exercising their formal authority and making decisions (principals). Others may be directing and coordinating the work of others (bursars). There may be many who have no formal authority but are fulfilling the expectations of a group or are exercising responsibility on behalf of a group (coordinators of program teams). Others may not have formal or informal authority but are able to influence colleagues through their technical, human or educational expertise (members of working parties or program teams). Many may be invaluable in that they help members of the group make sense of what they are doing, this being critical in times of continuing change, turbulence and uncertainty: 'Why do we have to change directions yet again?' 'Wouldn't it be easier if they simply told us what to do?' 'Why involve parents when they don't really know very much about this issue?' 'How will this improve the quality of learning in the school?'

A similar analysis may be made of leaders at the system level. In relation to the particular aspects of their work which relate directly to the notion of self-management, we would highlight especially those facets which are concerned with the influence of activities and helping others make sense of the changes which are occurring in the system: 'Why are we giving up responsibility in these areas?' 'Why decentralise when those in schools don't have the expertise or experience to make these kinds of decisions?' 'Where is the evidence that what we are doing is likely to improve the quality of learning in our schools?'

Attributes of the Leader in a Self-Managing School

Research over the years has not yielded a consistent set of findings about the personal attributes of leaders. Stogdill synthesised the findings of recent research and found a number of traits which consistently characterised effective leaders. These included a sense of responsibility, concern for task completion, energy, persistence, risk-taking, originality, self-confidence, capacity to handle stress, capacity to influence, capacity to coordinate the efforts of others in the achievement of purpose. These findings were general across many fields and we are not aware of any work which suggests that they do not apply to schools.

Some of the above would appear to be especially important, given the scope of change when a system and its schools move toward self-management. We would highlight persistence in the face of complexity and opposition from those who would prefer authority and responsibility to remain centralised; capacity to take risks and to handle stress under these circumstances; originality, especially in the early stages of the change; and self-confidence. Once some measure of stability is achieved, none would appear especially more important than any other.

Lists of attributes such as these provide only part of the picture when it comes to portraying what successful leaders do. A richer and more useful guide to what leadership entails has been furnished in recent studies of leadership. What follows is a review of generalisations which have emerged from such studies, adapted with illustrations to set the context of the self-managing school.

Focus on Transformational Leadership

The most helpful leadership concept derives from an important distinction between transactional and transformative leadership which was made by James McGregor Burns in 1978.[6] Expressed simply, transactional leadership is exercised when a leader and followers undertake, as it were, a transaction: from the followers, an agreement to work toward the achievement of organisational goals; from the leader, an agreement to ensure good working conditions or, in some other way, satisfy the needs of followers. This approach to leadership is, of course, important and necessary, but alone it may not ensure that the organisation achieves at a level of excellence or, if a change in direction or new levels of achievement are desired, that these will eventuate. Burns' comprehensive study of leadership over the centuries suggests that the most successful leaders in terms of bringing about changes in direction or new levels of achievement have, in addition, exhibited transformative or transformational leadership. Transformational leaders succeed in gaining the commitment of followers to such a degree that these higher levels of accomplishment become virtually a moral imperative. In our view a powerful capacity for transformational leadership is required for the successful transition to a system of self-managing schools.

In this section of the chapter we set out the fundamentals of transformational leadership as they apply to school self-management. In succeeding chapters we deal with four facets of the role of the transformational leader: namely, cultural leadership, strategic leadership, educational leadership and responsive leadership.

The fundamentals of transformational leadership

Beare, Caldwell and Millikan gleaned ten generalisations from recent research on leaders and leadership.[7] We have adapted, consolidated and focused these on the self-managing school, with simple illustrations from our observations and experience.

1 Leaders in the self-managing school have the capacity to work with others in the school community to formulate a vision for the school. In Chapter 2 we defined a vision as a mental picture of a preferred future for the school. We noted that, taken in its literal sense, those who hold a vision for the school are carrying around in their minds, and are able to give expression to, an image of the way they would like the school to be at some time in the future. We suggested that this image will be relatively explicit, with mind and word pictures of what students will be engaged in, what their accomplishments will be, what resources have been acquired, how these resources will be deployed, what processes of learning and decision-making will occur, how particular needs and problems currently experienced will be addressed.

This vision will contain several images. The most important is educational in nature, concerned with outcomes for students. The vision will also provide a picture of how the school will operate as a self-managing organisation: how will the principal, teachers, students, parents and others in the school community work together to manage the affairs of the school? In quite specific terms, what will be created and accomplished which is not evident now? Another image will be of the process to be employed in reaching this state of self-management and achieving these educational outcomes: how will particular problems, barriers or difficulties currently experienced be resolved? Underpinning these images is the capacity for strategic leadership which we take up in Chapter 5.

This generalisation differs in important ways from that which Beare, Caldwell and Millikan offered in respect to the leader's role in formulating a vision when they reported that 'outstanding leaders have a vision for their organisations.' This is unquestionably the finding of research, but it is a finding which is silent in respect to the manner in which the vision is generated. While a leader may bring a vision to the self-managing school or may formulate a personal vision once familiar with the setting, the essence of self-management is that, in general, the vision which is to shape the ordinary day-to-day activities in the school is formulated by the leaders and others together. We use the words 'in general' because we acknowledge that there are circumstances in which members of the school community will expect the leader to provide the vision. An implication of the foregoing is the need to establish a process wherein the leader can indeed work with others in the school community to formulate the vision. There is no one best way to do this. Indeed, in the early stages the principal or other person who has a vision of self-management will be concerned solely with bringing different individuals and groups together, creating a climate wherein an interest in and capacity for self-management can emerge. It may be several months before people are ready to formulate a vision for their school, and even then the process will not necessarily follow a rational or predetermined path. Clearly, however, the initiator here must be energised by a personal vision of what is possible.

This suggests a qualification of our generalisation in settings where a leader takes the initiative to transform the school or system of schools. Case studies of pioneering school systems, for example, suggest that the vision of the leader who took the initiative was not initially developed in association with others, although it may have required approval by a policy group. An example is the leadership of Michael Strembitsky who has been Superintendent of the Edmonton Public School District in Alberta, Canada since the early 1970s. His was a personal vision of school-based budgeting, now broadened to school-based decision-making, but he succeeded in articulating that vision in such powerful ways that it eventually became the shared vision of the school board and others, despite apparently strong opposition or scepticism from some individuals and organisations in the system. We will look more closely at Strembitsky's achievements in other chapters, especially Chapter 8, but note that, when an individual operates under such conditions, successful realisation calls for articulation and commitment by others. We take this up as our third generalisation below.

Thus far we have written of the leader as a particular individual, most likely the principal, but there are many leaders in a self-managing school. We would offer the same generalisation as a guide to their leadership. In a program unit, for example, the leader will work with colleagues in the unit to formulate a vision for their area of responsibility. This vision should be consistent with that for the school as a whole.

2 **Leaders in a self-managing school have a coherent personal 'educational platform' which shapes their actions**. The first generalisation addressed the importance of securing a shared vision for the self-managing school. This does not remove the need for each leader to have what Sergiovanni and Starratt have described as an educational platform, defined as the set of assumptions, beliefs, opinions, values and attitudes, not necessarily expressed in formal fashion, which guide the actions and

decisions of the leader. Included may be aims of education, expectations for students, social significance of schooling, image of learner, value of curriculum, image of teacher. Preferred pedagogy, language of discourse, preferred kinds of relationships, preferred kind of climate, purpose of leadership, preferred process of leadership.[8]

One can specify more precisely the planks of the platform for the leader in a self-managing school. As far as approaches to management and leadership are concerned, some key words might be 'community' (language of discourse); 'collegial' (preferred kinds of relationships); 'open' (preferred kind of climate); 'achievement of mission' (purpose of leadership); and 'empowering' (preferred process of leadership). We suggest some more detailed specifications in Chapters 4 to 7, commencing in Chapter 4 where we set out a view as to what constitutes excellence in education (in some respects, of course, this is a plank in *our* educational platforms).

What we are proposing, then, is that leaders at the school work with others to formulate the vision of the school or part of the school, but that each should have a coherent and well thought out educational platform of assumptions, values and beliefs which shapes decisions and actions. The platform may, of course, be tailored to the setting, but, in general, we see it as more fundamental and stable. On the other hand, because the vision must energise the work of all, it is best determined together and thus may differ in significant ways from some personal visions and may change over time.

3 Vision is communicated in a way which ensures commitment among staff, students, parents and others in the community. This generalisation has implications for leaders in any school, regardless of the extent to which there is a capacity for self-management. We know from the research findings of James Coleman and Thomas Hoffer that, all other factors being equal, schools with a high level of what they termed 'social capital' seemed to do better than others, with social capital considered to be an indication of the strength of mutually supporting relationships among principal, teachers, students, parents and others in the school community (including the church where the school is a church school).[9] We examine this notion of social capital in Chapter 4, in the context of school culture, and in Chapter 6, in the context of the empowerment of a school and its community. We note here, however, that one indicator of social capital is the extent to which there is commitment in the school community to the vision for the school. The level of this commitment is likely to be high where representatives of the community, defined broadly, have been involved in formulating that vision (even though, as noted in respect to the first generalisation, that vision may have emerged over time through a variety of means).

Vision may be communicated in a number of ways. Some will be formal in nature, in words both oral and written. The implication here is that leaders in the school should take every opportunity to bring the vision to the attention of others. To the extent that the vision is a picture of the particular ways in which the mission of the school will be brought to realisation over a period of time, this confirms the value of printing the school's mission statement in key documents which are widely distributed: including the school charter, the school prospectus, at the front of the school's policy handbook, program plan and budget, evaluation reports, student reports, advertisements and job descriptions. The vision can be communicated in speeches and other presentations, formally and informally.

We contend that this wide base of commitment is a necessary condition for success in a self-managing school. It may not be a necessary condition in schools which are not self-managing. Schools can, to a large extent, remain apart from their communities in systems where authority and responsibility for major decisions are retained at the central level and where schools continue to receive substantial support to the extent that their problems can be handled by others.

4 There are many facets to the leadership role: technical, human, educational, symbolic and cultural, with the higher order symbolic and cultural facets being especially important in the self-managing school. We are employing here the classification devised by Sergiovanni in his account of approaches to leadership in excellent schools.[10] In brief, technical leadership includes the capacity to plan, organise, co-ordinate and schedule. Human leadership involves the harnessing of available human resources in ways which include building and maintaining morale, encouraging growth and creativity, providing support for staff and empowering others in programs of development and through the creation of opportunities for participation in decision-making. Educational leadership involves the use of expert knowledge about education and schooling to diagnose students needs, develop curriculum, select appropriate approaches to learning and teaching, supervise and evaluate. Symbolic leadership involves focusing the attention of others on matters of importance to the school through the range of words, actions and rewards which are available to the leader. Cultural leadership involves the building of a strong school culture.

Sergiovanni suggested that technical and human facets of leadership, by themselves, may simply ensure that the school will not be ineffective. The presence of educational leadership may ensure that the school is effective, that is, it achieves its goals. To ensure the highest level of achievement over time, an important aspect of excellence, there must be symbolic and cultural leadership. The model for self-management provides a framework within which the technical, human and educational facets of leadership can be exercised. We develop further the educational facet in the section of this chapter which follows these generalisations.

In our refined model we would stress the importance of the capacity of leaders to focus on the symbolic and cultural. To illustrate the symbolic, consider again that aspect of leadership which calls for communicating vision in a way that ensures commitment among all in the school community. Our earlier illustrations were the formal use of words, both oral and written. Symbolic leadership includes the use of words which are, of course, symbols for the meanings and values we wish to communicate. But symbols also include actions and rewards. So we are considering here the wide range of words, actions and rewards which leaders can employ to communicate matters of value. Among the words we use, a powerful medium is the choice of metaphors. A variety of metaphors may be employed to describe the life of the school; these include military ('troops', 'parade', 'battle', 'chain of command'), business ('bottom line', 'clients', 'managers', 'shop front'); industrial ('productivity', 'chalk-face', probably derived from 'pit-face'); sport ('team', 'coach', 'game plan', 'players') and so on. Metaphors in relation to the processes of self-management will probably reflect the notions of team or family or community; those related to the outcomes of schooling or the students themselves will tend to reflect a focus on individuals and their empowerment through learning rather than a competitive situation where success is enjoyed by a few. Here again, however, fundamental views about the aims of education and schooling must be considered.

Actions are powerful symbols for communicating values. Values are communicated through ordinary, day-to-day choices. Important messages are sent, for example, by what activities a leader chooses to participate in or what events a leader chooses to attend, or which people a leader chooses to speak to, or how a leader conducts a meeting or other ceremony, or how a leader organises the office. Among actions one would expect in a self-managing school are participation in a wide range of activities or events in areas of the school program which highlight the particular aspects of excellence considered important in the school, a readiness to meet with and be seen to meet with a representative range of people from among the different groups which make up the school community or room arrangements for meetings which reflect the partnership of different groups in the school community.

Rewards, defined broadly, are also very powerful symbols for values. Leaving aside rewards for students which should, of course, provide recognition in matters related to the particular view of excellence which is embraced at the school, we would highlight those for teachers and others in the school community. What is required here is recognition for actions which are directed at the aforementioned view of excellence but also in the processes of self-management. The principal will wish to reward other leaders and others who accept responsibility in different school programs or who encourage the involvement of parents and the wider community in decision-making and other aspects of school operations. Rewards can come in a variety of forms including words of praise, further empowerment and recommendations for promotion.

Also important in the Sergiovanni framework is cultural leadership.

The importance of a strong culture has now been widely accepted in accounting for the success of schools and other organisations. In Chapter 4 we highlight some strategies which leaders in self-managing schools can employ to create and sustain a culture of excellence.

5   Leaders in self-managing schools keep abreast of trends and issues, threats and opportunities in the school environment and in society at large, nationally and internationally: they discern the 'megatrends' and anticipate their impact on education and in the school. The capacity for what we would call strategic leadership is an increasingly important requirement for leaders in schools, indeed in all organisations in the 1990s. It is, as with other generalisations, especially so in self-managing schools where leaders do not have others at the system level to do the strategic thinking for them to the extent that was assumed to be the case in times of more centralised control. In reality, it seems that leaders at the system level are only now coming to grips with the importance of the strategic aspects of their roles. In Chapter 5 we offer a model and some guidelines for the techniques of strategic leadership. The outcome is a set of priorities which take account of trends and their likely impact on the school. These priorities are constantly refined, suggesting that the capacities we describe involve much greater adaptability and flexibility than required in traditional approaches to long-term planning.

6   Leadership which empowers others is central to success in a self-managing school, especially in respect to decision-making. The model for self-management, including the refined version, calls for many leaders according to the number of program teams and more, where working parties are established for the analysis of policy issues and other matters. Sergiovanni's concept of 'leadership density' is an apt descriptor of what is required.[11] Research findings in a variety of fields, including education, also give support to a wider involvement in decision-making according to the expertise and stake of the people concerned.[12] In making provision for this involvement, leaders clearly need to avoid the situation of 'decision saturation', especially in times of continuing change as is being widely experienced in schools at this time. Not all teachers wish to be involved in all decisions, even when they have a stake in the outcome and have expertise which can be brought to bear. Sensitivity on the part of the leader is a requirement.

Providing people with the necessary knowledge and skills to participate in decisions is an important aspect of empowerment, hence the likelihood that the self-managing school will also be characterised by extensive school-based professional development programs. The image of 'the developing school' proposed by Holly and Southworth is what we have in mind here.[13] Another helpful image is that of 'deep coping' as described by Miles on the basis of research carried out in urban high schools in the United States which were highly successful in bringing about improvement.[14] Successful schools had a capacity for 'deep coping' as opposed to 'shallow coping' which characterised the efforts of schools which were unsuccessful. The former revealed a capacity quickly to assemble problem-solving teams to tackle projects for school improvement or to solve problems which had arisen in the delivery of the program for individuals or groups of students. These schools were also ready to organise small-scale training programs to assist staff in addressing these concerns. Where necessary, they were prepared to seek new staff to add to their capacity to bring about desired improvement. Given the wide base of involvement in decisions in the self-managing school, it is likely that training programs or professional development will be available for teachers, students, parents and others who have the opportunity to make a contribution.

The case for the empowerment of leaders, regardless of gender, can be made on grounds other than the desired conditions for self-management. On grounds of equity alone, then, we would expect to find men and women occupying in roughly equal proportions the range of leadership positions in schools and school systems. Yet we are mindful of the writing of people like Sarah Lawrence Lightfoot who suggested that what is important is the attributes of the leader, regardless of gender, which include the range of qualities that coincide with what have been traditional stereotypes. She called for leadership which offered 'a subtle integration of personal qualities traditionally attached to male and female images' on the basis of her research in 'good' high schools.[15] Naisbitt and Aburdene went further and suggested that conditions for leaders are emerging which suit both genders, in contrast to past practices which emphasised hierarchical controls and were dominated by men who had been socialised accordingly:

> The dominant principle of organisation has shifted, from management in order to control an enterprise to leadership in order to bring out the best in people and to respond quickly to change. This is not the 'leadership' individuals and groups so often call for when they really want a father figure to take care of all their problems. It is a democratic yet demanding leadership that respects people and encourages self-management, autonomous teams, and entrepreneurial units.[16]

The 1990s thus provide what Naisbitt and Aburdene call an 'equal [level] playing field' when it comes to leadership roles for men and women. They even suggest that women may hold a slight advantage since 'they need not "unlearn" old authoritarian behaviour'.[17] They wrote in the context of business in the United States in asserting that 'it is no longer an advantage [for a leader] to have been socialised as a male.'[18] While evidence for the 1990s being the 'decade of women in leadership' in education (the educational counterpart to one of the Naisbitt and Aburdene megatrends) is somewhat limited, we agree that the kind of leadership in a self-managing school is similar to the new 'dominant principle' described by these writers and, to that extent, should offer a level playing field for men and women.

Sergiovanni offers another perspective on empowerment with his notion of 'value-added leadership', essentially a development of Burns' notion of transformational leadership.[19] For Sergiovanni, the values to be 'added' are empowerment, ennoblement and enhancement. In examining emerging practices in school-based management, he expressed concern that decentralisation might end at the principal's desk or might involve taking power from one and giving it to another:

> However, empowerment can also be understood as the exchange of one kind of power for another — the exchange of *power over* for *power to*. Value-added leaders . . . are less concerned with controlling what people do, when they do it, and how; and more concerned with controlling accomplishments — the likelihood that shared values will be expressed and shared goals achieved. These leaders realise that to most effectively accomplish the latter, one must give up control over the former. When school-based management is understood in this way, the triangle is exchanged for the circle; a top-down management view of schooling is exchanged for a moral community built upon shared purposes and beliefs.[20]

In summary, taking all of these perspectives into account, this generalisation calls for empowerment in four major respects: empowerment of other leaders ('leadership density'); empowerment in decision-making, with avoidance of 'decision saturation'; empowerment through professional development and training programs so that all in the school community have the necessary knowledge and skills to participate in a self-managing school; and empowerment which acknowledges that requirements for leadership no longer emphasise roles for which males tended to be socialised in the past ('the level playing field'). Sergiovanni captures all with his notion of 'value-added leadership'.

Educational Leadership

In the final analysis, the case for self-management must be based on benefits for students in terms of gains in learning outcomes. Essentially, the issue is defined by the question: 'Will a capacity for self-management lead to benefits for students which would not have been possible under more centralised arrangements?' The case for self-management which we set out in *The Self-Managing School*, reiterated in Chapter 1 of this book, included the argument that resources, defined broadly, can be allocated in optimal fashion to meet the particular mix of priorities and learning needs that exist in a particular school. There is an increasing array of evidence that the conditions that may be created in a self-managing school are associated with school improvement. The key link in the chain of cause-and-effect will, however, be what happens in the classroom: will learning and teaching be enhanced under these conditions?

The central issue

The particular question addressed in this section of the chapter is: 'What is the role of the principal and other leaders in enhancing the quality of learning and teaching in the self-managing school?' We use as our starting point the state-of-the art review of research on instructional leadership offered by Murphy.[21] We then explore the implications in the context of the self-managing school. While some illustrations are offered, we take up related strategies and more detailed guidelines for action in Chapter 5.

The paradox

Murphy noted a paradox which is of central importance as far as self-management is concerned. He contrasted the normative account of the role of the principal ('what ought to be') and descriptions of the role which have emerged from studies of what the principal actually does ('what is'):

> Taken together, these studies present a picture of school adminis-
> trators whose time is heavily devoted to matters other than cur-
> riculum and instruction — to issues of student discipline, parent
> relations, plant operations, and school finance. . . . Most principals
> do not meaningfully supervise and evaluate teachers, plan and
> coordinate curriculum, actively monitor the technology of the
> school or the progress of students, or spend time in classrooms.
> In short, most administrators do not act as instructional leaders.[22]

While most of Murphy's extensive sources are from the United States, we do not believe that his generalisation would differ significantly if it purported to represent conditions in Australia, Britain, New Zealand and elsewhere.

A framework for the preferred role of principal

Murphy then provides a framework for the role of the principal as instructional leader drawn from more than 200 reports of research on school effectiveness, change and innovation, program implementation, outcomes

Figure 3.1. A Framework for Describing the Preferred Role of the Principal as a Leader of Learning and Teaching

MISSION AND GOALS

Formulating mission and goals of the school
Communicating mission and goals of the school

PROCESSES OF LEARNING AND TEACHING

Promoting quality teaching
Supervising and evaluating teaching
Allocating and protecting teaching time
Coordinating the curriculum
Monitoring student learning

CLIMATE FOR LEARNING

Establishing positive expectations and standards
Maintaining high visibility
Providing incentives for teachers and students
Promoting professional development

SUPPORTIVE ENVIRONMENT

Creating a safe and orderly learning environment
Providing opportunities for meaningful student involvement
Developing staff collaboration and cohesion
Securing outside resources in support of school goals
Forging links between home and school

Source: Adapted from a list in J. Murphy (1990) 'Principal Instructional Leadership', in P. Thurston and L. Lotto (Eds), *Advances in Educational Administration*, Greenwich, Conn., JAI Press, Vol. 1, Part B, p. 169.

of school reform programs over the last decade, instructional leadership in schools in general, instructional leadership in effective and ineffective schools, effects of instructional leadership on organisational outcomes, effective and ineffective principals and studies of school improvement. An adaptation of this framework is contained in Figure 3.1. We have replaced the term 'instructional leader' with 'leader of learning and teaching' and made other modifications to the terminology employed by Murphy.

Figure 3.1 classifies the preferred role under four broad types of activity: mission and goals, processes of learning and teaching, climate for learning, and supportive environment. For each of these are listed particular activities which research in the settings described above reveals as being carried out by principals. Several have already been discussed in the context of self-management, namely, activities related to the formulation and communication of the mission and goals of the school, maintaining high visibility, providing incentives for teachers and students, promoting professional development, developing staff collaboration and cohesion, securing resources in support of school goals, and forging links between home and school. Of special interest here are those activities which focus on learning and teaching and a supportive environment: promoting quality learning, supervising and evaluating teaching, allocating and protecting teaching time, coordinating the curriculum, monitoring student learning, establishing positive expectations and standards, creating a safe and orderly learning environment, and providing opportunities for meaningful student involvement. Murphy draws from the research in providing a range of sample behaviours for each of these activities.

Barriers to adoption of the preferred role

Murphy proceeds to an exploration of barriers to the adoption of the preferred role. He includes shortcomings in training and preparation, with few programs in the United States calling for studies in learning and teaching; practices at the system level and norms of the profession that downplay direct involvement in learning and teaching on the part of principals; and the nature of the role itself, with its traditional focus on 'managerial' or 'administrative' aspects of the role, the variety of small activities which hinder attention to learning and teaching, the absence of a system of rewards and sanctions which the principal may utilise in relation to learning and teaching, and the influence of teacher unions which have resulted in matters related to learning and teaching becoming, increasingly, the subject of award negotiations and collective agreements.

These barriers suggest strategies to redress the disparity between actual and preferred roles of the principal as a leader in learning and teaching where such disparity exists. There are major implications for universities and other institutions which provide pre- and in-service training for principals, for school system policy-makers and for teacher unions. To some extent these place the solution in the hands of people other than those in schools. There is, however, some promise within the model for self-management itself, and it is here that we turn to an analysis of the role of principal offered by Michael Fullan in his thought-provoking monograph entitled 'What's worth fighting for in the principalship?'[23] He offers strong affirmation of key elements in the model in suggesting a course of action.

Fullan believes that the task for the principal in implementing all centrally determined policies 'is clearly impossible, creates overload, confusion, powerlessness, and dependency or cynicism',[24] an observation which confirms Murphy's view that, by attempting to cope with continuous change by addressing all expectations, principals are generally unable to tackle key elements of their role as leader of learning and teaching. Fullan contends that 'there is no point in lamenting the fact that the system is unreasonable, and no percentage in waiting around for it to become more reasonable. It won't.'[25] Fullan then draws on recent research on leadership, and views about leadership and management advanced by Patterson, Purkey and Parker in the educational setting and by Block in the business setting, to describe a set of conditions which principals should help create within the school.[26] These have much in common with the refined model for self-management we outlined in Chapter 2. He urges a view of the principalship which places emphasis on vision, autonomy, courage, empowerment of others, strategic planning and development of self, and then offers guidelines for action along the following lines:[27]

- avoid blaming others outside the school; work with colleagues to assume control of an agenda within the school;
- while having a large vision, take small steps without excessive planning and management;
- focus on important matters like learning and teaching;
- focus on fundamental matters like the professional culture of the school: empower others and build visions, making the curriculum the focus of professional activity;
- take risks, but be selective and begin on a small scale;
- empower others in the decision-making process on matters of significance, something that will require support in the form of time, money and personnel; build teams of leaders;
- build a vision which includes desired outcomes as well as processes through which those outcomes will be realised;
- set priorities and exclude action on those in the lower order: 'decide what you are not going to do';
- build networks of support inside and outside the school;
- know when to be cautious, especially 'when we don't know the situation, when survival is at stake, following periods of risk and expansion, and when we are in a zero trust environment.'[28]

While Fullan is essentially offering encouragement for principals to work with others in the school community to take charge of their own destiny, a parallel course is for leaders at the centre of a school system to provide the conditions in which this initiative can be taken (although principals should not wait around for this to happen). Thus, in system policy-making, Fullan urges leaders to 'err on the side of autonomy over dependency.'[29]

Summary

Our purpose in this chapter was to highlight some of the major concepts, perspectives, generalisations and theories which are relevant to leadership in a self-managing school and, at the central level, where the intention is to create a system of self-managing schools. Our starting point was to observe the variety of definitions of leadership and concluded, in the words of Duke, that leadership was 'a gestalt phenomenon, greater than the sum of its parts', including the traditional notions of exercising authority and directing others, but also influencing and making activity meaningful. Efforts to identify traits of leaders have turned up a relatively small number which appear to have special significance in the context of the self-managing school: sense of responsibility, concern for task completion, energy, persistence, risk-taking, originality, self-confidence, capacity to handle stress, capacity to influence, and capacity to coordinate the efforts of others in the achievement of purpose. Burns' notion of transformational leadership was embraced. We set out the fundamentals of transformational leadership by adapting and refining some generalisations on leadership which were proposed by Beare, Caldwell and Millikan following a review of recent research. The result was six generalisations which have special relevance to leaders in self-managing schools.

1 Leaders in the self-managing school have the capacity to work with others in the school community to formulate a vision for the school.
2 Leaders in a self-managing school have a coherent personal 'educational platform' which shapes their actions.
3 Vision is communicated in a way which ensures commitment among staff, students, parents and others in the community.
4 There are many facets to the leadership role: technical, human, educational, symbolic and cultural, with the higher order symbolic and cultural facets being especially important in the self-managing school.
5 Leaders in the self-managing school keep abreast of trends and issues, threats and opportunities in the school environment and in society at large, nationally and internationally: they discern the 'megatrends' and anticipate their impact on education and in the school.
6 Leadership which empowers others is central to success in a self-managing school, especially in respect to decision-making.

We then focused our attention on the core activities in the school, namely, learning and teaching, and drew on the state-of-the-art work of Murphy and his framework for specifying the role of the leader of learning and teaching. Murphy described the difference between the actual role of the principal, as described in published accounts of practice in general, and the preferred role as it has emerged in research on practice in 'good schools'. This preferred role was contained in the aforementioned framework. He identified barriers to the adoption of the preferred role, including shortcomings in training and preparation; practices at the system level and norms of the profession that downplay direct involvement in learning and teaching on the part of principals; and the nature of the role itself, with its traditional focus on 'managerial' or 'administrative' aspects, the variety of

small activities which hinder attention to learning and teaching, the absence of a system of rewards and sanctions which the principal may utilise
in relation to learning and teaching, and the influence of teacher unions
which have resulted in matters related to learning and teaching becoming,
increasingly, the subject of award negotiations and collective agreements
(thus tying the hands of principals and other leaders).

We found the approach of Fullan appealing, essentially proposing that
principals and their colleagues at the school level take charge of their own
agenda rather than continue in a state of dependency as they addressed the
virtually impossible task of responding to a constantly changing and complex agenda determined at the central level. He offered some guidelines
for action which, in many respects, provide support for the major elements
of the refined model for self-management.

The framework for the exercise of leadership set out in this chapter
is, on the one hand, a more detailed specification of the refined model and,
on the other, a reaffirmation of its major themes. It is within this framework
that leaders can address the major features of the refined model; thus we
turn in Chapters 4 to 7 to the particular ways in which this can be done.

Part B

Leadership in the Self-Managing School

4 Cultural Leadership: Creating and Sustaining a Culture of Excellence

Moving from near dependency under a centralised arrangement toward autonomy in a system of self-managing schools means a significant change in the way things are done at the school and central levels. This amounts to a change in culture at both levels.

Our purpose in this chapter is to highlight the major characteristics of a school's culture and the role of the leader in creating and sustaining it, and to suggest some strategies for leaders in carrying out this task in a self-managing school. This purpose implies that the culture of a self-managing school differs in important ways from the culture which has sustained schools in the recent past. This may indeed be the case in many settings but no sweeping generalisations of this order are offered. Indeed, two observations should be made at the outset. First, it is unlikely that there will be any change to the core values and beliefs which determine the culture of an already excellent school. Second, any implication of change does not necessarily represent an adverse judgment on accomplishments in the past. On the contrary, the achievements of systems of government or public schools should be the subject of celebration. These achievements have been underpinned by a strong culture which is founded in values and beliefs which should surely be sustained.

Our first task is to provide a framework for describing and analysing the culture of a school. We will then identify what we believe are the characteristics of a culture of excellence in a self-managing school and of those other parts of a school system (centre, region, district) which provide direction and support to self-managing schools. Key concepts in the core of a culture of self-management are defined and some new patterns of leadership behaviour are outlined. The latter are concerned with marketing, efficiency and accountability. Marketing is selected for a detailed illustration of how the culture of a school can be changed in a manner which has educational integrity. We conclude the chapter with ten implications for leadership in the self-managing school.

Describing and Analysing the Culture of a School

Expressed simply, a school's culture is 'the way we do things around here'.[1] One does not search for and then find the culture of a school, one experiences it in ordinary day-to-day activities. In recent years much has been said and written about the topic, but school culture is not a new phenomenon. In many respects we are rediscovering the importance of culture as a factor in accounting for excellence in schools. When considering the leader's role in creating and sustaining a culture, we are to some extent re-focusing on higher order acts of leadership after years of preoccupation with lower order, though nonetheless important, managerial activities.

The recent interest in school culture is, however, based on a rich array of research, and we are now able to describe and analyse the phenomenon using language and a degree of precision which was not readily available in the past. Above all, we can offer some guidelines for those who have the opportunity to exercise leadership.

The notion of culture as 'the way we do things around here' is, of course, just a starting point. We do things in our schools because we have particular values and beliefs about what ought to be done in our schools. These are the intangible foundations of culture. Then there are the tangible manifestations of culture: the words we use, the behaviours we engage in, and buildings and other facilities and artifacts we construct and gather. A more detailed specification of the tangible and intangible provides a framework for describing and analysing the culture of a school. The specification which follows is that proposed by Beare, Caldwell and Millikan and illustrated in Figure 4.1.[2]

The foundations of school culture are defined by answers to questions such as the following. What are the purposes of education? What is the role of the school in achieving these purposes? What knowledge, skills and attitudes are worthy of being addressed in the educational program of the school? What is the relationship between a school and its community; between a school and government? To what extent should the school cater for the needs of all of its students? How should a student learn? What behaviours and relationships are desirable among different members of the school community?

Values, philosophies and ideologies — as reflected in answers to questions such as these — are manifested in a variety of ways. In a verbal sense these include statements of aims and objectives, the curriculum, the language that is used in every day discourse, metaphors, organisational stories, organisational heroes and organisational structures. They are also manifested in behaviour: in rituals, ceremonies, approaches to teaching and learning, operational procedures, rules and regulations, rewards and sanctions, psychological and social supports, and parental and community interaction patterns. Manifestations in materiel include facilities and equipment, artefacts and memorabilia, crests and mottoes, and uniforms.

Figure 4.1. A Framework for Describing and Analysing the Culture of a School

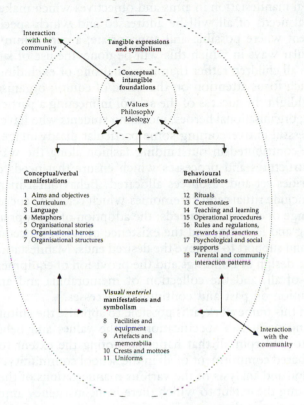

Source: H. Beare, B.J. Caldwell and R.H. Millikan (1989) *Creating an Excellent School*, London, Routledge, p. 176.

We now have the means to describe, in a basic sense, the culture of a school. There are other considerations which may help us determine the strength of a school's culture. Important here is the extent to which different individuals and groups share values and beliefs and are committed to seeing their manifestation in forms such as those listed. Also important is the degree of consistency between values and beliefs and their different manifestations. A strong culture is indicated by all in the school community sharing the same values and beliefs. There will be similar answers to questions such as those we posed earlier, and there will be consistency in the ways these values and beliefs are manifested in a verbal, behavioural or material sense. A weak culture is indicated by fragmentation of values and beliefs and inconsistency in their manifestation.

The strength of a school's culture may be illustrated with reference to equity; that is, the belief that all students ought to receive an education which enables their full potential to be realised, taking account of particular individual circumstances. A strong culture which reflects this belief would see all members of the school community committed to this value, with verbal manifestation in aims and objectives which make clear that the educational needs of all will be addressed and which specify targets for achievement where possible and appropriate; a curriculum which shows the particular ways in which this will be done; the use of language which recognises all children rather than marginalising or excluding some; metaphors which focus attention on the value of equity; organisational stories which highlight the success of the school in meeting a particular challenge in the past; organisational heroes, including students who have, for example, been successful in overcoming some particular disadvantage, and teachers who have contributed in outstanding fashion along the way; and organisational structures and processes which ensure that needs can be identified, priorities set and resources allocated. Behavioural manifestations of strength include rituals and ceremonies which celebrate success in meeting the full range of educational needs; the adoption of appropriate approaches to teaching and learning; and the existence of rules, procedures, rewards, sanctions and support to achieve the desired ends. Manifestations of materiel include the design of buildings and the provision of equipment to cater for the needs of all, and the collection of memorabilia and artefacts which focus attention on past and continuing successes.

Given this framework, it is possible to appraise the culture of a school. The starting point is a specification of the values and beliefs which are intended to underpin all that happens, noting the extent to which these have the shared commitment of all in the school community. Then follows a description and analysis of the various manifestations of these beliefs and values, noting the extent to which there is inconsistency among them. An agenda for action is then set where there is evidence of fragmentation and inconsistency. Some guidelines for action along these lines are offered in another section following consideration of the particular characteristics of culture which are called for in a self-managing school.

A Culture of Excellence in a Self-Managing School

At the heart of a culture lie core assumptions, values and beliefs about things that are important in education and schooling. Most important, of course, will be those related to the very purpose for the school's existence. We believe that this purpose is concerned with the achievement of excellence so the starting point in exploring the role of a leader in creating and sustaining a culture of excellence in a self-managing school is an examination of what is meant by excellence. What follows is, in many respects, the personal educational platform of the authors. There will, of course, be widely differing assumptions, values and beliefs as to what constitutes excellence. The point we make here is that these must be shared and clarified in the school setting. What follows is offered as an illustration.

Values and beliefs

What are the core values and beliefs which underpin the culture of excellence in a self-managing school? Five are identified, with three concerned with ends and two concerned with the means to achieve those ends.

The key values which define ends are quality, effectiveness and equity. An excellent school offers a *quality* education, that is, it pursues goals of great worth. Which goals are of great worth will, of course, be a matter for resolution in each school and school system. Our view is that these goals should include those related to:

- the basics;
- the new basics, including a capacity for problem-solving, creativity, and the capacity for and love of life-long learning and re-learning;
- the arts, defined broadly to include music, drama, dance, song, story, poetry and more;
- spiritual development, also defined broadly, including fundamental considerations of purpose in life and our relationship to others and to our environment;
- personal development; and
- physical development.

In all of these, there is:

- connectedness, reflecting an holistic approach to curriculum design and delivery;
- coherence, in respect to a unifying set of core values; and
- continuity in the sense that the school is a 'centre for communicating civilisation'.[3]

But while there is continuity, there is also responsiveness, locally and nationally: the particular configuration of goals to be addressed in a particular school at a particular time in relation to other places of learning, including the home, will be determined at the school level taking account of 'the larger picture'. This capacity for responsiveness is, of course, one of the features of a self-managing school.

The second key value is *effectiveness*. An excellent school is an effective school; that is, goals of great worth are achieved. But an excellent school must be more than an effective school: there must also be *equity*; that is, goals of great worth are achieved by all, regardless of circumstance. For this we need a framework of policies at the national and state level to ensure that issues of equity are addressed throughout the nation.

These three key values — quality, effectiveness and equity — are concerned with outcomes or ends. There are two key values which are concerned with means — efficiency and empowerment. An excellent school places value on *efficiency*. Such a concern acknowledges that resources are limited, so there must be a capacity to set and re-set priorities, monitor what is accomplished, and make appropriate changes. Some people may be astonished that considerations of efficiency are associated with excellence, but it should be remembered that equity may be at risk if efficiency is ignored: every instance of wastefulness, duplication or unnecessary expenditure may mean that the educational needs of one or more students may not be met. A self-managing school has the capacity to be efficient in this positive sense.

An excellent school will place value on empowering its staff, students, parents and the wider community. Such *empowerment* calls for appropriate involvement in decision-making and decision implementation and the acquisition of knowledge and skill so that involvement will be fruitful.

These five values underpinning a culture of excellence may be incorporated in an 'equation of values', based on a formulation of Fantini:[4]

$$\text{Excellence} =$$
$$\text{Quality} + \text{Effectiveness} + \text{Equity} + \text{Efficiency} + \text{Empowerment}$$

Self-management enhances a school's capacity for responsiveness in addressing issues of quality, provides a framework for achieving efficiency in the allocation of resources, and specifies a role for the community in the decision process.

Tangible manifestation of values and beliefs

As noted in the first section of this chapter, a school's culture is experienced in the tangible manifestation of values and beliefs in words, behaviours and materiel. A strong culture calls for a shared commitment among individuals and groups in the school's community and a high degree of consistency among the different manifestations of culture.

Having defined the key values in a culture of excellence in a self-managing school — quality, effectiveness, equity, efficiency, empowerment — we turn now to the tangible ways in which these may be manifested. To do so in exhaustive fashion would be tedious and unnecessary. An illustration was provided at the outset of the tangible manifestations of equity. A further illustration may be offered for two facets of the values of quality and empowerment:

- in respect to quality, '. . . the particular configuration of goals to be addressed in a particular school at a particular time in relation to other places of learning, including the home, will be determined at the school level'; and
- in respect to empowerment, 'an excellent school will place value

on empowering its staff, students, parents and the wider community. Such empowerment calls for appropriate involvement in decision-making and decision implementation and the acquisition of knowledge and skill so that involvement will be fruitful.'

Examples of the ways in which these values may be manifested include the following, with words in parenthesis referring to the various tangible manifestations of culture:

- a school council has been established, with powers which include the setting of goals, policies and priorities reflecting local needs and opportunities [organisational structures; parent and community interaction patterns];
- elections for school council and the occasion of the first meeting each year receive extensive publicity and are the subject of special celebrations [rituals, ceremonies];
- the aims, objectives, curriculum, policies and priorities of the school reflect the outcomes of decisions by school council and are made available in easily understood form to all with an interest in the program of the school [aims and objectives, curriculum, language];
- staff and parents are involved in professional development programs to ensure that knowledge and skill are acquired for successful involvement in decision making and in the instructional program of the school [psychological and social supports, teaching and learning];
- stories are told and written of outstanding contributions by individual parents and teachers, with buildings and other facilities or special awards named in their honour [organisational stories, organisational heroes, artefacts and memorabilia];
- a special room is set aside for meetings of school council, with appropriate displays of a functional and symbolic nature [facilities and equipment, artefacts];
- the principal establishes procedures to secure the wide involvement of staff in planning and resource allocation [operational procedures];
- the principal recommends a teacher for a senior appointment on the basis of outstanding leadership in fostering community involvement [rewards and sanctions]; and
- the metaphor of community shapes the structures and processes of the school [metaphor].

A Culture of Self-Management

The previous section dealt with what we called a culture of excellence. Except for the attention we gave to empowerment, the major features could be addressed in any school or system, regardless of the extent to which authority or responsibility had been decentralised. We now turn our attention to the questions: Is there a culture of self-management? What are the core assumptions, values and beliefs which underpin such a culture? How is such a culture manifested in a tangible sense? What role can a leader play in fostering a culture of self-management?

We believe that it *is* appropriate to refer to a culture of self-management. Expressed simply, 'there is a way of doing things around here' in a self-managing school and at the central level, in a system of self-managing schools, which is different from the way things are done in schools and school systems where there are more centralised arrangements. The tangible manifestations of a culture of self-management include the various documents which have been prepared in the school setting through collaborative arrangements: charter, mission, vision, policies, plans, budgets and curriculum. One may observe the people at work in these collaborative arrangements. Leaders will utilise different symbols compared to former times or to those in evidence in other places: the words which are used, the behaviours which are manifested, the rewards which are offered reflect the core assumptions, values and beliefs which underpin the culture. Over time these will become routine so that they are, indeed, 'the way we do things around here'. The new teacher or parent or student will become socialised in this way.

Core of the culture of self-management

Underpinning these tangible manifestations of a culture of self-management is a set of assumptions, values and beliefs about the way a school should be managed. These are mainly concerned with relationships: the relationship between a school and government, between a school and its community, between the principal and staff of the school, and among all who make up the school community.

At the core may be something which transcends schools and education, something which is contained in that mysterious word 'subsidiarity'. The principle of *subsidiarity* has been expressed in classical form as follows: 'It is unjust and a gravely harmful disturbance of right order to turn over to a greater society of higher rank, functions and services which can be performed by lesser bodies on a lower plane.'[5] This principle may be a driving force for self-management. Leaders of some school systems which have pioneered the approach seem to have subscribed to it, notably Michael Strembitsky in Edmonton: '. . . whatever can best be done at the school level should be done at that level, as opposed to having those functions performed from a centralised location removed from the scene of the action.'[6]

Another underpinning is the notion of *empowerment*, both as an end and as a process: a leader is committed to providing all in the school community with an opportunity to influence decisions and contribute to the day-to-day activities in the school, according to their interest, expertise or stake in the outcome. Such empowerment is, in itself, a manifestation of an end in education: the full development of each individual. Participation in the processes of decision-making is one tangible manifestation of this element in the core; others include providing people with information and the knowledge and skills so that they can fruitfully and satisfyingly make a contribution.

Trust is a fundamental attitude in self-management. Leaders at the centre and in schools have the confidence that people will be able to contribute to the achievement of educational goals when they are given the opportunity, authority and responsibilities of self-management. There is also acceptance that there will be occasions when errors will be made, failures will be encountered and harm will be done.

A fourth fundamental in the culture of self-management is associated with the notion of *synergy*, another mysterious word which is generally understood to mean, in simple organisational terms, that a group working together can achieve more than individuals working separately. Whether it is an assumption or a value or a belief is unclear, but in a culture of self-management a commitment to the notion seems to underpin the behaviour of the leader. The tangible manifestation is that 'the way things are done around here' includes the ready formation of problem-solving teams, working parties and the like to address key issues which arise from time to time.

Finally, there is acceptance of *responsibility*. Leaders at the school level in a system of self-managing schools are, of course, accepting a higher level of responsibility than their counterparts in more centralised arrangements. The tangible manifestations of responsibility are many and these are reflected in the different phases of the refined model for self-management. Interestingly, these leaders accept that there is a complementary response of accountability.

Some patterns of behaviour reflecting the core

These core assumptions, values and beliefs are manifested in different ways in the various tangible manifestations of the culture of self-management. Some examples were offered above. In all of these there seems to be a spirit of 'we will solve this problem ourselves', or 'we will set our own agenda for action', or 'we can do it' rather than 'let "the system" sort it out', or 'we can't do it'. Once this spirit is manifested, patterns of behaviour which were formerly frowned upon or were regarded as inconsistent with the ideals of education, or were simply never considered at all, become desirable and possible, even though new terminology may be needed in some instances. Three instances are considered here — marketing, efficiency and accountability — three concepts which educators associate with the business sector but which, with a different orientation, may become 'the way things are done around here', with the outcome being a contribution to excellence as conceived in the first section of the chapter.

Marketing.   Consider the concept of marketing. Educators, at least in government or public schools, have generally rejected it or, at most, have been lukewarm. There is, however, a contemporary view of marketing which seems to suit the times and is relevant to self-management. Kotler and his colleagues described five philosophical positions or concepts which might underlie an approach to marketing: the philosophical concept, the product concept, the selling concept, the marketing concept and the societal marketing concept.[7] Most are likely to draw a negative response from educators, especially the selling concept and the marketing concept; the former assuming 'that consumers will either not buy, or not buy enough of, the organisation's products unless the organisation makes a substantial effort to stimulate their interest', the latter assuming 'that the key to achieving organisational goals consists of the organisation determining the needs and wants of target markets and adapting itself to satisfying these more effectively and efficiently than its competitors.'[8]

Kotler and his colleagues acknowledged that traditional views of marketing may be inappropriate 'in an age of environmental deterioration, resource shortages, explosive population growth, world wide inflation and neglected social services' and proposed a 'societal marketing concept' which takes account of the current environment:

> The societal marketing concept holds that the key task of the organisation is to determine the needs, wants and interests of target markets, and to deliver the desired satisfactions more effectively and efficiently than its competitors in a manner that preserves or enhances the consumer's or the society's well-being.[9]

A capacity for marketing along these lines is consistent with patterns of educational management which are emerging around the Western world. At the school as well as system level, educators are being encouraged to determine 'needs, wants and interests' and to design and deliver educational programs which will satisfy these 'in a manner which preserves or enhances the consumer's or the society's well-being.' In the broad sense our 'competitors' are international, given the relationship between education and the economy, but more immediately, they are other school systems or other schools, even other schools within a single system of education. We should be comfortable with this view of 'competitors' if we accept that there should be diversity to meet different 'needs, wants and interests', and if we wish to effect the best possible match between these and the educational programs in a particular system or school. We have devised the following view of marketing in the educational setting, based on the societal marketing concept of Kotler and his colleagues:

> The educational marketing concept holds that a key task of a school system or school is to determine the needs, wants and interests of potential students and their parents, and to design and deliver educational programs more effectively and efficiently than other school systems, where competition for students is occurring or is desired, or among schools within a particular system where such competition will not produce demonstrable harms, all in a manner that preserves or enhances the student's or society's well-being.

This concept of marketing is entirely consistent with a culture of excellence in a self-managing school as we outlined it in the first section of the chapter. An implication for leaders is a capacity to understand and articulate such a view and work accordingly with colleagues and others in the school community. The metaphor of the market may still be a stumbling block; the alternative may be not to label the process at all but to make activities along the lines described a part of normal, day-to-day and year-to-year planning: the needs of potential students are the foci, communication of information is crucial. The important thing is to ensure educational integrity in the day-to-day activities associated with the marketing effort. Over time, people will accept it as 'the way things are done around here'.

We return to this issue in the next section of the chapter, providing guidelines for leadership in changing the culture of a school to accommodate the marketing concept in education.

Efficiency. We included efficiency in our 'equation for excellence' in the first section of the chapter. From our experience it is a notion which is generally rejected by educators who contend that 'educational rather than efficiency criteria should be employed in decision-making in our schools.' Efficiency is associated with cost-cutting in an era of economic rationalism and excessive influence on the part of ministers and treasury officials. Yet the analysis we offered earlier suggests that we must embrace efficiency if we are to achieve equity and effectiveness, given multiple and complex priorities to be addressed with limited resources.

The implication here is that leaders must be able to explain why considerations of efficiency are crucial to the achievement of excellence. In other words, the intangible manifestation of a culture of excellence, as reflected in goals of effectiveness and equity, must be manifested in tangible ways through management processes which ensure that the school is able to identify its priorities, allocate scarce resources, monitor processes and outcomes and, in general, ensure that there is minimum duplication and wastefulness. As we expressed it earlier, every instance of duplication and wastefulness may mean that the needs of one or more students may not be met.

As with the concept of marketing, the terminology may get in the way. It may be preferable simply to describe and practise the process without the image of efficiency. In any event, an understanding of what is involved, a capacity to articulate its purpose, and the ability to implement along the lines illustrated will mean, over time, that there is efficiency in 'the way things are done around here': it becomes part of the culture.

Accountability.   Another tangible manifestation of the culture is accountability, considered here to be a willingness to acquire information about the processes and outcomes of self-management and to share this information with others who are then able to make judgments in the light of expectations as these are reflected in the school's charter, mission, policies, priorities and so on. Like marketing and efficiency, educators have generally reacted negatively to the notion of accountability. In a self-managing school, however, it is a complement of responsibility, and we have incorporated it from the outset in the evaluation phase of the model for self-management. We proposed that schools carry out an annual cycle of major and minor evaluations, with members of program teams playing an important role in the gathering and analysis of information and the writing of simple one- or two-page evaluation reports which are then utilised in identifying needs, setting priorities, formulating plans and allocating resources in the following year.

The intention is to make these simple and manageable approaches to evaluation and accountability such acceptable and normal processes in the school that they become 'the way we do things around here'; that is, they become part of the culture of self-management. From our experience all of this can occur without the use of words like accountability yet, when there is the expectation that schools 'be accountable', those schools which have made the process a part of the culture seem to have no difficulty in responding. Leaders and others should be able to articulate what they are doing in educational terms and to acknowledge, at the same time, that they are accountable. We examine the issue of responsibility and accountability in more detail in Chapter 7.

Changing the Culture at the School Level:
Marketing with Educational Integrity

We return here to the marketing concept to provide an illustration of cultural leadership in the self-managing school. An opportunity for appraisal of a school's marketing capacity is provided. Reference is also made to a recent study in Australia to suggest how a capacity for entrepreneurship may enhance a capacity for marketing.

Becoming comfortable with the concepts of marketing and entrepreneurship

In the last section we adapted a definition of Kotler and his colleagues to offer a contemporary view of the marketing concept in education. Educationists may be concerned about also incorporating the concept of entrepreneurship, given the shoddy view of the entrepreneur which has emerged in recent years. Why, it may be asked, would one wish to advocate an approach to the management of schools which has failed in the manner of many high profile entrepreneurs of the 1980s? On the contrary, an appraisal of the current context of schooling suggests that entrepreneurial schools and entrepreneurial leaders are precisely what are called for. However, we return to the original meaning of the term 'entrepreneurship', one which emphasises creativity, confidence and an enduring contribution to the community. Campbell and Crowther offer the following: 'An entrepreneurial school is one in which there exists a passionate commitment to use all available resources to create new ideas and actions that will enrich the quality of education, and life generally, within the school and its community.'[10]

Nurturing a marketing culture

Using these concepts as a starting point, and adding the approaches to self-management and leadership for self-management that we have developed thus far, it is possible to offer guidelines for the nurturing of a marketing culture in schools that has a high level of educational integrity. We have chosen to present these guidelines in the form of sets of questions which embody the approach we advocate, but which are expressed in a form that invites self-appraisal of a school of interest. These questions are set out in Figure 4.2.

What is suggested here is that marketing and entrepreneurship, two concepts which apparently had little or no place in the lexicon of educational leaders in public schools in the past, are appropriate in the context of schooling in the 1990s. There are strategies available which are not only workable but also eminently desirable to the extent that they have educational integrity. The intention is to enhance the quality of education. The processes involved should enrich the work of educational leaders and create opportunities for educational leadership. They should pervade the self-managing school.

Figure 4.2. Appraising the Marketing Culture of Your School

APPRAISING THE MARKETING CULTURE OF YOUR SCHOOL

SCALE

Rate your school for each of the ten sets of questions according to the following ten-point rating scale:

1–2   A strongly negative response to all questions
3–4   A mixed but mostly negative response
5–6   A mixed but mostly positive response, with matters for major improvement readily apparent
7–8   A positive response to all or most questions, with matters for minor improvement readily apparent
9–10 A strongly positive response to all questions

While the total of your ratings may be of interest, it is the item-by-item analysis which may be of value as a starting point in planning the manner in which the marketing capacity of your school may be enhanced.

1 *EXPECTATIONS OF THE COMMUNITY*

Are the expectations of parents of current and potential students in your community known to the policy group, principal and staff? Are there clearly defined processes for monitoring these expectations?

[RATING FOR OUR SCHOOL =]

2 *MISSION AND PROGRAM*

Does your school have a statement of mission (or equivalent), setting out the primary purpose for the school's existence in your community? Is this statement clearly understood and accepted by the policy group, principal and staff? Is it consistent with the expectations of parents of current and potential students in your community? Is the educational program of your school consistent with the statement of mission and the expectations of parents of current and potential students? Are there clearly defined processes for ensuring alignment of these?

[RATING FOR OUR SCHOOL =]

3 *COMMUNICATION*

Are details of mission and program communicated to parents of current and potential students in an effective manner which makes clear how these are consistent with expectations? Are printed materials and other means of communication of the highest quality or at least consistent with the standard set by competitors?

[RATING FOR OUR SCHOOL =]

4 *SPECIAL AND ORDINARY ACTIVITIES*

Is attention paid to the marketing potential of special events and, especially, ordinary day-to-day activities, including the manner in which students, parents and others in the school community are welcomed; ceremonies are conducted; mail and telephone calls are initiated and answered?

[RATING FOR OUR SCHOOL =]

5 *UNIQUENESS*

Has the uniqueness of your school been identified and addressed in marketing efforts? Have efforts been made to align interests and expertise of particular members of staff with particular facets of the educational aspirations of parents of current and potential students? Where the opportunity arises for the development of school traditions, have appropriate priorities been set as far as attracting staff is concerned⁻

[RATING FOR OUR SCHOOL =]

Figure 4.2. (Cont.)

6 *WIDER COMMUNITY*

Have the interests of the wider community of your school been taken into account in the marketing effort? Have all businesses and industries been included? Is corporate citizenship in education encouraged? Are other agencies in the public sector involved? Old Scholars? Is communication frequent, varied in intent and two-way? Are financial contributions, sponsorship and other forms of support sought in an appropriate manner?

[RATING FOR OUR SCHOOL =]

7 *STRATEGIC LEADERSHIP*

Is there a capacity for strategic leadership among members of the policy group, principal and staff? Are priorities set and re-set according to a continuing appraisal of opportunities and threats; strengths and weaknesses? Does your marketing reflect the outcomes of these analyses? Is there ongoing appraisal of the school program and of the marketing effort?

[RATING FOR OUR SCHOOL =]

8 *HUMAN RESOURCE MANAGEMENT*

Is the development of a capacity for marketing a priority in human resource management in your school? Have those with particular flair and expertise been identified and appropriately involved? Do all members of the policy group and staff, including the principal, appreciate that they have a role to play in the effort? Are marketing implications considered as a matter of course in the planning processes of the school? In these and other respects, is marketing seen as a continuous, ongoing activity rather than a discrete event of short duration for a particular purpose such as increasing enrolments or raising funds?

[RATING FOR OUR SCHOOL =]

9 ENTREPRENEURSHIP

Does the culture of the school foster 'a passionate commitment to use all available resources to create new ideas and actions that will enrich the quality of education, and life generally, within the school and its community'? Is this entrepreneurial spirit encouraged in the marketing effort? Is there a budget allocation for marketing? Is there a sharing of resources among schools which may be viewed as collaborators in a combined marketing effort?

[RATING FOR OUR SCHOOL =]

10 *INTEGRITY*

Is there integrity in the marketing effort? Is there consistency among the values evident in marketing and those underpinning the culture of the school? Is this consistency clearly evident?

[RATING FOR OUR SCHOOL =]

[TOTAL RATING =]

The focus for marketing is the student

To many people, marketing is synonymous with the raising of money, fostering images of fund-raising campaigns, door-knocking, school fairs and other efforts to solicit funds from parents and business. Some teachers do not wish to be involved in such work, finding it inconsistent with what they value in education and a distraction from what they believed to be the most important ways they can make a contribution. We tend to agree with them.

We believe that the primary marketing effort should be focused in very powerful ways on ensuring that each student and, through the student, the parent, receives the very best of educational services. All the guidelines in Figure 4.2 are intended to bring this about. We highlight that concerned with 'ordinary activities', the everyday, ongoing, routine interactions between teachers and students, teachers and parents. If all of these reflect the values embodied in the mission of the school and are appreciated as such by students and their parents, then the reputation of the school will surely grow. In other words, the most important marketing function which can be carried out by teachers is related to learning and teaching.

In many contexts it is possible to demonstrate that more money can be raised through a focus on learning and teaching than through time-consuming and often educationally distracting efforts to raise funds and sponsorship from business and industry. The reason will be apparent from the manner in which schools should be funded in a system of self-managing schools. Depending on the extent to which budgeting has been decentralised to schools and the overall cost of educating a child in a particular nation, school and program, the money brought to the school by the attendance of a single additional student is likely far to exceed that which will be raised by the investment of far greater effort in raising funds by other means. For example, the enrolment of a student may bring an extra $5000 through formulae-driven budget allocations to a school. A modest marketing effort one year may result in the enrolment of ten more students than would otherwise have been expected in a primary school with declining enrolments with current attendance of one hundred. The additional income for the school is thus $50,000. Even allowing for the fraction of an additional teaching position which may be required, the cash in hand is still likely to be far greater than most schools of this size will raise in a relatively sophisticated fund-raising effort in the local community. Of course, in systems where budgeting is still centralised, with grants to schools for school-based budgeting relatively small (for example, $100 per student), one can understand why principals and their colleagues frequently feel the need to spend time and effort in raising funds from other sources.

Accordingly, we invite the reader with an interest in securing additional resources for a school to review the questions set out in Figure 4.2

and note how few, if any, need involve fund-raising in the usual sense. For teachers, they may suggest nothing more than doing the very best job in activities they value most, but to do it in a manner which will make the school an exceedingly attractive place to attend.

Guidelines for fund-raising when appropriate or necessary

We do not suggest that schools should not engage in raising additional funds through donations and sponsorships where this is possible and efforts can be mounted without distracting from learning and teaching. In some places it may be very difficult, if not impossible, to increase enrolments. In other places it may be relatively easy to secure funds from other sources. Our purpose here is simply to shift the focus since, in our experience, many have come to expect that a shift to self-management implies a refocusing of the work of teachers to replace funds which formerly came from government. This expectation has emerged, unfortunately, we believe, when restructuring has occurred in times of financial difficulty and reductions in resource allocations to schools would have occurred regardless of the extent to which self-management had been encouraged.

The two questions in Figure 4.2 which explicitly mention financial contributions and sponsorship are as follows:

- Are financial contributions, sponsorship and other forms of support sought in an appropriate manner?
- In these and other respects, is marketing seen as a continuous, ongoing activity rather than a discrete event of short duration for a particular purpose such as increasing enrolments or raising funds?

We believe that, where necessary, these aspects of the marketing effort can be carried out with the highest educational integrity, maintaining a focus on the central purposes of schooling. The following additional guidelines are offered.

- Identify a range of business and industry which you feel should be part of the school's community. Forward at least one school publication each year. Invite representatives to contribute their expertise in the form of educationally relevant presentations to classes and assemblies. Arrange field visits by students in like manner. In other words, contact and communication should be ongoing; in many instances there will be no request for financial or other material support. The pay-off will be the positive image of the school which, directly or indirectly, may lead to additional enrolments.

- Financial contributions may be sought from time to time but in the context of ongoing linkages of the kind described above. Contributions or sponsorship should preferably link the donor to the school in matters of mutual interest. For example, a company associated in some way with the publishing industry may sponsor the publication of the school charter.

A Culture of Excellence at Central, Regional and Other Levels

While the focus of this chapter is the culture of the school, it is important to note that a culture of excellence in a self-managing school must be supported and sustained by complementary changes at the central, regional and other levels outside the school.

One of the most powerful expressions of this need appeared recently in the review of education in the state of New South Wales in Australia. The government accepted the major recommendation of Brian Scott, who conducted the review, 'to make all schools well-managed, self-determining, self-renewing centres of educational quality'.[11]

It is interesting to highlight statements by Scott in his recent and comprehensive report on school-centred education in New South Wales which make clear that there must be a change in culture at central, regional and other levels outside the school:[12]

- ... the assumption that has guided the development of the New South Wales school system for more than 100 years — namely, that the quality of school education is best achieved through a centralised system — is no longer valid for a modern, technologically-advanced state.

- The inflexibility of the Department's structures and procedures has made it unresponsive to the real educative needs of students and teachers.

- [The Department] ... should be well capable of adapting to the rate of change prescribed. To put the point metaphorically, it *is* possible to teach the elephant to dance, even though a quick-step may be out of the question.

- [The seniormost officers] ... will be agents of change during a fundamental redefinition of corporate culture. Such a role will not come easily to those who have been part of a different culture, in some cases for more than 30 years.

- The past era of highly paternal and protective leadership is no longer culturally appropriate or relevant.

- [There is] . . . a need to turn the Department responsible for school education 'downside up'.

- The Review recommends that the term 'Head Office' should no longer be used, and that 'Central Executive' should be adopted as a more appropriate label . . . .

The cultural dimensions of these statements are evident, especially in respect to values and beliefs, organisational structures and processes, language and metaphor. Notwithstanding the need for a centrally determined framework, the essence of the change may be summarised in the language of a single word, a shift from 'direction' to 'support'. Citing an earlier briefing paper, Scott asserted that: 'The objective of the system's policy-making functions and administrative operations should be to provide excellent support for the classroom teacher. Activities which do not support this objective should be severely questioned.'[13] We return to the nature of change at the system level in Chapter 8 where our concern is how the system can be transformed.

Implications for School Leaders

Several implications for school leaders will already be evident from the illustrations offered thus far. The following list of ten is not exhaustive. It incorporates some guidelines and strategies for those with an opportunity to exercise leadership in creating and sustaining a culture of excellence in a self-managing school.

1 School leaders should be able to describe and analyse the culture of their school. Figure 4.1 may be used as a checklist to carry out this task. The sections of this chapter which dealt with the culture of excellence and the culture of self-management may also be useful in commenting on the extent to which a strong culture has been achieved.

2 In creating and sustaining a culture of excellence, school leaders should be able to work with others in the school's community to define elements of excellence which are relevant to their setting, and to identify and resolve inconsistencies between these and the various manifestations of culture in their schools. They should ensure that the underlying values and beliefs are reflected in a consistent manner in the various tangible manifestations of the school's culture. Here again, Figure 4.1 furnishes a systematic view of the manifestations of culture and may assist in the identification of inconsistencies. For example, a core value in the particular view of excellence in a school may be a quality education along the lines we set out in the first section of the chapter. Yet a review of the awards which are made at the end-of-year graduation may not include recognition of achievement in the arts. The process for determining awards may not yet reflect the value placed on empowerment, suggesting that a more representative awards committee be struck in the following year.

3 **The creation or changing of a school's culture will take time**. Culture is not formulated and implemented like a policy or procedure. School culture is not school climate which can be transient in nature. A strong culture involves a shared commitment and concerted action among individuals and groups in the school's community, and the time for its development will more likely be measured in years or months than in weeks or days. The reasons are evident if we return to the basic notion of school culture as 'the way we do things around here'. We are referring to tangible manifestations of assumptions, values and beliefs in the ordinary day-to-day activities of the school.

4 **Creating or sustaining a school's culture will be more difficult in some settings**. Difficulties may be experienced, for example, where for a variety of reasons the school community is fragmented in its assumptions, values and beliefs about schooling, or when mutually supporting relationships among principal, staff, students, parents and others in the school community are not strong. In these situations we describe the 'social capital' of the school as low. Additional resources, including a commitment of time on the part of the school's leaders, may need to be invested to build the social capital of the school. We take up this issue in more detail in Chapter 6 in the context of educational leadership and the empowering of a community.

5 **School leaders should be able to 'see the larger picture' — discern the megatrends — appreciating that elements of a school's culture are in many respects determined by forces which are shaping society as a whole**. The trend to self-management is itself a reflection of a number of broader trends, or megatrends, in the manner we outlined in Chapter 1. One may not necessarily subscribe to the same view as Naisbitt and Aburdene,[14] but some of the megatrends they see for the 1990s will have a profound effect on schools in the years ahead, especially those concerned with the renaissance in the arts, the role of women in leadership, a wider interest in spirituality and 'the triumph of the individual'. While trends which are more local in nature will be of more immediate importance, the leader in the self-managing school will likely be exploring the various scenarios for the years ahead. This is an aspect of strategic leadership which we describe and illustrate in Chapter 5. We also offer some scenarios in Chapter 9.

6 While our personal view of excellence outlined earlier referred to certain enduring goals in a quality education ('the school is a centre for communicating civilisation'), **the culture of a self-managing school**

must incorporate the need to manage continuing change. Scott acknowledged this reality in making recommendations for change in New South Wales, asserting that' . . . in the modern world we now live in, school education — its curriculum, its teaching and learning processes, and its delivery systems — should be in a continual state of adaptation'.[15] Schools leaders will thus ensure that appropriate structures and processes are in place to manage this state of affairs. The rapid formation of a working party or problem-solving team, even if the response is to buffer the school against a particular change, is simply part of 'the way we do things around here'.

7   While the development of a school's culture calls for the exercise of higher order leadership, **attention must also be given to technical, human and educational facets of leadership**. If the values and beliefs which underpin the culture of the school are indeed to shape day-to-day activities and outcomes for students, then (i) suitable curriculum and approaches to learning and teaching must be devised to meet the full range of student needs, (ii) the resultant educational program must be timetabled and coordinated, and (iii) processes must be put in place to ensure the appropriate involvement of members of the school community in decision-making processes. These are demanding times for those who work in schools, and the necessary psychological support must also be provided. Indeed, the culture of the school should incorporate the value of caring; and 'the way we do things around here' should include a range of pro-cedures, rituals and ceremonies to help people cope. In Chapter 8 we deal with the perils of restructuring in education and show how the culture of the school can be used in this fashion.

8   It is clear that **all of these facets of cultural leadership cannot be exercised by one or a small number of people**. The principal and other leaders should be adept at empowering others. A culture for excellence in a self-managing school will nurture leadership on the widest possible scale. There will be an element of risk-taking in the management of human resources.

9   **School leaders should also be adept in the way they manage symbols**. In this context symbols are those words, actions and rewards which focus the attention of members of the school's community on matters of importance. Opportunities abound if one considers the various tangible manifestations of culture, especially in respect to rituals, ceremonies, stories, heroes, artifacts and memorabilia. In each instance the words or actions or rewards may not, in themselves, contribute in a substantive way to the achievement of educational goals, but they may do so, in an indirect manner, through the meanings they convey. For example, the events school leaders choose to attend send messages to others about what is valued in the school. The words school leaders use in speaking to students and staff have the same effect. Likewise, the manner in which a school receives its visitors — a mental rehearsal of what visitors see and hear

when they arrive at the school and meet its leaders and others — will reveal much about the values of the school and may suggest ways in which changes might be made to reflect a culture of excellence in a self-managing school.

10 'Dramatic consciousness' is important in the exercise of cultural leadership. Leadership of the kind outlined here places an emphasis on the cultural as much as the managerial. Indeed, it is appropriate to broaden our language, including our metaphors, and select from the cultural in the broad, everyday sense of the word. Robert J. Starratt has done this in a recent book in which he introduced the metaphor of drama. He had this to say about the need for a different perspective:

> The language of efficiency and effectiveness cannot be thought to encompass the essence of schooling . . . The perspectives on schooling derived from organisation and management theory need to be seen against a broader and deeper landscape. Such a fresh perspective of schooling emerges when we conceive of schooling as drama. The argument . . . unfolds the human drama inherent in schooling, a drama not only of the individual person attempting to fashion an identity, but a drama of a community in the process of defining itself. The schooling process can be described as drama, not only because of the stakes involved for the players, but also because of the stakes for society.[16]

Starratt utilised this metaphor in suggesting that 'dramatic consciousness' is a requirement for leadership. In brief, this requires a leader to be conscious of the manner in which even the simplest word or action in the course of ordinary, everyday activities can be full of meaning for those who hear or observe. The long-term impact may be profound. The parallels with the so-called 'butterfly effect' in chaos theory are palpable.[17] There is a strong element of dramatic consciousness in our guidelines for marketing in the culture of a self-managing school, especially that which focused on ordinary day-to-day activities: 'Is attention paid to the marketing potential of special events and, especially, ordinary day-to-day activities, including the manner in which students, parents and others in the school community are welcomed; ceremonies are conducted; mail and telephone calls are initiated and answered?'

Summary

Let us return to our opening theme. Expressed simply, a school's culture is 'the way we do things around here'. That way in a self-managing school is likely to be significantly different from that in a school which has not been empowered for self-management. While many manifestations of culture will remain unchanged, we have proposed that the core values underpinning a culture of excellence in a self-managing school should be quality, effectiveness, equity, efficiency and empowerment. The particular way in which these values will be manifested in a particular setting is a matter for decision at the local level. A strong culture will emerge when shared commitment has been achieved and there is a high degree of consistency among the different tangible manifestations of these core values. We then outlined some major features of a culture of self-management, referring to assumptions, values and beliefs related to subsidiarity, empowerment, trust, synergy and responsibility. We suggested that patterns of behaviour which educators have often rejected can become part of this culture, in particular those concerned with marketing, efficiency and accountability. We selected one of these, marketing, to illustate an approach to changing the culture of the school in a manner which has educational integrity.

Ten implications for leaders were identified. In summary, these were concerned with a capacity to describe and analyse a school's culture; a capacity to work with others to build a shared commitment to the cultural underpinnings of the school; recognition that the development of a school's culture will take time; acknowledgment that development of a school's culture will be difficult in some settings; the importance of discerning megatrends and 'seeing the larger picture'; establishing structures and processes to manage continuing change, deploying a wide range of approaches to leadership with the managerial supporting the cultural; empowerment of others and the achievement of 'leadership density'; a capacity to manage symbols to focus attention on matters of importance; and 'dramatic consciousness' in the exercise of leadership.

The power of a school's culture is evident, not only in helping to achieve excellence but also in the manner it provides a buffer against the harmful effects of continuous change. There is thus a challenging and enriching opportunity for cultural leadership in a self-managing school.

5   Strategic Leadership: Taking Charge of the Agenda

In this chapter we focus on the role of the leader in a major process in the refined model for self-management, namely, strategic planning. The outcome is a development plan, often referred to as a strategic plan, a corporate plan or an improvement plan.

As set out in Chapter 2, we found in much of our work in different settings that schools were experiencing difficulty in coping with continuous change and complex agenda, much of which was set outside the school and its community. Our observations in these settings, ongoing experience at Rosebery, and research findings suggest that schools which are coping best have developed a capacity for setting their own priorities.[1] They use a variety of structures and processes which are, essentially, a form of school-based strategic planning. Their response is consistent with Fullan's call, noted in Chapter 3, for initiatives to break the chain of dependency on centrally determined *prescriptions* for change.[2] We acknowledge, of course, that centrally determined *frameworks* are necessary and desirable; we are referring to what is possible when systems of schools are committed to the approach we describe as self-management and when schools seize the opportunity which is thereby afforded to 'take charge of their own agenda'.

Our first task is to define in operational terms what we mean by strategic leadership. We turn then to a model for strategic planning which is suitable for use in schools. We provide illustrations from our own work and offer guidelines for others who may wish to adapt the approach to their own settings.

Strategic Leadership

Strategic leadership is distinguished from ongoing, routine, day-to-day leadership on three dimensions: time, scale of issue and scope of action. As far as time is concerned, strategic leadership is more concerned with the longer term than the shorter term. Issues tend to be national and international as well as local in their scale. Scope of action tends to be more school-wide than program-focused. By implication, the outcomes are strategies for action, being more at the policy level in respect to their specification of broad guidelines for action.

Strategic leadership is best defined in operational terms, that is, by listing what leaders actually do when they are engaged in strategic leadership. For the school as a whole, principals exercise strategic leadership by:

- keeping abreast of trends and issues, threats and opportunities in the school environment and in society at large, nationally and internationally; discerning the 'megatrends' and anticipating their impact on education generally and on the school in particular;
- sharing their knowledge with others in the school's community and encouraging other school leaders to do the same in their areas of interest;
- establishing structures and processes which enable the school to set priorities and formulate strategies which take account of likely and/or preferred futures; being a key source of expertise as these occur;
- ensuring that the attention of the school community is focused on matters of strategic importance;
- monitoring the implementation of strategies as well as emerging strategic issues in the wider environment; facilitating an ongoing process of review.

Leaders other than principals will exercise strategic leadership in a self-managing school, especially leaders of program teams. The scale of action may have a focus on individual programs, but school-wide considerations are paramount.

Structures and Processes for the Exercise of Strategic Leadership

We have observed a variety of approaches to strategic planning in schools. In *The Self-Managing School* we described a rudimentary form in use at Rosebery, essentially the setting of priorities among different policies and programs according to an appraisal of local needs and expectations at the system level. Since the time of publication, as we noted earlier, centrally determined expectations have tended to overwhelm the local agenda. Some schools have adopted approaches to strategic planning which have been used in the private sector. In searching for a framework to guide schools in general, we have found the approach advocated by John Bryson to be most helpful. His interest was in the needs of public and non-profit organisations.[3]

We have made adaptations to Bryson's approach so that it is consistent with our refined model for self-management. There are seven stages in the adaptation as illustrated in Figure 5.1.

- formulating a plan for strategic planning;
- reviewing the school charter to clarify mission;
- reviewing the school charter to clarify authority;
- identifying scenarios for the likely impact on the school of changes in its external environment, and the threats and opportunities associated with each;
- appraising resources, current strategies and recent outcomes to determine strengths and limitations;
- generating a list of strategic issues, in order of priority, on the basis of strengths, limitations, opportunities and threats;
- formulating strategies for action for each of the strategic issues;
- describing a vision for the school when all strategies have been successfully implemented.

Two matters are noteworthy before we describe each stage of the approach. The first is related to purpose. The process should not be viewed as an additional demand on schools which are already overloaded. The intention is to lighten the load and reduce dependency on others; it should foster a sense of regained control and empowerment. If these are not the effects, then whatever procedures have been employed should be refined or replaced. Consistent with our guidelines in *The Self-Managing School*, there should be a minimum of paperwork. The second is related to the nature of the model. We describe eight ongoing interrelated tasks rather than eight discrete, linear events. While particular activities involving a limited number of people might be organised from time to time to focus attention on each of these tasks, it is desirable, indeed inevitable, that informal discussions involving many people occur continuously.
What follows is a brief description of the eight stages of the process, with particular attention being given to the role of the principal and other leaders. Illustrations in two settings will then be provided.

Formulating a plan

The first stage is the formulation of a plan for strategic planning. Given that this is a policy-level task, it is likely that this will be prepared for and be approved by the policy-making group. Like any other plan, it will specify what will be done, when it will be done, by whom it will be done and with what resources. Implied here is that the outcomes of the process will be determined at this point. In general, we recommend that the written outcome, which we describe as a development plan, be a relatively short

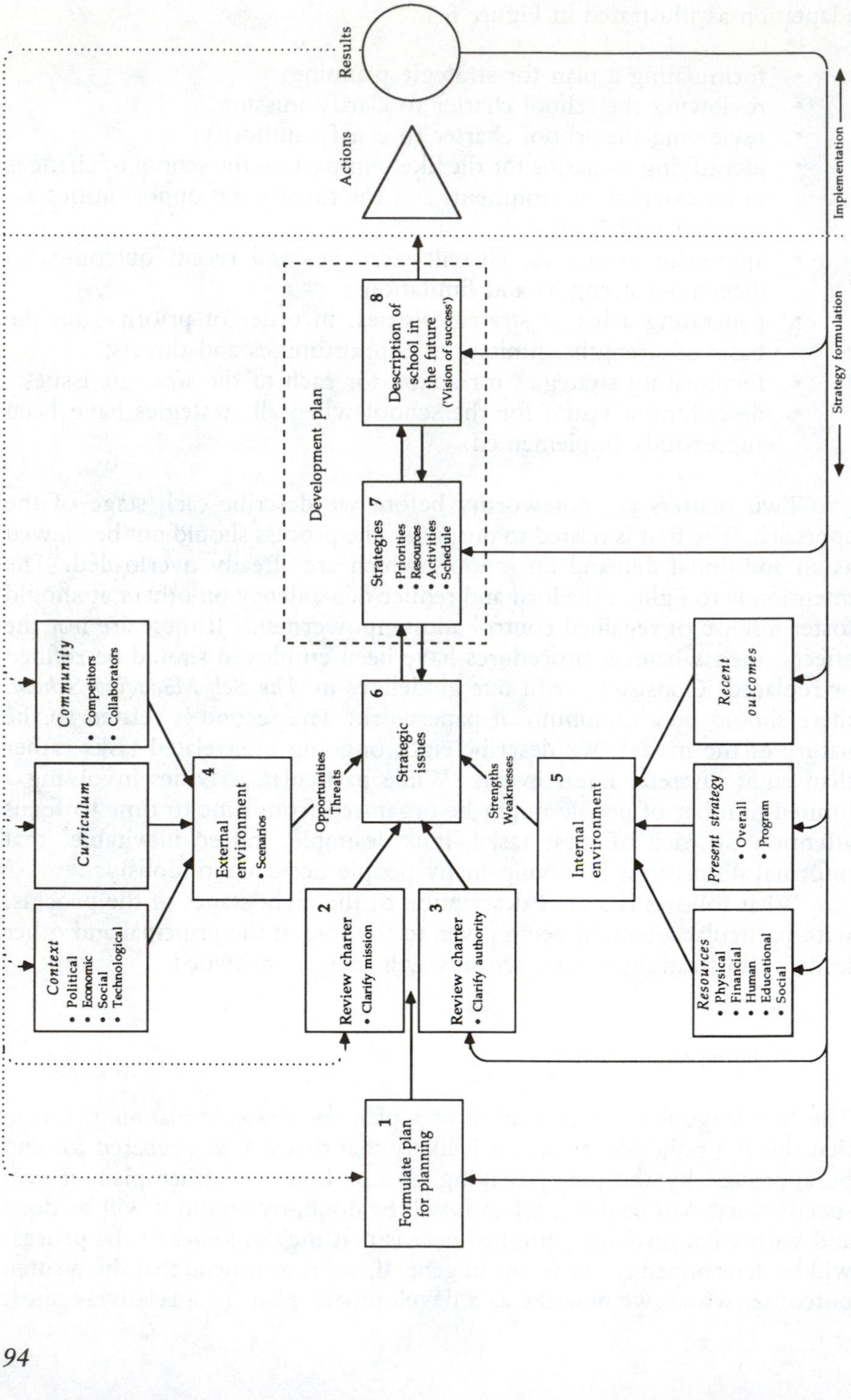

Figure 5.1. A Process for Strategic Planning

Results

Actions

Implementation

Strategy formulation

Development plan

8 Description of school in the future ('Vision of success')

7 Strategies
- Priorities
- Resources
- Activities
- Schedule

6 Strategic issues

Opportunities / Threats

Strengths / Weaknesses

4 External environment
- Scenarios

Community
- Competitors
- Collaborators

Curriculum

Context
- Political
- Economic
- Social
- Technological

2 Review charter
- Clarify mission

3 Review charter
- Clarify authority

5 Internal environment

Recent outcomes

Present strategy
- Overall
- Program

Resources
- Physical
- Financial
- Human
- Educational
- Social

1 Formulate plan for planning

Source: Adapted from Bryson's model for public and non-profit organisations; J. Bryson (1988) *Strategic Planning for Public and Non-profit Organisations*, San Francisco, Jossey Bass, Ch. 3.

document, no longer than about ten pages, with a single-page summary for easy communication to all in the school community. This document will describe in general terms the issues to be addressed and the strategies to be employed, including specification of responsibility, estimates of resource needs, and schedules for implementation. A brief description of what the school will be like when the strategies are successfully implemented should also be included. There is no place for detailed prescriptions of particular courses of action; indeed, much of this sort of detail need never be committed to paper. There should also be agreement about the language of the development plan. We suggest simple descriptions of unresolved matters of concern (issues) and courses of action (strategies) in language which will be readily understood by all in the school community.

It is important in this initial planning stage to determine who will be involved and the manner of their involvement. We recommend the same criteria we offered for determining involvement in working parties during the policy-making process: 'Who has a stake in the outcome?' and 'Who has expertise to offer?' A relatively small group may coordinate the process and prepare drafts plans, but there should be consultation with different individuals and groups in the school community, either with the whole or with representative samples of the whole when numbers are large. Key events such as strategic planning seminars should be scheduled. It is intended that strategic planning be dynamic, so the schedule should include the period of time each year when the development plan will be refined and updated.

The roles of key people should be specified, especially those of the principal and other leaders who will be expert sources of information as well as participants in the decision-making process.

Reviewing the charter of the school

Bryson suggested two stages following the formulation of the plan for strategic planning. One is to review the 'mandate' of the organisation, that is, to review the extent to which the school has authority and responsibility. This constitutes a preliminary examination of the external environment. The second is to review the mission of the school, constituting a preliminary examination of the internal environment. In our refined model for self-management, we have proposed a charter which will integrate these considerations, with a school charter defined in Chapter 2 as a document to which both government and school policy group (council, board) have given their assent, containing a summary of the centrally determined framework of priorities and standards; an outline of the means by which the school will address this framework; an account of the school's mission, vision, priorities, needs and programs, together with an overview of the strategies which will be followed in addressing them; reference to key decision-making processes and approaches to program evaluation; all reflecting the culture of the school and an intended pattern of action in the medium to longer term. We should note here that the strategic plan differs from the charter in one important respect: the former is intended to address issues in the medium term, with priorities reviewed and refined annually; the latter is intended to be relevant for a longer period, say three to five years or more, without annual review.

We acknowledge that most schools will not presently have a document along the lines of a school charter, so our description of this stage of the process will consider the two stages which were identified by Bryson.

Clarifying Authority and Responsibility. The purpose of the whole endeavour is to help schools 'take charge of their own agenda', within a centrally determined framework of goals, priorities and requirements for accountability. The extent to which a school has the authority and responsibility to do this must be made clear to all at the outset, and throughout the process as different people become involved in the process. The principal is likely to be the most appropriate person to brief other leaders and participants in general. These other leaders will, in turn, brief members of their groups and organisations.

Reviewing the Mission of the School. In similar fashion, it is important that participants in the process are aware of the school's mission, defined in Chapter 2 as its purpose for existence in a particular community. A statement of mission usually includes major beliefs about the particular kind of schooling to be offered and the broad goals which will give shape to its program. It will preferably contain some words which establish its context, noting particular characteristics and educational needs of the community in which it is located. Mission statements come in various forms but, in our view, are best expressed concisely, in less than one hundred words, so that they can be reproduced easily to provide a focus of attention in important documents and at times and places which will gain the interest of all in the school community. The formulation of a development plan is one such occasion when the mission statement should be the focus of attention.

A review of mission is important in strategic planning because it provides a starting point for participants to identify those aspects of the school's current operations which may no longer be of sufficient priority to warrant a commitment of resources. It may also help identify gaps in the program which need to be addressed in the development plan. It may also give rise to a review of the mission statement itself and, in the longer term, the school charter, something which participants may feel needs to be done before work on the development plan can proceed. Major refinements can, of course, be time-consuming, and it may be appropriate to proceed with a draft of a refined mission statement or charter.

Some schools may not have a mission statement or charter. Instead, there will be a variety of documents containing goals or aims of the school, statements of philosophy or belief, or a collection of policies. These may serve the same purpose as far as offering a starting point for strategic planning is concerned. If the school has none of these documents and no mission or charter, we recommend that time be invested at the outset in formulating at least a draft mission statement so that the strategic planning process can proceed. We have found in our work in different settings that much progress can still be made with informal understandings and loosely worded statements, even gaps which, in a rational sense, appear serious. In fact, the formulation of a mission statement might come easily after a strategic plan has been formulated. The various discussions, debates and decisions may focus the attention of participants on matters of importance in a much more effective manner than attempting to prepare a mission statement before participants have had a chance to come to grips with the purpose, priorities and programs of the school.

Identifying scenarios: threats and opportunities in the external environment

The first three stages are essentially laying the foundation for the strategic planning process. The first major task is likely to be the identification of scenarios which arise from a scanning of the external environment, and it is in this area that strategic leadership is required of the principal. Environmental scanning occurs in three interrelated areas we will describe simply as context, curriculum and community.

1 **Context**. Scanning the context for education calls for the principal and other leaders to take account of trends and issues which may be broadly described as political, economic, legal, technological, cultural and demographic. Strategic leadership calls for awareness of the ways in which changes in the political-governmental sphere may affect the school. Related to these will be the likely impact of economic factors. At the time of writing Australia is in the most serious recession since the depression. There have been general effects experienced by all schools but also local effects associated, for example, with the collapse of financial institutions which served large numbers of people in particular towns and cities, major job losses in the automobile and mining industries, and a collapse in the international wool market. Local effects have included loss of enrolments, increase in transiency rates, and inability of parents to meet the costs of books and other materials. These may not, however, constitute long-term trends. Those which have long-term significance include major changes in political and economic alignments such as the emergence of the European Economic Community and nations in the Pacific Rim as powerful associations of interests. There may be long-term implications of the Gulf War

as far as schools are concerned, including changes to curriculum and changes to attitudes and patterns of student behaviour in relation to nations and students from nations which participated in or were affected by the war.

Legal factors include matters related to family law and the implications of equal opportunity legislation. Political, economic and legal factors combine in matters broadly described as industrial. It seems that schools in most countries under consideration in this book are constrained in their planning by an increasing array of conditions which serve, on the one hand, to ensure uniformity in efforts to provide teachers with a secure and safe working environment but, on the other hand, to limit the degree of freedom in school self-management. In the United States there is a trend toward relaxation of these constraints, with provision for 'waiver' under clearly defined circumstances in school systems which have embraced the notion of self-management. We take up these matters in Chapter 8 in the context of system-level change.

Technological developments relate especially to computers and telecommunications and the opportunity they provide for enhanced management of information in learning and teaching and the support of learning and teaching. Cultural and demographic changes may be local in their effects, but there are broader trends about which principals and other school leaders should be aware, including the values, beliefs and practices of people from different ethnic and religious backgrounds and long-term demographic trends and associated enrolment projections for particular communities as well as the nation in general.

In general, the scanning of the context for education calls for a capacity to discern what were described in Chapter 1 as megatrends as well as particular trends and issues which are affecting a nation, state or local community. The implication is that principals and other school leaders will read widely, will have a wide range of other sources of information, and will engage their colleagues and others in the school community in discussion of these matters and their likely impact on the school. Special seminars, workshops, meetings or retreats which form part of a plan for strategic planning provide opportunities for the formal presentation of information along these lines.

2 Curriculum. Most of these contextual factors have a direct impact on education. For example, technological developments have major implications for the curriculum and approaches to learning and teaching. International developments in matters related to the economy have major implications for the responsiveness of business and industry which call, in turn, for responsiveness in schools. These relationships were explored in more detail in Chapter 1. However, principals and other school leaders should be knowledgeable about trends and issues in education in a more specific sense, especially in relation to learning and teaching. There have been major advances in knowledge in recent years of a kind which makes it possible to bring rhetoric to reality as far as meeting the needs of all students is concerned. For many school leaders, the preparation for teaching received in pre-service programs is inadequate, and ongoing in-service or staff development programs are required to update their knowledge. We explore needs and programs in more detail in Chapter 6. What we describe here is essentially the enhancement of the professional culture of the school so that the principal and others are continually learning about their profession, consistent with Holly and Southworth's image of 'The Developing School'.[4]

A plan for strategic planning should include events where advances in knowledge about learning and teaching are shared and addressed in the setting of priorities. However, if what we describe is to become part of the culture of 'the developing school', these activities should be more or less continuous in the day-to-day life of the school.

3 Community. Our view of the self-managing school includes the immediate community of principal, teachers and other staff, students, parents and others who live or work in the neighbourhood. We include matters related to their interests in an appraisal of the internal environment of the school. As far as the external environment is concerned, scanning of community refers more broadly to the attitudes of the community towards education and schooling in general. A characteristic of society in the later years of this century in most countries under consideration is a more active involvement of members of the community. In some instances this is a return to relationships which prevailed in the past. Indicators of change include the emergence or re-emergence of school councils or school boards, and a removal of enrolment or zoning restrictions which require students to attend particular schools, regardless of their interests and wishes or those of their parents. At a central level, governments are generally more responsive than before to the concerns of parents and other interest groups such as business and industry, in contrast to a situation which prevailed for much of this century when ministers relied on the permanent head of the school system to provide policy advice. The implication for principals and other school leaders in the self-managing school is the need to keep abreast of community interests and concerns as they relate to education and schooling.

Included in the community aspect of this scanning of the external environment are other schools and organisations which provide support. Like Bryson, we classify these broadly as competitors and collaborators. What occurs in other schools in systems of government and non-government schools as well as in independent schools is relevant to the self-managing school. To express it bluntly, many of these schools are competitors. If the self-managing school has a mission which makes it special within the community of schools in a particular town or city, it is important to know about the programs in other schools so that points of similarity or difference can be addressed and appropriate marketing initiatives can be prepared. We take a positive view of marketing here, one which has educational integrity in the manner described in Chapter 4. In similar fashion, leaders in the self-managing school need to take account of trends and issues in their educational communities as they concern the work of organisations which can provide support for schools: these might be viewed as collaborators. In some countries there is a decline in the provision of such services, described in Chapter 1 in the context of declining resources and, in some instances, budgetary crises. Monitoring such developments, identifying other sources of potential support and identifying likely future developments are all part of this aspect of strategic leadership.

So far we have referred to the need for school leaders, especially the principal, to engage in environmental scanning in three areas described simply as context, curriculum and community. Essentially this is a matter of being knowledgeable about trends and issues in these areas and bringing these to the attention of others in the school's community. In order to make use of this information in a development plan, it is important to sense the extent to which these represent threats or opportunities to the school as far as the achievement of its mission is concerned. Some are clearly threats, for example, a decline in enrolments and resources arising from an economic recession. Advances in technology present opportunities for schools to improve the management of information in learning and the support of learning. The extent to which these constitute threats and opportunities is aided by the process of scenario writing. Essentially this involves asking a series of questions such as 'If this happens, what is the effect on our school?' For example, 'if the nation continues to experience an economic recession, if the mining industry which supports our community remains in decline, if non-government schools continue to lose students to government schools, then the effect on our school will be. . . .' The outcome of this kind of analysis will be a series of strategic issues which may be addressed in the development plan. These issues will also be shaped by an appraisal of the school's internal environment in the manner described below.

An analysis of threats and opportunities and the identification of strategic issues are tasks which lend themselves to a seminar or workshop style of activity. As we have made clear in several places, it is important that discourse on these matters be ongoing, but a formally organised event of this kind provides a focus for deliberations and a further opportunity to bring together key representatives of different groups in the school's community.

Appraising the school's resources, current strategies and recent outcomes: strength and limitations in the internal environment

An intention of strategic planning is to identify issues, set priorities and formulate strategies to assist the school address its charter or fulfil its mission. A critical consideration will be the extent to which the resources of the school, the strategies currently in place and its achievements to date make a contribution to this end.

Resources. In appraising the resources of the school, the principal and other leaders will take account of the various kinds of capital: physical, financial, human, educational and social. Physical capital refers to the buildings, grounds and equipment. Financial capital includes the reserves built up by the school including, where appropriate, any foundations which have been established, current and anticipated levels of fees and grants, including recurrent grants from governments and other public authorities. Human capital refers to the knowledge and skills of teachers, support staff and others who are in a position to assist the school. Educational resources include the library and other learning support services, computers and telecommunication facilities inside the school and elsewhere in the wider educational community. Social capital, a concept popularised in recent years by Coleman and Hoffer,[5] was defined in Chapter 4 in terms of the strength of mutually supporting relationships among principal, teachers and other staff, students, parents and other members of the school's community.

Current Strategies. Current strategies include the curriculum of the school; approaches to learning and teaching; structures and processes for planning, problem-solving, decision-making and evaluation, including the organisational structures of the school; and how the services of individuals and units elsewhere in the system and in the wider educational community are utilised.

Recent Outcomes. Information about the manner in which the school is currently achieving its mission, in a general sense and in the various learning programs in the school, is important in the strategic planning process. In addition to results on a variety of internal and external tests, reports of minor and major program evaluations conducted on a cyclical basis as outlined in *The Self-Managing School* will also be utilised. A variety of other indicators may be utilised, including retention rates, absentee rates, staff turnover, measures of school climate, placement and further education of graduates. Matters related to the use of indicators are explored further in Chapter 7; the point we make here is that there will be an array of information about recent outcomes which will assist those involved in strategic planning to identify issues to be addressed in the next stage of the process.

It will be apparent that a number of leaders will be involved in appraising the internal environment of the school. In addition to the principal, leaders of all program units and others with special responsibilities across the school will be able to contribute. Much of the information described above will be known to many on a more or less continuous basis, but, as in the appraisal of the external environment, it is worthwhile to include in the plan for strategic planning one or more seminars, workshops or retreats when all of this information is brought together in formal fashion. The intention is then to assess the current strengths and limitations of the school.

Establishing a priority among issues of strategic significance

At this stage of the process those engaged in strategic planning will have at hand a variety of scenarios, being the outcome of an appraisal of the external environment, with attendant threats and opportunities for the school; and some sense of the strengths and limitations of current operations, being the outcome of an appraisal of the internal environment. The task now is to make a list of strategic issues which are essentially a set of unresolved matters of concern which may warrant action in the future according to the priorities attached to each. These issues may take several forms, implied by descriptions of strengths, limitations, opportunities and threats. Expressed in the form of questions, these issues may be identified in the following manner. In the light of the information gathered thus far:

- What opportunities are presented to the school arising from changes in context (political, economic, legal, technological, cultural and demographic), curriculum (including approaches to learning and teaching and the support of learning and teaching) and community (including matters related to current and potential competitors and collaborators) which can be taken up by the school to enable it more effectively to achieve its mission?
- What threats are presented by changes in context, curriculum and community which must be countered or buffered by the school in order that it can maintain its progress in achieving its mission?
- What internal limitations are evident among resources, current strategies and recent outcomes which may serve to place boundaries on the extent to which the school can take up opportunities or counter threats?
- What internal strengths will assist the school in taking up opportunities or countering threats?

Responses to these questions might be invited from all who have participated in the process thus far, but a crucial task of the principal and other school leaders will be to formulate a concise list of issues which should be addressed in the strategic plan and to establish an order of priority for action. The criteria for establishing such an order may include urgency, especially in relation to countering a threat or overcoming a limitation, and potential contribution to the achievement of the school's mission, especially in relation to opportunities and strengths. The views of a wider group might be sought in establishing an order of priority. In the final analysis, the decision on the order will be taken by the policy group, but leaders will play a crucial part because of the expertise they will bring to bear.

While there are no hard and fast guidelines on the matter, we do not recommend a long list of priorities. Very stringent tests should be applied to keep these to a minimum, especially in respect to those issues arising from demands outside the school's community which are not related in a significant way to the achievement of the school's mission. A maximum in the range of five to eight is offered as a rough guide to what can be managed in addition to meeting the ongoing routine needs of the school.

Formulating strategies for action

The next task is to formulate strategies for each of the issues for which a priority has been set. In each instance there will be appraisal of alternatives in the light of available resources and, for the preferred alternative, the formulation of a broad plan for action with the usual specification of what will be done, by whom it will be done, when it will be done and so on. It is likely that, for some issues, action will proceed in stages over several years.

We stress that this need be only a broad plan, with detailed specifications worked out as part of the annual planning process. The intention at this point is to prepare the strategic plan which, as stated at the outset, is a relatively brief document of no more than ten pages, capable of summary in a maximum of one page.

It is possible and desirable to involve a number of people in this task. Small working parties can be formed to prepare the broad plan for each of the strategic issues. The same guidelines offered for working parties in the policy-making process might be followed: a maximum of six to eight chosen or volunteered according to stake and expertise, with information gathered from others when necessary. Given that the development plan for the school as a whole should normally not exceed ten pages, then each broad plan need not exceed one page if, say, six strategic issues have been included among priorities to be addressed. The remaining pages are devoted to a summary of strengths, limitations, opportunities and threats identified in earlier work, together with other contextual information and a concluding statement of a visionary nature.

Describing the future: vision in strategic planning

The final task is to describe what the school will be like when all of the strategies have been successfully implemented. This is an important part of the process because it will demonstrate the worth of the plan, build confidence in the capacity of the school to 'take charge', and foster commitment to the ongoing activities which follow adoption. What we are describing is, essentially, a vision within a vision.

The task of writing this vision can be given to a small representative group or to a single individual. The outcome should be a concise, well-written, attractive and reassuring statement, thus strong writing skills will be required. It will be incorporated in the development plan, possibly as a concluding statement, as it is adopted by the policy group.

The Dynamic Nature of Strategic Planning

Thus far we have considered the process of strategy formulation. Strategy implementation and strategy review are also included in the total process for strategic planning as illustrated in Figure 5.1. We do not go into the details of these aspects of the approach since they do not differ in any significant respect from policy implementation and program evaluation. We do, however, wish to draw attention to the dynamic nature of strategic planning.

Once approved, the development plan will provide a framework for annual planning for whatever period of time is covered by the former. It may be three to five years. It should be understood, however, that the development plan can be reviewed at any time, certainly annually, given that change in both external and internal environments are likely to be continuous. New issues may arise, new priorities may need to be set. Herein lies the merit of a relatively short document and a widely dispersed capacity for strategic leadership. The task of ongoing review and refinement should not be a burden; indeed, as noted from the outset, the intention is that the process is a means of helping cope with continuous change by affording an opportunity for the school to 'take charge of its own agenda'. The point is that, at any moment in time, the school has before it a development plan which provides a framework for the annual plan.

Managing the process of review will be a key responsibility for the principal or another leader to whom such responsibility has been delegated. All leaders will be exercising strategic leadership in an ongoing fashion by continuously focusing the attention of all in the school community on matters of strategic importance.

Illustrations of Strategic Leadership

Two illustrations of strategic leadership are provided. The first is contained in an account of the preparation of a development plan at St Anne's and Gippsland Grammar School in Sale, Victoria, Australia. The second is set at Rosebery District High School in Rosebery, Tasmania, the school which pioneered the approach incorporated in the model for self-management.

St Anne's and Gippsland Grammar School

St Anne's and Gippsland Grammar School is an independent, non-government school in the Victorian country town of Sale. It is, by its nature, a self-managing school, although it must operate within government guidelines in respect to the use of public funds it receives and to the registration it must secure. The school is incorporated as a company. Its governing body is a council which is responsible for property, financial management and policy direction. The principal is responsible for the implementation of policies and decisions of council and for all activities associated with the internal management of the school. The school was established in 1971 with the amalgamation of St Anne's Church of England Girls' Grammar School, founded in 1924, and Gippsland Grammar School, founded in 1961. It is a co-educational school with an enrolment in 1990 of 817 students, 243 in the Junior School (Preparatory to Year 6) and 574 in the Senior School (Years 7–12).

The school is selected for illustration because it utilised an adaptation of the Bryson approach in the preparation of a development plan (known at St Anne's and Gippsland Grammar School as the strategic plan) as illustrated in Figure 5.1. In our view, this adaptation, along with the style of strategic leadership adopted by the principal and others, is an exemplar for any self-managing school. What follows is a brief account of what took place, with illustrations of key outcomes, including a summary of the development plan as it was approved by the school council.

In 1988 the school council, through its chairman, The Right Reverend Colin Sheumack, Bishop of Gippsland, expressed its wish for a development plan, but plans for its preparation were not fully realised until the appointment of a new principal, Campbell Bairstow, in 1990. The adaptation of the Bryson approach was selected after consultation with Brian Caldwell, who served as facilitator of the process. Caldwell met initially with Campbell Bairstow and the Head of Junior School, Mrs Elizabeth Board. A time frame was established, commencing with a one-day seminar in late August, concluding with the adoption by the school council in mid-December of a development plan for 1991–95.

The starting point was a one-day residential strategic planning seminar which commenced on a Friday evening and concluded on Saturday evening.

Participants included fifteen members of the school council, the principal and other senior school leaders, and representatives of teachers, old scholars and the school foundation. Including a secretary and facilitator, a total of thirty-two people attended. A process similar to that illustrated in Figure 5.1 was carried out in seven sessions, each of one and one-half hours duration. The following is a summary.

- The chairman of the school council opened the seminar with a statement on the decision to prepare a development plan and a summary of preparations for the event. (This was in essence a report on the stage described in Figure 5.1 as 'formulating a plan'.)
- A review of 'The Nature and Purposes of the School' was carried out in groups broadly representative of the school community. When combined with the articles of incorporation, this statement matches what we described in Chapter 2 as a school charter. (This activity corresponds to the stage described in Figure 5.1 as 'reviewing the charter of the school'.)
- The principal gave a presentation in which he highlighted features of the external environment, dealing mainly with political, economic, social, technological, demographic and cultural factors from a national, state and local perspective. Participants then worked in their groups to prepare scenarios which summarised their views of the likely impact on the school of threats and opportunities that may arise from these factors. Three scenarios were prepared and shared. (The presentation and subsequent activity correspond to the task described in Figure 5.1 as 'identifying scenarios: threats and opportunities in the external environment'.)
- The principal and five other senior school leaders then gave short presentations on the internal environment of the school, these corresponding to matters classified in Table 5.1 as resources, current strategies and recent outcomes. Participants were then invited to identify strengths and limitations which should be taken into account in listing issues to be addressed in the development plan. A classification was provided, namely, curriculum, teaching, learning, climate, culture, finance, staff and buildings. (These presentations and activities correspond to the task described in Figure 5.1 as 'appraising the school's resources, current strategies and recent outcomes: strengths and limitations in the internal environment'.)
- Participants were then invited to identify issues to be addressed in the development plan, taking account of discussions related to external and internal environments. Six sets of issues were identified in the broad areas of finance, curriculum, facilities, marketing, teaching and learning, management and structure. These issues were expressed in the form of questions, for example, 'How can the transition between Junior and Senior School be managed more

effectively?', 'How can the curriculum in Years 7 and 8 be designed and delivered more effectively?' and 'How can communications within the school and between the school and community be enhanced?' (This activity corresponds to the task described in Figure 5.1 as 'establishing a priority among issues of strategic significance', although a priority order was not nominated at this point.)

- Participants then re-formed in teams according to their expertise (in contrast to the previous grouping which furnished a representative cross-section of interests in each group). Issues were assigned for the preparation of draft plans for action. Particular attention was given to targets, sequence of activities, responsibilities, time line and, where possible, estimated costs. These drafts were expressed in point form in about half a page in each instance. (This task corresponds to that described in Figure 5.1 as 'formulating strategies for action'.)

- The final task in the one-day seminar was to prepare vision statements describing what the school would be like when strategies had been successfully implemented. Each of five cross-sectional teams prepared such statements. This activity, coming near the end of an intensive day, tended to be uplifting and celebratory, with the outcomes symbolising the success of the event and confidence that the venture would bear fruit. (This activity corresponds to that described in Figure 5.1 as 'describing the future: vision in strategic planning'.)

A small team consisting of the chairman of the school council, the principal, the head of the junior school and the facilitator, prepared a plan for taking the draft development plan forward, culminating in submission of a final draft to the school council some ten weeks later. It was agreed that the draft would be circulated among all participants, refined, then circulated among all staff. Working parties would be formed to prepare a more detailed specification of development plans, with the principal and a representative working party to review all and establish an order of priority.

These plans were followed in the manner described. A final meeting of the principal, the head of the junior school and facilitator resulted in a one-page summary of the development plan which was approved by the school council. Details in plans for implementation are considered the responsibility of the principal. An excerpt from the one-page summary setting out the major strategies is contained in Figure 5.2. The total length of the development plan, including the one-page summary, is nine pages. Each element in the plan consists of brief statements on expected outcomes, proposed action, responsibility and cost. Expected dates of completion are provided.

Figure 5.2. Excerpts from Summary of Development Plan at St Anne's and Gippsland Grammar School

---

THE ST ANNE'S AND GIPPSLAND GRAMMAR SCHOOL
DEVELOPMENT PLAN 1991–95

SCHOOL DEVELOPMENT

A School Development Officer will be appointed in 1991 to manage the tasks of public relations, fund-raising, coordination of activities of Foundation and Old Scholars that are relevant to development, quality communication with the school community, and development of community support for the school and for education.

CURRICULUM DEVELOPMENT

A Director of Studies will be appointed in 1992 to carry out the tasks of curriculum coordination across the school and to manage the curriculum to meet the needs of all students in the years ahead.

FACILITIES

There will be improvement to facilities in the Library, Junior School, school grounds and areas for individual work by staff and students. These will be carefully phased in over the next five years according to priorities and availability of resources.

TEACHING AND LEARNING

A range of activities will be carried out to develop approaches to teaching and learning to ensure that the needs of students will be met, that transition to Year 7 will be enhanced, and that staff have support through professional development programs. These will be carefully sequenced over the next three years according to the availability of resources and the priorities set.

FINANCIAL MANAGEMENT

A range of policies and procedures will be put in place in 1991 to ensure that the financial resources of the school will be planned and managed efficiently and effectively.

MANAGEMENT STRUCTURE

The management structure of the school will be refined over the next two years to ensure that it more closely matches our curriculum and learning needs, providing opportunity for more staff to exercise leadership, minimising hierarchical levels, consistent with exemplary practice for schools and other organisations in the 1990s.

Different individuals and groups are involved in implementing the plan, the outcomes of which are continually monitored, with refinements as necessary. The plan provides the framework for the annual planning process in the school. It is, as intended, a dynamic and concise document which focuses the attention of all on important matters as they are continuously identified and reviewed in a climate of continuing change.

The development plan was implemented in the first year in the manner intended. After one year the same group that came together to prepare the initial plan gathered again to review progress in implementation and to make refinements for the year ahead. This half-day meeting included brief reports by the principal and other leaders which provided summaries of achievements as well as new threats and opportunities which presented themselves due to changes in the school's external environment (these being mainly a consequence of the severe recession in Australia at the time). There was some fine tuning of the development plan, mainly in the form of a reordering of priorities. The impression received by Brian Caldwell, who served as facilitator of this review meeting, was of a school in charge of its agenda to the extent possible under difficult economic conditions, with an air of determination and optimism apparent among participants in the process.

This account highlights the importance of strategic leadership, exercised in the main by the principal, but with very important contributions by the chairman of the school council, the head of the junior school and others who contributed in special ways at the seminar and in the subsequent deliberations of working parties.

Rosebery District High School

Priority setting occurs at two points in the cycle of self-management at Rosebery District High School: one during the process of preparing a development plan, with refinements annually; the other annually in preparation for the process of program planning and resource allocation. Consideration is given here to the first of these; we describe and illustrate the other in the section which follows.

Rosebery District High School has utilised a form of strategic planning since 1986, taking the initiative at the outset 'to take charge of its own agenda' in the midst of more or less continuous change. The focus has been on setting priorities for managing changes to curriculum and certification requirements, paralleled by changes which will help teachers acquire the knowledge and skills successfully to manage these changes. Given this focus on curriculum and approaches to learning and teaching, the preparation of the strategic plan has normally been the responsibility of the principal and leaders of program units, in consultation with their colleagues. The endorsement of school council is obtained.

A simple five-step process is used at Rosebery.

- Issues to be addressed in the development plan are identified, these being the outcomes of internal and, especially, external forces which are analysed in similar fashion to that described in relation to Figure 5.1. These issues are described as 'planning elements'.
- Action to be taken in addressing each planning element is then specified. Several years are invariably required, so the concern here is to determine a realistic time schedule, with responsibility for implementation allocated among staff.
- The action to be taken at the start of the schedule is specified in some detail.

- The development plan is then prepared, summarising the planning elements and a timetable for addressing each element over the several years required for implementation. The strategic plan, once endorsed by school council, is made available to all who will be involved in implementation and to others on request.
- The development plan is reviewed annually, with more detailed specification of action in the year ahead, but with changes to priorities as necessary as a result of changes in the external and internal environment.

With relative stability as far as its community is concerned, the school has been able to devote its energies in strategic planning to the afore-mentioned matters related to curriculum and teaching. It has been able to establish a five-year time frame for its development plan, with annual revisions ensuring that there is always a schedule for the next five years. Extensive system restructuring in 1990 and a further thrust toward self-management in Tasmania, combined with sharply declining enrolments which will accompany an anticipated cut-back in the town's mining in-dustry, will almost certainly mean that the development plan in the early years of the decade will deal with a wider range of issues, with a three-year time horizon rather than five years as was possible in the late 1980s.

One noteworthy feature of the development plan at Rosebery is its length, with only three pages required to summarise planning elements and a timetable for action over a five-year period. For 1987–91, six planning elements were identified in response to state-wide initiatives related to a new curriculum framework at the secondary level and the introduction of a Tasmanian Certificate of Education. Planning elements were described in single sentences in relation to curriculum, assessment techniques, student profiling, professional development, management structures and programs to communicate developments to all in the school community. The time-table for each year contains single sentences for each of the six planning elements. Consistent with guidelines we have offered for school self-management, the document is concise and is expressed in simple language that can be understood by all.

Setting Priorities in the Annual Planning Process

The development plan serves as a framework for the annual planning cycle because, as illustrated above for the approach used at Rosebery District High School, each year in the timetable for action in addressing particular priorities contains activities which must be carried out in order that the longer-term outcomes can be achieved. Account must be taken of these activities in preparing program plans and program budgets in the year under consideration. They must take their place among other priorities which arise from the findings of major and minor evaluations as well as the maintenance of ongoing programs for learning and teaching and the support of learning and teaching. In this section we describe and illustrate the approach to priority setting used in the annual planning process at Rosebery District High School.

At Rosebery a priority is placed on every policy which, by implication, covers all programs and elements in strategic plans. These priorities are reviewed annually. There is frank acknowledgment that equal priority cannot be given to all, even though all may have value and all may be considered important. Four general principles are followed in setting priorities. First, wherever possible, priorities are expressed in terms of intended outcomes for students rather than resources to be acquired. The statement, 'To ensure that all students are "computer-literate", commensurate with age and ability' is more appropriate than 'To purchase eight personal computers and to place one in each classroom.' Second, developing this principle further, the process of priority-setting is separated in time from that of resource allocation. Unnecessary and potentially damaging conflict can arise if priority-setting is left to the time when efforts are being made to reconcile budget proposals and available resources. We recommend that priority-setting occur in the first months of the school year, for the following school year, with planning for resource allocation taking place in the last months of the school year. The principal and other school leaders will identify priorities after consultation with members of program units, with the policy group (the school council at Rosebery) responsible for the adoption of priorities, which then provide the framework for planning and resource allocation in the year to follow. There will thus be several months for priorities to be highlighted in general discourse, a desired outcome being understanding and, it is hoped, acceptance of their good sense. A third principle, given limited resources, including the time and energy of teachers, is that the addition of a new priority or an elevation of a policy to a higher priority must result in the deletion or lowering of a priority of another policy. A fourth principle, evident throughout the description thus far, is that the process of priority-setting is open and collaborative. The particular ways in which these principles are reflected in the processes of priority-setting will vary from school to school. In Figure 5.3 we summarise guidelines based on those in use at Rosebery, as developed under the leadership of Terry Brient, Acting Principal. They are set out in what is essentially a policy on priority-setting.

Developing a Foresight Capability

We have described a capacity for strategic leadership on the part of the principal and other school leaders which differs in very significant ways from capacities in systems which are relatively centralised, or which

Figure 5.3. Guidelines for Priority-Setting in Annual Planning Based on Those in Use at Rosebery District High School

---

GUIDELINES FOR PRIORITY-SETTING

1 Teams engaged in program evaluation are encouraged to suggest priorities for attention in the year ahead.

2 The policy group will take account of recommendations by teams engaged in program evaluation in formulating priorities to serve as a framework for planning and resource allocation.

3 Priorities are best expressed in terms of expected outcomes for learning and teaching and the support of learning and teaching.

4 Each new policy is assigned a priority in its first year of implementation, with annual review of this priority in the years to follow.

5 Policies (which include, by implication, programs and elements in development plans) are assigned a priority by number, with these being Priority 1, Priority 2 and Priority 3 in order of relative importance. It is acknowledged that all are important; the order reflects relativity.

6 Priority 1 is allocated where a major impetus is desired in the year ahead or when a new policy, program or element in the development plan is to be implemented.

7 Priority 2 is assigned to all other policies, programs or elements that are essential to maintain the school program in the year ahead.

8 Priority 3 is allocated to those policies, programs or elements which are desirable but not critical to the maintenance of the school program in the year ahead unless their resourcing falls below a specified level; resourcing at least to this level is assured with a Priority 3 rating. Some policies, which might otherwise be assigned a Priority 3 rating, might be deleted altogether if new policies have been implemented or if some policies have been raised in priority.

9 Priorities for the year ahead are determined by the middle of the preceding year.

10 Draft priorities are widely circulated for comment and recommendation for change prior to formal approval by the policy group.

---

prevailed in most public or government systems until recently. In the latter, leaders could maintain a relatively closed outlook on the world when all that was required was 'running a tight ship', faithfully implementing a centrally determined curriculum with a prescribed syllabus of study, a compliant community, and promotion by seniority in lock-step fashion. There were visionary leaders, to be sure, but they tended to be the exception. Now there is the expectation that all school leaders will be visionary leaders, and certainly that is the case for self-managing schools.

Our descriptions and illustrations have noted the manner in which leaders in self-managing schools can scan the external environment of the school, noting emerging trends and issues, discerning the megatrends, and working with their colleagues and others to set priorities and determine strategies for action which take account of these matters as they work toward the fulfilment of the school's mission. In many ways, however, this strategic leadership is still rooted in the present: 'noting emerging trends and issues, discerning the megatrends' does not necessarily mean that the leader can think through the possible scenarios for how events will or should unfold in the future. It is in this connection that we conclude the chapter by exploring the possibility of the school acquiring a capacity for what is described in the futures literature, as in ordinary everyday discourse, as foresight. Richard Slaughter of the Foresight Research Unit at the University of Melbourne's Institute of Education describes foresight as 'a conscious effort to expand awareness and clarify the dynamics of emerging situations'.[6] The approaches we have described and illustrated in this chapter are examples of foresight.

If we proceed further into the futures field, we find a range of techniques which might be included in the school's repertoire in order that it may 'take charge of its own agenda'. One is the QUEST (*Qu*ick *E*nvironmental *S*canning *T*echnique) process which has five stages: preparation, an environmental scanning workshop, intermediate analysis and report, a strategic options workshop and follow-up work. Slaughter summarises the argument behind the process, which was pioneered by Burt Nanus.

1 Organisations need efficient and cost-effective ways of dealing with uncertainty and rapid change.
2 To assume that the future will be like the present, or that decisions can be deferred until the environment is better understood, increases the risk of failure.
3 The future cannot be predicted. However, alternatives can be systematically explored.
4 Top executives already possess a view of the dynamics of their organisations' environments. This view can be made clearer and more explicit.
5 Techniques from futures research can be combined to provide a coherent picture of alternative future environments.
6 This picture can be used as a basis for strategic planning.[7]

The argument set out above and the QUEST process are consistent with what we have described in this chapter, but much higher levels of sophistication are possible. This raises the desirability of including units on futures in pre- and in-service programs for school leaders. We resist the temptation to suggest that the foresight capability for schools be developed at the system level, with information shared among schools which would, in turn, acquire the same capability over time with the assistance of centrally or regionally based consultants. Similarly with pilot schemes and 'cascade models' for dispersing the capability. These approaches have been typically adopted when an innovation is to be taken up across a system of schools. Consistent with the concept of subsidiarity, as described in Chapter 4, and the general approach we have taken as far as empowerment in self-managing schools is concerned, we suggest that individual schools should, from the outset, develop the capability themselves, utilising, where it is efficient and effective to do so, the expertise of people in other schools, and elsewhere inside and outside the system. There are several strategies which might be employed.

- The principal or other school leader might bring together a small foresight team to develop the capability.
- The foresight team might work with the assistance of an expert consultant in the early stages to acquire some of the skills of scenario writing and cross-impact analysis (which underpin QUEST and the approach we described and illustrated in this chapter).
- The school might subscribe to publications and other services which will assist members of the foresight team and others keep up-to-date with trends, issues and scenarios, especially as they may relate to schools.
- The foresight team might foster an ongoing discourse in the school's community on matters of strategic importance and make specific contributions during strategic planning and priority-setting.

While this capability will enhance strategic leadership — our major concern in this chapter — it will also enhance educational leadership and the development of a school's community. We take up this notion of educational leadership in Chapter 6, focusing on learning and teaching and the support of learning and teaching.

6 Educational Leadership: Nurturing a Learning Community

In this chapter we are concerned with educational leadership and the particular ways in which teachers, parents and others can play their part in achieving excellence in a self-managing school. The focus is on learning and teaching and outcomes for students; the image is that of school leaders engaged in 'nurturing a learning community'.[1]

Chapters 4 and 5 also dealt with educational leadership but our concern there was the role of the leader in establishing the very best conditions that are possible so that the real work of the school can proceed. In Chapter 4 our concern was the cultural underpinnings of the school; in Chapter 5 we offered guidelines on how schools can 'take charge of their own agenda' and ensure that, at any point in time, the priorities they are addressing are optimally matched to opportunities and threats (external) and strengths and limitations (internal). We turn now to 'the real work of the school' that occurs on a day-to-day basis in classrooms and wherever students learn and teachers teach and parents support.

In many respects a school is a community of communities. We consider three: the community of teachers, the community of parents and the community of students.[2] We deal with each in turn, although it is the synergy of the three which we are seeking. In each instance, we briefly review the findings of recent studies to demonstrate that the debate about whether self-management has educational benefits should now be laid to rest. We then offer guidelines for school leaders who are engaged in this nurturing aspect of their roles. Illustrations from a variety of settings are provided. Our starting point, however, is an examination of the centrally determined framework which will allow these educational benefits to be attained; these being the 'preconditions' for success in educational leadership.

Preconditions

In Chapter 1 we described the trend to self-management and explored some of the underlying factors. Two questions are frequently raised: '*Why* shift authority and responsibility to the school?' and 'What benefits will accrue to *students*?' A strong case has often been argued in reports that led to restructuring and self-management, with recent examples being those by Picot in New Zealand and, especially, Scott in New South Wales.[3] However, critics continue to press: 'Where is the evidence that radical decentralisation has led, in direct cause-and-effect fashion, to educational benefits, including measurable gains by students?'

We are not aware of neat research designs showing before and after effects of restructuring and self-management. Given the time required for significant effects to be demonstrated in any large-scale change in education, it is unlikely that policy-makers would wait for the outcomes of controlled experiments over a number of years. There is, however, another genre of research for which the body of findings has become so powerful a policy indicator that it is difficult to ignore. Two examples of this kind of research are reviewed here. The first, alluded to in earlier chapters, is that undertaken by Matthew Miles and his colleagues in urban secondary schools in the United States.[4]

Case studies were completed following a nation-wide survey of schools which had shown major educational gains in the wake of system- and school-initiated improvement projects. Researchers identified sixteen factors which contributed in a cause-and-effect manner to school improvement. Four of these were preconditions to the extent that a system-wide policy was required to set them in place. These were the appointment of strong educational leaders, essentially demonstrating the capabilities we have explored in earlier chapters; a relatively high level of school autonomy, especially in relation to the allocation of resources; appointment of staff to help ensure a high level of staff cohesiveness; and the decentralisation of decision-making to the extent that the principal and staff have the opportunity to adapt the program of the school to meet the needs and interest of the local community. The remaining twelve factors were addressed by the principal and staff. These included power sharing or the empowerment of staff, the provision of rewards for staff, vision, the exercise of control over staffing, the exercise of control over the allocation of resources, staff willingness and initiative in the management of change, evolutionary program development, the building of external networks, evidence of 'deep' rather than 'shallow' coping in addressing problems which arise in school improvement, good strategies in the implementation of change, the institutionalisation of change, and change in organisational structures and processes. It is the preconditions that we wish to highlight here: these were centrally determined policies which fostered a capacity for self-management. The factors which more directly contributed to school improvement were the last twelve, but they required a certain style of leadership, a level of staff cohesiveness and a relatively high degree of autonomy in respect to program and resources in order to be fully effective.

Other examples of research which point to the importance of pre-conditions are those undertaken over the last decade by Sizer, Goodlad and Johnson.[5] The widely reported work of Sizer and Goodlad followed long-term study in a large number of schools. Particular attention was given to conditions for learning and teaching. In each instance the researchers found that tight, centralised controls on schools placed constraints on teachers, limiting the extent to which they could address the range of student needs with available resources. Conclusions were unmistakable in their implications for self-management and the need for preconditions of the kind identified by Miles. Sizer concluded that 'one imperative for better schools' was to give teachers and students room to take full advantage of the variety among them, a situation which 'implies that there must be substantial authority for each school. For most public and diocesan Catholic school systems, this means the decentralisation of power from headquarters to individual schools.'[6] Goodlad concluded that there was a need for 'genuine decentralisation of authority and responsibility to the local school within a framework designed to assure school-to-school equity and a measure of accountability.'[7]

The work of Sizer and Goodlad was undertaken in the early 1980s and was reported in *The Self-Managing School*. Recent research extends their approach by examining more closely the actual day-to-day work of teachers. The study of Susan Moore Johnson in the late 1980s was along these lines, being motivated by the general lack of success in the first wave of reforms in the United States, including those which involved an increase in centrally determined rules and regulations such as licensing examinations and merit pay schemes for teachers, centralised curriculum and competency tests for students.[8] Johnson described what followed in these terms:

> As it became clear that these regulatory reforms not only evoked anger and resistance among teachers but also failed to increase test scores, policy analysts tendered a new explanation of the schooling problem, one that also centred on teachers and their work . . . The strategy of these so-called second wave reformers was to transfer authority for educational design to teachers, making them the agents rather than the objects of school reform.[9]

To Johnson, however, the problem was still not focused as it should be: 'These policy analysts, like the architects of earlier changes, approached the problem as a political one, the issue being who was to have the power over the direction of schooling.'[10] While the thrust of the second wave was consistent with what was known about the needs of professionals to have control over their own work, it still, in Johnson's view, 'begs the question of how schools should be organised for better teaching and learning. What structures, standards, norms and practices enable and encourage teachers to do their best work?'[11]

Johnson sought an answer to this question by interviewing a representative sample of 115 teachers in public and private (independent and church-related) schools from school districts in eastern Massachusetts. These teachers were nominated as 'very good' by their principals. Questions ranged over almost every aspect of the workplace. Analysis of responses revealed the same kinds of constraints on teachers as were identified in earlier studies but suggested that the solution was more complex than might have been envisaged initially:

> There is no magic bullet, and those who would improve schooling must approach their task with respect to its complexity. This study suggests that improving the school as a work-place will involve many persons on many fronts — legislators to influence salaries; leaders from private industry to enrich school resources and opportunities for professional development; union leaders to encourage teachers to assume greater responsibility for their profession; administrators to make the central office a resource centre rather than a control centre; and parents, teachers and principals to collaborate and ensure that their schools are responsive to students' needs.[12]

To some extent, Johnson has come full circle since her solution is, to a large extent, cast in terms of a shift in the locus of power. It is, of course, a reaffirmation of the concept of self-management. However, she took the case further by drawing attention to the large number of actors who must be engaged, ranging over policy-makers, principals, teachers, parents, business leaders, central administrators and union leaders. She makes specific recommendations for policy and practice and these are listed in Figure 6.1. Again, they are consistent with earlier recommendations by Sizer and Goodlad and with the practices we describe in the refined model for self-management, especially in respect to the opportunity teachers should have to influence what they teach and how their schools are run. Noteworthy are her recommendations related to accountability, cautioning against narrow measures of productivity, but acknowledging the need for peer assessment on the part of teachers and their leaders. We take up this issue in Chapter 7. She called for a greater commitment of resources to schools but, given the economic circumstances which prevail in the early 1990s, this may not be possible. The alternative, instances of which were cited in Chapter 1, is for a re-allocation of resources within the field of public education. If this re-direction is to favour schools, then there must be a reduction at the central level, the outcome of which will be a further thrust to self-management and an imperative for quality in the delivery of service by those who remain at the centre.

In general, we believe that there is little value in extending the debate about the merits of self-management unless it is to question the capacity of schools to take up the opportunities which are provided. The findings

Figure 6.1. Implications for Policy and Practice Arising from Johnson's Study of the Teacher's Workplace

---

KEEPING GOOD TEACHERS TEACHING

1 Policy-makers must secure sufficient funds to ensure that public schools are well-financed.

2 Public schooling should be decentralised and deregulated so that the school site, rather than the district, becomes the primary unit of organisation and so that teachers, principals and parents can institute practices that address the needs of the school community.

3 Policy-makers should abandon industrial models of schooling that prize standardisation or promote narrow measures of productivity; they must direct their attention to improved teaching and learning for inquiry and higher-order thinking.

4 Public schools must engage parents more meaningfully in the education of their children and coordinate public services on behalf of children and their families.

5 Schools should rely more on the professional expertise of teachers by granting them greater influence in what they teach and how their schools are run. In turn, teachers and their leaders should take steps to increase their responsibility for managing their schools and assessing the performance of their peers.

Source: S. Johnson (1990) *Teachers' Work: Achieving Success in Our Schools*, New York, Basic Books, pp. 332–339.

of Miles, Sizer, Goodlad and Johnson, all eminent scholars in their field, are consistent and are supported by others, although, as acknowledged in Chapter 1, we support Malen, Ogawa and Kranz in their call for ongoing research on school-based management.[13] In the remaining sections of this chapter we explore ways in which teachers, parents and students can indeed take up these opportunities. We include further evidence in support of the argument that educational benefits will accrue from a shift to self-management.

The Community of Teachers

We now examine more closely how the workplace of teachers can be enhanced within the framework of the revised model for self-management. It is clear that this model affords an opportunity for the implementation of Johnson's fifth recommendation, namely, 'Schools should rely more on the professional expertise of teachers by granting them greater influence in what they teach and how their schools are run.'

Restructuring the workplace of teachers

The model for self-management provides teachers with the opportunity to influence the nature of their work in very powerful ways. Teachers are

119

represented on the policy group of the school which is responsible for approving the school's charter, mission, policies, priorities, strategic plan and budget. While the policy group is responsible for approving decisions on these matters, our guidelines have made clear that there should be appropriate involvement of teachers in the events leading up to decisions. Included here are working parties to conduct policy analyses and prepare options on policy for consideration by the policy group. Teachers are engaged in program teams, essentially teams which reflect the interests of teachers in areas of teaching and learning and which support teaching and learning. Here they provide input in the policy process, being especially influential since they are a major source of expertise in curriculum policies in their areas of interest; in devising strategies for longer-term curriculum change; in preparing plans and priorities for the year ahead and proposing budgets; and in program evaluation on a cyclical basis. Central to their role, of course, is teaching and the implementation of curriculum according to priorities, plans and available resources.

These activities of teachers become routine over time; they are the tangible structures and processes of a culture of self-management. There are also the non-routine activities which provide a further opportunity to address Johnson's fifth recommendation. We refer here to the capacity of teachers and their leaders to tackle quickly and skilfully problems which arise in the course of their work. The formation of small teams for trouble-shooting and problem-solving is an important aspect of this capacity. Essentially, it is what Miles called 'deep coping', acquiring whenever necessary additional knowledge and skills to enable them to address the problem at hand.[14] This capacity contrasts with 'shallow coping', where problems are not addressed or are down-sized, or where for one reason or another teachers are unable or unwilling to develop the capacity to be effective.

Ongoing acquisition of knowledge and skill

So far we have simply confirmed that the refined model for self-management provides a framework for taking up Johnson's recommendation on the workplace for teachers. For benefits to be realised, teachers must be successful in the various tasks. What follows are some descriptions of approaches whereby these capacities can be acquired. We are not concerned with the detail of curriculum or the detail of how teachers should teach and students should learn. Such a treatment is beyond the scope of the book. Our chief concern is strategies for leadership.

Professional development is the key since pre-service programs for teachers typically have little to say about the processes in the model for self-management, except that phase concerned with implementation in the classroom and that is, to some extent, the way things should be. So a first consideration is the manner in which practising teachers can acquire the knowledge and skill to make a worthwhile contribution in the *processes* of self-management as they were outlined above. One cannot contribute in these processes unless one has knowledge in matters related to *curriculum* and *learning and teaching*.

There are several approaches to acquiring these capacities which may be pursued singly or in combination: formal in-service training programs organised by the school system or the school, participation in postgraduate award courses, and informal on-the-job learning as teachers go about their work.

In-service Training Programs Organised by School Systems. We see a place for system-wide initiatives in professional development programs despite the trend to self-management, especially in the time of transition from a relatively centralised to a relatively decentralised operation, or when a major curriculum change is made and it is simply more efficient to organise from the centre a program for all schools. Increasingly, however, we see these as the exception, with most professional development programs becoming school-based or district-based.

As far as acquiring knowledge and skills in the processes of self-management is concerned, we offer three examples from our own experience. We included a brief description in Chapter 2 of our work in Victoria where the model for self-management was utilised in the introduction of what was described in that state as school-level program budgeting. A strategy for in-service training was devised centrally, in consultation with representatives from each of twelve regions in the state. We worked over a three-year period in a series of one- and two-day workshops for principals, parents, teachers and, in some instances, students. Each school was represented in these seminars by a small team, usually three or four, which was representative of these groups. Over the course of each workshop, participants had the opportunity to acquire knowledge about the different phases of the model for self-management and to apply it in a series of policy and planning simulations. Beginning with about fifty trial schools in 1984, by 1986 we had worked with about 5000 people from about 1100 schools. In addition, we had assisted central and regional officers to acquire the capacity to conduct their own training programs. In some instances we worked in individual schools with the principal, staff and the school council, often with as many as 100 people. The intention, however, was for the principal, with the assistance of a regional consultant in the early stages, to organise school-based training programs. The goal set initially was for all schools in the state to acquire the capacity by the end of the 1980s. Evidence suggests that this expectation has been satisfied in large measure, although, as noted in Chapter 2, it has been a case of 'mutual adaptation', with a host of local variants of the practice.

We were engaged in similar activities in New Zealand in 1988 and

1989 following adoption of the major recommendations of the Picot Report. Our work was of shorter duration than in Victoria, but more people were involved. Over a six-month period we worked in all parts of the country with about 10,000 people in events ranging in length from a one-hour presentation to two-day workshops. For single presentations, our aim was to describe developments in New Zealand in the context of similar changes elsewhere, with a short overview of the model for self-management. For the workshops, we followed the same approach as in Victoria, with presentations and simulations of key phases of the model. There was one major difference in New Zealand: we tended to work with principals and other school leaders in separate events from those organised for parents. Our preference is for groups which are broadly representative, modelling the kind of relationship which should be created within a self-managing school.

Jim Spinks' work in England and Wales over an eighteen-month period in 1989 and 1990 involved similar numbers of people as in New Zealand. One- or two-day events combining presentations and simulations were the major feature. Participants were mainly principals, leaders of boards of governors, and officers of local education authorities. For Britain and New Zealand, the intention was that training capacities should be quickly acquired by officers or staff in universities and colleges, who would then serve as consultants to schools in the early stages. Thereafter, the capacity would be developed through school-based activities. In many instances, however, schools proceeded directly with their own adaptation of the model.

We offer the following guidelines based on these experiences.

- It is desirable, at least in the early stages, for parents and, where possible and appropriate, students, to join teachers and principals in workshops which introduce the processes of self-management. Simulation exercises should model the kind of relationship which will characterise the approach in the school setting. At the very least this will ensure that representatives of all groups will receive information about the nature, purpose and general approach at the same time.
- Training programs should be conducted from the outset with people employed centrally or regionally who can assist schools in the early stages of transition to self-management. However, this period of dependency should be relatively short since the aim is to have a capacity for self-management in schools as soon as possible.
- Consultants should not be specially designated as consultants in self-management, giving the impression that self-management is a process which is separated from curriculum and teaching. It is preferable that all central and regional consultants have the capacity to support schools in the transition to self-management.

- The principal is the key person in the adoption of approaches to self-management and should be involved in all training programs, taking the lead with other school leaders in developing understanding and skill at the school level.
- Training programs should include sessions that provide participants with an opportunity to plan in preliminary fashion the manner in which self-management will be introduced in their own settings. Account should be taken of the time required; our initial recommendations for three to five years to develop the capacity are now somewhat generous given the pace of change, but one to three years will be required in most instances.

The most comprehensive system-initiated program for development in curriculum and teaching that we observed was in the Pittsburgh School District in Pennsylvania. It arose from general concerns about the quality of education in this large urban system in the early 1980s. An assessment of needs resulted in the identification of a number of priorities, foremost of which was the development of knowledge and skills among teachers. The needs assessment and subsequent design of program were carried out with the full support of the teachers' union and wide involvement of teachers throughout the system. The outcome was a program involving every teacher, with an eight-week mini-sabbatical for secondary teachers conducted at the Schenley High School Teachers Centre, an inner city school refurbished for the purpose, and a four-week experience for all elementary (primary) teachers at the Brookline Elementary School Teachers Centre. By the end of the decade all teachers had participated, and ongoing programs had been institutionalised at the school level.

The focus of these programs was the acquisition of knowledge and skill in a repertoire of approaches to teaching based on the Madeleine Hunter model of clinical teaching. Participants also had the opportunity to update knowledge in areas of the curriculum. Following training at the teachers' centres, programs continued at the school level, with principals and teachers assisted by centrally based 'coaches'. The program was evaluated regularly by a panel representative of the different perspectives on evaluation with highly favourable judgments being received. The outcomes in relation to problems which gave rise to the initial assessment of needs were very positive, since the Pittsburgh school system under the leadership of its superintendent, Dr Richard Wallace, is now generally considered one of the best urban jurisdictions in the United States.

Three other matters are noteworthy in respect to the Pittsburgh experience. First, there was significant support from business, there being a general view that the future well-being of the city depended, among other things, on a strong school system. Support from business is now more widespread in the United States. Second, a parallel development was the introduction of Principals' Assessment Centres, based on the approach of the National Association of Secondary School Principals. These had a strong thrust toward the professional development of principals. Third, what occurred in Pittsburgh was not associated at the time of its introduction with a major initiative in self-management; in contrast, the implementation of a system-wide teacher effectiveness program in the Edmonton Public School District in Alberta, Canada, was seen as a valuable complement to that system's pioneering effort in school self-management.

David provided accounts of system-initiated programs in three districts in the United States which have recently taken the initiative in restructuring, with school self-management a major component in each instance.[15] Features included:

- in Dade County, Florida: training in the processes of school self-management in three-day conferences for teams of principals and teachers; mini-sabbatical programs of seminars, professional clinics and research for teachers;
- in Jefferson County, Kentucky: an Academy funded primarily by the Gheens Foundation which employs a staff of sixty to work with teachers on a broad range of professional development programs; working with representatives of teachers' union, central administrators and university staff to design and implement the notion of the 'professional development school', with twenty-four schools initially involved in programs to re-design the workplace for teachers;
- in Poway Unified School District (California): this system had a form of self-management throughout the 1980s to the extent that it is now part of the culture of the system, with every job description throughout the system described in terms of support for student learning; a feature is the comprehensive professional development program with a focus on learning and teaching.

It is clear that system-initiated professional development programs play an important part in school self-management, with the focus being curriculum and teaching, although training in the processes of self-management is evident in the early stages. David identified three themes in efforts to restructure education in the United States, each of which has implications for system-initiated professional development.

1 The goal of school restructuring is long-term change guided by a conception of schools as stimulating workplaces and learning environments.
2 School staff members need the skills, authority and time to create new roles and environments appropriate to them.
3 Restructuring schools requires building new coalitions of support and creating new conceptions of accountability.[16]

Participation in Postgraduate Award Courses. Another opportunity for teachers to acquire knowledge and skill is through postgraduate award courses. In Chapter 3 we cited Murphy's view that such courses in the United States do not adequately prepare principals for the role of leaders of learning and teaching because of their focus on management. This short-coming needs to be addressed in the first instance so that principals and other school leaders who undertake postgraduate work are broadly prepared in at least the three areas of curriculum, teaching and management.

The courses which hold the most promise for principals, other school leaders and teachers in general would appear to be those which give par-ticipants an opportunity to integrate their formal learning with on-the-job work. We have been involved in what we believe is a model arrangement in this respect in Tasmania, Australia. The Centre for Continuing Education of Teachers (CCET) in Tasmania is a consortium of the Department of Education and the Arts and the University of Tasmania. It has been in existence for nearly twenty years and provides a framework for the design and delivery of a range of award and non-award programs. A feature is that it has a very small core staff, fewer than five, with most of the teaching being done by university staff, officers of the school system and private consultants. The award programs are for various bachelors degrees, postgraduate diplomas and masters degrees. In most instances the courses of study are designed by small teams representing practitioners and aca-demics, with formal approval required by the school system, which provides a substantial level of resource support, as well as the university, since the program must have appropriate academic rigour. Of particular interest is the fact that papers and other assignments are based on the application of knowledge acquired to the work setting of the participant. A variety of modes is offered, including release from employment in blocks of time during the school year, summer school, late afternoon and breakfast seminars. Reviews of in-service and professional development programs in Australia have invariably praised this approach to the acquisi-tion of knowledge and skill by practising teachers. In recent years, several of the CCET programs and similar university-school system partnerships have responded to the needs of practitioners as the system moved to self-management.

In 1990 the CCET was incorporated in a new structural arrangement called the Centre for Advanced Teaching Studies (CATS), with an enlarged program which included the encouragement of research on problems in teaching, again with a partnership between system and university, extended now to doctoral degrees. Regrettably, the financial crisis in Tasmania in the early 1990s led to uncertainty about the long-term future of this initi-ative. Success to date and the general principles on which the program was founded in the early 1970s are, in our view, exemplary, and are similar to the thrust in the United States toward professional development schools and various consortia of university-school partnerships.[17]

Teachers as reflective practitioners

Thus far we have examined some promising developments which, on a system-wide or postgraduate award basis, enable teachers to acquire the knowledge and skill to succeed in restructured workplaces, including those in the self-managing school. We now address two critical considerations. How will this knowledge and skill be incorporated into the day-to-day work of teachers? How will teachers learn on the job, in the absence of externally organised programs? Donald Schön's notion of 'reflective practice' is helpful.[18] In addition to offering a brief explanation of the concept, our purpose is to show that the self-managing school is the optimal setting, all other factors being favourable. We then combine the concept with practices described variously as mentoring and coaching to suggest the way in which school-based and teacher-based programs can be implemented.

Schön argued that professional education offered in universities, which is largely theory-based, falls short of what is required for the professions. Without challenging the validity of theory, Schön pointed out that situations encountered by professionals rarely fall into the neat categories defined by particular theories. Expressed another way, professional problems rarely occur singly; problems are multiple and complex. The practitioner uses a variety of hunches and intuition, often on a trial and error basis, to deal with these problems. Perceived cause-and-effect relationships in accounting for success or lack of success then become part of the repertoire of knowledge. Theory is helpful to the extent that it helps organise experience, but by itself is an insufficient guide to practice. Schön argues for professional preparation which enables the prospective practitioner to encounter problems and develop the capacity for reflective practice; similarly for programs of professional development. The notion of 'reflective practice' is similar to Starratt's notion of 'dramatic consciousness' and Argyris' notion of 'double loop learning'.[19] Reflective practice was evident in the postgraduate award programs offered by the Centre for Continuing Education of Teachers in Tasmania described earlier.

What is needed, then, is an organisational culture which allows reflective practice. Such a culture affords an opportunity for teachers to deal with problems as they arise, reflect on cause and effect possibilities, design alternative approaches for addressing the problem, take note of the outcomes and so on. We suggest that the culture of self-management provides this opportunity. Indeed, Schön sketches some optimal conditions for reflective practice that closely parallel what we have in mind:

> In contrast to the normal bureaucratic emphasis on uniform procedures, objective measures of performance, and centre/periphery systems of control, a reflective institution must place a high priority on flexible procedures, differentiated responses, qualitative ap-

preciation of complex processes, and decentralised responsibility for judgement and action. In contrast to the normal bureaucratic emphasis on technical rationality, a reflective institution must make a place for attention to conflicting values and purposes. But these extraordinary conditions are also necessary for significant organisational learning.[20]

A self-managing school meets these conditions except to the extent that it must work within a centre/periphery system of policies, priorities and frameworks for accountability.

Mentoring and coaching

Mentoring and coaching have been practised in schools for many years but they appear to be coming into their own in times of restructuring and educational reform. Writing in the context of the United States, for example, Healy and Welchert have observed that:

> In an effort to revitalize our nation's competitive vigour, the school reform movement has co-opted a strategy of the ancient Greeks: mentoring . . . The desire to enlist mentors in optimising career development and more recently in promoting excellence in education has inspired a flurry of research and development projects on mentoring.[21]

Mentoring, coaching and practices such as the unfortunately named clinical supervision are characterised in the school setting by a relationship between two teachers (including school leaders), the purpose of which is development and improvement in practice, and which normally but not exclusively involves the collection of information on mutually agreed criteria by one person for feedback, reflection and decision by the other. A school where these are part of the culture, that is, where these are 'the way things are done around here', has developed in part the capacity which Miles called 'deep coping'. The supervisory pattern in these practices has replaced the traditional hierarchical pattern with a collegial approach which is consistent with the reforms to the workplace of teachers advocated by Johnson and others. It also sits comfortably with the culture of self-management.

Expressed another way, if the intention is to help all teachers acquire the repertoire of knowledge and skills to meet the needs of all of their students, then patterns of development and supervision which rely comprehensively and permanently on system-initiated training schemes or on the exclusive involvement of the principal and other school leaders, are unlikely to prove equal to the task. Empowering teachers to work with teachers is a better way. The problem for educational leaders is how to ensure that teachers have the knowledge and skill to support each other in this fashion.

Paradoxically, it seems that system-initiated programs are needed to develop this school-level capability. Coaching was the key strategy in the program in Pittsburgh described earlier. Every teacher at the elementary (primary) and secondary levels, as well as principals and other school and system leaders, learned the skills of coaching. Seminars were followed by classroom experience at the two teachers' centres which were also operating schools. Once back in their schools, teachers were expected to continue the coaching arrangements, with subsequent surveys revealing a high level of implementation. There was a team of centrally-based consultants who served as coaches to the principals as they went about their work in this facet of their roles as educational leaders.

It is clear from the Pittsburgh experience that substantial resources are required to develop a coaching capability across a system of schools. The key question is: 'Does the coaching have the desired effect?' In the case of Pittsburgh: 'Did teachers acquire the knowledge and skill in the Pittsburgh adaptation of Madeleine Hunter's model of clinical teaching?' Subsequent evaluations suggest an answer in the affirmative. Bruce Joyce, generally regarded as a pioneer of contemporary approaches to coaching in the educational setting, has reported high levels of success compared to outcomes when staff development has not been followed by coaching:

> without coaching for application, the success of staff development efforts is often as low as 10 per cent professional implementation rate . . . by adding coaching for application and related activities the success level can be raised well above the 75 per cent professional implementation rate.[22]

Mentoring is related to coaching as an approach to collegial support. In one important respect, however, it is broader than coaching, since coaching is one of several ways in which the mentor can give support. Following the model of Gray and Gray, other roles include leader, role model, instructor, demonstrator, motivator, supervisor, counsellor and resource linker (to others with expertise).[23] In another important respect it is narrower than coaching, since the mentor is a colleague with a particular set of attributes and interests which differ from those of the protege. The definition of Healy and Welchert illustrates:

> we consider mentoring to be a dynamic, reciprocal relationship in a work environment between an advanced career incumbent (mentor) and a beginner (protege) aimed at promoting the career development of both. For the protege, the object of mentoring is the achievement of an identity transformation, a movement from

the status of an understudy to that of a self-directing colleague. For the mentor, the relationship is a vehicle for achieving mid-life 'generativity' . . . meaning a transcendence of stagnating self-preoccupation. . . .[24]

There is a rich literature which describes mentoring practices with high levels of success reported in different settings.[25] Like coaching, however, there must be a high investment of resources in developing the necessary capabilities at the school level. Training of mentors and protégés is a critical part of the process.

In concluding this overview of coaching and mentoring, we draw on two experiences in Tasmania, Australia to demonstrate that there is some urgency in developing school-level capability through system-wide initiatives along the lines of those undertaken in Pittsburgh. This urgency arises from pressures to reduce expenditure on education, especially at the central level, along the lines we described in Chapter 1. Under these conditions, programs of the kind we have described are under threat. Our first example is of an initiative in Tasmanian primary and secondary schools, the general purpose of which was to improve the processes of learning and teaching by forming pairs of teachers who would work together to investigate a particular aspect of practice. Training was provided by two centrally-based officers. An evaluation of the program revealed a high level of success:

> Overwhelmingly participants pointed to a supportive workplace 'culture' and compatibility with their collaborating partner as significant features of the school in enabling development to take place. In partnerships which prized open and forthright communication, encouraged risk taking, celebrated successes and saw every encounter as an opportunity for learning, participants reported significant improvement in skill level, in enthusiasm for teaching and in their desire to continue learning.[26]

Central to success was the support of the principal. Regrettably, funding for central support of the project ceased after two years. All but one of the participating schools continued, albeit on a limited scale. It seems that a critical mass of practice around the system had not been developed so the nurturing of the approach will be dependent on networking of leaders in a small number of schools.

Another instance in the Tasmanian setting is a mentoring program which commenced in 1989 for which Brian Caldwell served as consultant.[27] In this instance it was part of a management development program for the Division of Technical and Further Education in the Department of Employment, Industrial Relations and Training. All newly appointed leaders in technical and further education colleges and central services participated in this program, a feature of which was a mentoring arrangement over the two-year course. Particular attention was given to the selection of mentors; training of mentors and protégés; coaching of mentors and protégés during the first year of on-the-job application; regular monitoring and the use of input, process and outcome indicators; and securing the visible support of the senior officer in the division, as well as the principal of each college. The model of Gray and Gray was adapted to serve as a guide to mentoring.[28] Very high ratings were received on all indicators, with a noteworthy outcome being an indication in the first year of the wider adoption of mentoring practice in some colleges and central service units. However, as with the previously cited initiative in Tasmania, there was a danger that the mentoring program would founder before a critical mass of practice had developed.

The two Tasmanian examples illustrate that there is a critical 'window of opportunity' for programs of central support but it is likely to be relatively small, especially in times when resources are limited and the balance of priorities is being tipped in favour of direct support to schools.[29] In any event, the aim must be to develop capacities at the school level as quickly as possible rather than foster a dependence on central arrangements.

The Community of Parents

We turn now to the second of the three communities we included in the community of communities which constitute the school, and take up the fourth recommendation of Susan Moore Johnson cited earlier, namely, that 'public schools must engage parents more meaningfully in the education of their children.' While Johnson uses the word 'engage', we see the need to be more precise, distinguishing between 'participation' and 'involvement' in the manner proposed by Marsh. Whereas involvement usually occurs as a matter of course, participation implies a stronger role, 'a partnership between parents and school staff in various domains of decision-making, including curriculum.'[30]

We begin with a short review of recent research by Coleman and Hoffer which suggests that the role of parents is crucial in achieving a high level of social capital, considered by these writers to be important in securing educational benefits for students. The specific dimensions on which participation by parents might be sought are suggested in further research undertaken by Chrispeels and Pollack. We then turn to a review of those features of the refined model for self-management which provide structures and processes for parental participation. We conclude this section of the chapter by exploring the manner in which parents can acquire the knowledge and skills to participate effectively.

The educational benefits of parental participation

The case for parental participation has been argued in comprehensive fashion by Marsh, who offered a range of reasons for encouraging it, although he acknowledged that problems may result.[31] He proposes a continuum of participation from passive to active (reporting students' progress to parents, special events which are attended by parents, activities to inform parents about the educational program, assistance by parents in non-instructional activities, assistance by parents in the instructional program, participation in decision-making processes).

Our purpose here is to review recent research which casts a new light on the issue of parental participation. This reveals that the educational benefits which arise may be more a product of the interaction of parents with others in the school community than the outcomes of parental participation as a practice in its own right. Expressed another way, the key to achieving educational benefits is to secure a synergy of communities: ensuring that the effect of the whole is greater than the effects of each group considered separately.

Coleman and Hoffer's research in public and private high schools in the United States suggests that schools where there are strong supporting relationships among principal, teachers, students, parents and other members of the school community, including, for many private schools, the church, are likely to be more effective than schools similar in all other respects but which lack such support.[32] Coleman and Hoffer used the term 'social capital' to describe these relationships. High social capital is indicated when students encounter the same set of reinforcing values no matter where they move in the school community: the values espoused by the school are supported by the principal, teachers, parents, students, the church and the wider community. This research was the culmination of a series of studies throughout the 1980s in which student achievement in public and private high schools was compared. Among other things, their purpose was to determine the reasons why some types of schools, notably Catholic schools, seemed to secure higher achievement and higher growths of achievement in a number of areas of learning. Their conclusion was that it was not so much the catholicity of the schools as the particular attributes of their communities. Various implications arise from these findings, but we turn to a second study before addressing them.

The particular dimensions on which mutually supporting relationships might be built are a matter of some importance for schools which seek to develop their social capital and thereby increase their effectiveness. Recent research by Chrispeels and Pollack yielded findings which are helpful in specifying the mutually supporting role of parents and teachers.[33] Their starting point was earlier research by Hallinger and Murphy which revealed that certain characteristics of effective schools, or effective schools' correlates as they described them, are embedded in the community in some instances, most notably in high socio-economic status (SES) communities where 'the community . . . infuses the correlates into the school.' These correlates are the setting of high expectations, an academic focus, providing rewards for success, a high external opportunity to learn and commit time to task, the existence of a safe environment, strong home-school relations, and the monitoring of progress. The existence of these correlates in high SES communities still demands, of course, strong support by the principal and staff of the school if the school is to be effective. The earlier research cited by Chrispeels and Pollack suggested that principals and staff in schools in low SES communities buffered the school against the influence of the community where the aforementioned effective schools' correlates were not embedded; where, in many instances, the opposite characteristics were evident. In other words, the principal and staff had to make their own special efforts to develop these correlates in their schools and overcome the potentially negative impact of the community.

Chrispeels and Pollack then conducted their own research in ten primary schools in San Diego County, reflecting a broad cross-section in terms of size, geographic distribution, and ethnic and SES composition of the student population. The majority of schools increased their effectiveness over time but, significantly, no school made efforts to buffer the influence of low SES communities. Indeed, schools which served such communities 'made considerable outreach efforts to their community in an effort to raise parental expectations and involve parents more actively in the learning process with their students.' Chrispeels and Pollack concluded that, rather than buffering, 'a more promising approach may be to assess the degree of presence or absence of the effective school correlates in the community and design intervention programs that help to embed the correlates in the community.'

The significance of this research lies in the specification of factors or correlates which are important as far as community impact on schools is concerned. These have often been vague and ill-defined. Moreover, it acknowledges the limitations of the community in low SES populations and suggests that the principal and staff of a school should take the initiative to develop the community. Following the work of Coleman and Hoffer, this sets an agenda for some schools in terms of the building of social capital. It identifies some particular directions a school council may take in setting school policy in low SES communities.

An implication of these findings is that structures such as school councils, by themselves, will not guarantee an improvement in outcomes for students. The work of such bodies must be focused and, while the research reported here suggests some ways in which this focus can be achieved, the particular approaches must be determined in the local setting.

Structures for parental participation

The refined model for self-management offers many opportunities for parents to participate in the decision-making processes of the school and for parents and teachers to interact in ways that will help build the social capital about which we have written.

We advocate a strong role for parents as members of the policy group in the school, thus securing their participation in such matters as charter, mission, goals, policies, priorities, strategic plan, budget approval and cyclical evaluation of programs. In the policy-making phase, in particular, parents can directly participate as members of working parties, or can provide information as working parties go about their task of generating options for consideration by members of the policy group. They can participate in program evaluation in similar fashion.

The model for self-management thus provides a structure and suggests processes for participation at the active end of the continuum proposed by Marsh (reporting students' progress to parents, special events which are attended by parents, activities to inform parents about the educational program, assistance by parents in non-instructional activities, assistance by parents in the instructional program, *participation in decision-making processes*). In a self-managing school it is expected that parents will participate in other less active roles in this continuum, but the particular ways in which this might be done are beyond the scope of this chapter. Marsh provides a range of possibilities and illustrations.[34] Taken together, a self-managing school provides the setting in which Johnson's fourth recommendation can be implemented ('public schools must engage parents more meaningfully in the education of their children').

Parent development programs

Parent development is as important as staff development in the view of self-management we have presented thus far. There would appear to be three key values underpinning programs of parent development. First there is the value of providing information about education in general and school in particular. Concern is often expressed that parents lack the knowledge to make a worthwhile contribution, and that may be the case in many settings. An implication of research reported here is that the principal and other school leaders should work with teachers to ensure a regular flow of information to parents on matters of substance. The guidelines we provided in *The Self-Managing School* are helpful in respect to school policies. We suggested that each school policy be presented in no more than one page and be free of jargon, expressed in language that all in the school's community can understand.

A second value underpinning the development of parents is a commitment to growth in parental attitudes and knowledge about matters which are crucial to the educational achievement of students. We refer here to what Chrispeels and Pollack called the 'effective schools' correlates', notably the fostering of high expectations for all students, a focus on educational goals of great worth (see Chapter 4), providing rewards for success, a good environment for learning at home, a safe environment, fostering strong relationships between home and school, and providing regular reports on student progress. For some schools, these correlates (attitudes, knowledge and supportive practice) are already embedded in the community; for others, there will need to be special effort on the part of schools to develop these, something which will invariably call for additional resources and/or a re-allocation of priorities.

A third value is acceptance of partnership in development. We refer here to the desirability, wherever possible, of parents and teachers learning together in matters related to the structures and processes of self-management and in matters more directly related to the educational program of the school. We cited earlier what we consider to be exemplary practice in Victoria which is now part of the culture of development in that state. Wherever possible, principals, teachers, other school leaders, representatives of teachers and leaders of school councils participated together in programs designed to assist the acquisition of knowledge and skill in school council operations, school improvement, school-level program budgeting, and the manner in which parents and teachers can work together to support student learning.

Community of Students

The third community in this community of communities is the students. Providing an excellent education is the primary purpose of a school and the end for which the notion of self-management is but a means. Since the theme of this chapter is educational leadership and the nurturing of a learning community, all that we have written thus far is directed to that end. One special matter we take up at this point, however, concerns the contribution of students in the process of self-management and the need for an appropriate program of development to equip them for this role.

It is normal in Victoria for students to be represented on the council of a secondary school. While not a prerequisite in the model for self-management, we can see merit in their inclusion on the policy group, at least at the secondary level, since they have an interest or stake in the outcomes of most decisions and have expertise to offer on many issues. Even if there is no place for them here, there will be a variety of issues for which it will be helpful to have student representatives on working parties or at least be the source of information as a working party carries out a policy analysis. Consistent with the value of partnership we described earlier, there is merit in having student representation in programs for the development of knowledge and skills in self-management.

Setting aside the matter of student participation in policy-making or elsewhere in local adaptations of the model for self-management, there remains the need for the development of leadership for those involved in student representative councils and other organisations and groups with student leaders. We recommend leadership development programs for students, with schools working together in such ventures where this is advantageous for the schools concerned. Marsh takes up the issue of student involvement, presents arguments for and against, and offers guidelines for development along these lines.[35]

Extending the Learning Community

There are underlying tensions in a number of issues raised thus far. Susan Moore Johnson called for a greater commitment of public funds to education, yet all nations under consideration are experiencing economic downturns and, for other reasons, are winding back central and bureaucratic arrangements, including some that provide support for schools. Acquiring the capacity for self-management and the nurturing of learning communities has required some large-scale programs of development for teachers and parents which, in the early stages, have been organised from the centre or the region. Recently, however, some have had a relatively short time frame for the aforementioned economic and organisational reasons.

Johnson suggested one way of resolving these tensions which, if implemented, extends the notion of community and builds even further the synergistic gains we described earlier. She called for 'leaders from private industry to enrich school resources and opportunities for professional development.'[36] We cited examples of private sector support for system-wide professional development programs in Pittsburgh, Pennsylvania and Jefferson County, Kentucky. Indeed, private sector support seems to be gathering momentum on many fronts in the United States as well as in Britain and Australia.

Many views about support from the private sector seem no longer relevant. These include the expectation that private support will only be directed to schools which are already advantaged (in fact, support seems to be evenly distributed across all types of school and community); and that business, in particular, will seek to advertise in a manner inconsistent with values held in the school (in fact, much of the 'promotional' material refers to programs and outcomes for students which have been planned independently of the source of support, with simple and usually unobtrusive reference to that source).

What emerges is the possibility that, while support from the private sector may be a source of financial capital, it may be viewed just as much as an addition to social capital. It seems that attitudes on the part of all leaders, in schools as well as in the private sector, must be transformed; indeed, it is a potentially productive field for the exercise of transformational leadership as this concept was defined in Chapter 1.

Guidelines for Educational Leadership

We offer ten guidelines for educational leadership in the self-managing school.

1   For leaders of school systems, work with policy-makers to create the preconditions for self-management, that is, to establish a policy framework within which the principal and others in the school community can take up the opportunities which self-management provides. We refer, in particular, to those identified in research: a capacity to adapt curriculum to meet the educational needs of students in a particular community; the appointment of strong educational leaders as principals; a high degree of autonomy, especially in relation to the manner in which resources are allocated within the school; and staffing arrangements which will ensure placement of a cohesive team, committed to the mission of the school.

2   For leaders at all levels, understand the case for self-management in terms of educational benefits for students and an enhanced workplace for teachers, appreciating that the major issue is ensuring that schools can develop the capacity to take up the opportunities afforded by self-management.

3   For principals and other school leaders, adapt the refined model for self-management to the needs of the school, thus establishing structures and processes wherein teachers, parents and (where appropriate) students have the opportunity to participate in decisions on substantive matters related to the educational program of the school.

4   System-wide programs of professional development have proved valuable for teachers and parents, but 'the window of opportunity' appears to be closing for their long-term operation, especially where financial resources are severely constrained and, for other reasons, there are pressures to cut back on central and regional support services. **For system-wide programs of professional development**, plan for a well-resourced, short-term initiative with a team of people who share the vision of self-management and are committed to ensure a school-level capacity at the earliest possible opportunity. Long-term career prospects should not be encouraged for those wishing to work centrally and exclusively on matters related to self-management.

5   Wherever possible and appropriate, **professional development programs for teachers, parents and students should be conducted**

simultaneously, modelling the kinds of relationship and experience which are part of the culture in a self-managing school.

6   The core of professional development programs for teachers must be the acquisition of knowledge and skill in matters related to curriculum, learning and teaching.

7   Award-based programs in universities should be planned and delivered in a partnership arrangement between institution and practitioner, with assignments and papers centred on school-based experiences. Consortium arrangements between universities and school systems are recommended.

8   Traditional top-down approaches to supervision of teachers are neither desirable nor feasible for self-managing schools in the 1990s: **collegial approaches such as coaching and mentoring are recommended**. All other conditions being favourable, the self-managing school offers an optimal setting for 'reflective practice'.

9   The concept of capital should be extended to include social capital, the aim being to build the strongest possible mutually supporting relationships among principal, teachers, parents, students, other members of the school community and, where appropriate, the church. In some communities additional resources and/or a re-ordering of priorities will be necessary as teachers work with parents to build common understanding and mutually supporting home and school practices on key factors identified in effective schools research (the fostering of high expectations for all students, a focus on educational goals of great worth, providing rewards for success, a good environment for learning at home, a safe environment, fostering strong relationships between home and school, and providing regular reports on student progress).

10   Extend the learning community to include the private sector in order that an even wider basis of support can be secured. This support will include financial support, since there is every indication that public funds will prove inadequate for the task. Promising practices in several countries dispel many of the fears traditionally held by educationalists: leadership of the transforming kind is called for in schools and in the private sector.

This chapter is subtitled 'Nurturing a Learning Community'. This conveys the notion that considerable patience and care are required if all of the communities in the school community are to come together in a mutually supporting fashion. We have also mentioned in several places the concept of synergy, implying that accomplishing the task will yield benefits beyond those which might be achieved with fragmented arrangements. The leadership required may be described as transformational, nurturing and empowering, underpinned by a vision of excellence and a commitment to self-management, and energised by knowledge about learning and teaching.

There is a beautiful Kiswahili word, 'harambee', which means 'let us pull together'. It was used by Mzee Jomo Kenyatta, the first president of an independent Kenya, during his inaugural speech in which he called for all people to contribute their resources for the benefit of all.[37] Educational leadership of the kind we have described here is a call for harambee.

7 Responsive Leadership: Coming to Terms with Accountability

Our concern in Part B is the leader's role in the self-managing school. In Chapter 4 we dealt with cultural leadership and the manner in which the leader works with others to create and sustain a culture of excellence. In Chapter 5 we were concerned with strategic leadership and the importance of taking charge of the school's agenda, addressing simultaneously external threats and opportunities and internal strengths and limitations. The focus in Chapter 6 was on ways in which school leaders can nurture the entire community in matters related to learning and teaching and the support of learning and teaching. Implicit in all of our illustrations and guidelines was a leader who is responsive to the needs of students, the local community and society at large; that is, while the decentralisation of authority is the essence of self-management, the exercise of that authority calls for a high level of responsiveness.

In Chapter 7 we take up the issue of responsiveness and examine ways in which leaders and others can demonstrate that they have indeed been responsive to the needs of the student, the local community and society at large. We describe this as responsive leadership, thus completing our classification of four facets of the role of transformational leader in a self-managing school (cultural leadership, strategic leadership, educational leadership and responsive leadership). In doing so, we deal explicitly with the demand for accountability which characterises the delivery of public services in the 1990s.

In a general sense accountability refers to a process of providing information to others, enabling judgments to be made about a particular phenomenon. More specifically, there is accountability in a self-managing school when processes have been established to provide information internally, to the local community, and externally, to the school system and others, to enable judgments to be made about the extent to which the school is responsive to the needs of students, the local community and society at large. Included here are relatively narrow but nevertheless important aspects of accountability such as the manner in which money has been used or laws have been obeyed.

Our starting point is a summary of major issues in accountability as these are emerging in the 1990s. We then outline the approach to program evaluation advocated in *The Self-Managing School*. This dealt with the gathering of information and the making of judgments on the extent to which the school addressed its goals and needs, implemented its policies and used its resources in the various programs of the school. Our main concern was accountability in the local setting. We then demonstrate how this approach can be incorporated in a model for accountability which addresses the aforementioned issues of the 1990s. We describe broad strategies for accountability at different levels of a school system, making reference to the comprehensive approach in the system of self-managing schools in the Edmonton Public School District in Alberta, Canada. We comment on transitions in approaches to accountability in Australia, Britain and New Zealand, focusing in particular on changes in the role of the inspector which have been foreshadowed in Britain following publication of *The Parent's Charter*.[1] Some implications are drawn for the appraisal of principals and their schools. We conclude with a listing of attributes of the responsive leader in the self-managing school.

Issues in Accountability

Five major issues in accountability are evident in the several countries identified in this book: purposes to be addressed, testing of students, roles in accountability, appraisal of staff, and feasibility of approach. Debates are frequently conducted in a highly charged and heavily politicised manner.

Purposes to be addressed

Accountability has only recently become a major issue in schooling. In Australia, for example, a common pattern in the past involved the testing of students at primary and secondary levels, with outcomes communicated to parents and students in a regular report. So-called external examinations were conducted at the senior levels of secondary schools, with public reporting of results for individual students in some places. Schools with high levels of success in external examinations were sometimes identified. Inspectors moved from school to school on a cyclical basis. In recent years external examinations were abandoned at all but the most senior level and, at that level, were retained with the addition of a major component of school-based assessment. Until recently the word 'accountability' was not used, but the purpose of accountability, as far as it was implied, was largely related to the furnishing of information on the achievements of individual students and, in general and somewhat ill-defined terms, on the performance of schools. Accountability of the school to the system as implied in the inspectorial approach was weakened when the inspectorate was phased out in many places.

The explicit use of the word 'accountability' has accompanied such developments and concerns as the introduction of special purpose grants, with governments seeking information about the extent to which the purposes of these grants were achieved; concern on the part of parents that schools were providing a good education; a broad-based concern in society about the quality of education, especially in respect to the acquisition of basic skills or core competencies, and the manner in which these matched the economic needs of the nation; concern at disparities among schools and school systems across the nation; and concern for efficiency, especially at a time of great pressure to reduce expenditure on public education. As a result, there has been a growing expectation that schools and school systems should be able to furnish information on many matters to different individuals, groups, organisations and levels of government for a variety of purposes.

The purposes of accountability, as they have emerged in the 1990s, may be expressed in terms of the intended target and the nature of information to be provided. Each implies a 'right to know' as far as that target is concerned:

1   accountability of the school to the student and parent, with regular reports of student progress and achievement during each year of schooling;
2   accountability of the school to parents and the local community, with reports of a general nature being furnished from time to time in relation to the achievement of expectations;
3   accountability of the school to the school system, with reports of varying specificity on the achievement of goals, priorities and standards, including the manner in which resources have been deployed;
4   accountability of the school system to the government, being a consolidation of information on the achievements of the system;
5   accountability of state governments to national governments, as national strategies for educational reform have emerged, with reports on the extent to which school systems have attained targets or standards which have been mutually agreed or are a condition of funding;
6   accountability of governments and systems of education to the community, especially in respect to the extent to which resources have been provided to enable schools to achieve expectations which have been set for them.

The means by which these purposes are to be addressed are currently the subject of discussion and debate in most places, with no standard patterns emerging. Preferred approaches are, in many instances, limited by the availability of resources to collect and analyse information. The key issue in the context of this chapter is the extent to which these multiple purposes of accountability can be consistent with and addressed in a self-managing school. In this chapter we comment on all, but give particular attention through explanation and illustration to the second and third purposes in the above list.

Testing of students

There is widespread interest in the testing of students at different levels of schooling and the public reporting of results, often on a school by school basis. Such practices extend those often associated in the past with external examinations at the senior secondary level. Testing along these lines has been under way for a number of years in most states of the USA and has now made its appearance in England and Wales. In Australia it has been introduced in New South Wales, with national approaches foreshadowed in late 1991.

The arguments advanced for testing are generally based on the economic imperative, that is, concern that the schools of the nation must provide students with the knowledge and skills that will enable them to participate fruitfully in a labour force which matches the needs of the nation within a global economy. Arguments in favour of assisting student and parent choice of school are also evident, as is the case based on increasing mobility of families. In summary, it is asserted that information about the performance of schools, generally and individually, should be made available publicly to enable decisions of one kind or another to be made about the quality of education.

There are limitations in these approaches to testing, not the least of which is their narrow focus and the resultant distortion which may occur in learning and teaching, especially for testing at the primary level. Highly valued goals may be devalued. Serious concerns have properly been raised about the validity of school-by-school comparisons when the results are made available to the public and no account is taken of the characteristics of the school and its community. Those who make decisions based on the published results have no means of determining the 'value added' component of the school's contribution.

The issue is whether national, state or system-wide testing can be accommodated in the concept of the self-managing school. We believe that they can be, but point out that the results constitute just one of many sets of indicators in a framework for accountability.

Roles in accountability

Another issue is the roles of different individuals and groups in the collection, analysis and interpretation of information. At the local level, for example, who is responsible to whom when we refer to the school being accountable to its community? On the one hand, it may be vague and ill-defined if parents and others are simply left to form their own judgments and take their own actions on the basis of an annual report delivered in general terms on a particular occasion by the principal, with no specification of procedures on how that report may be taken up. On the other hand, there may be a clearly defined expectation that the principal will report outcomes for a number of matters, including reports on specific initiatives which have been undertaken in a particular year, as well as more or less standard forms of reporting on matters of recurring interest such as academic achievement.

The issue here is the extent to which the role of principal, other school leaders and the policy group should be specified in terms of the kind of information to be gathered, the form in which it should be reported, and the actions to be taken after reports have been made.

Accountability of the school to the school system is more complex and problematic, especially where the traditional inspectorial role has been phased out. Two approaches characterise what is emerging in different countries. One is the expectation that schools will have a charter or a development plan which includes information about the manner in which centrally determined priorities are to be addressed. These plans are made available to personnel at the district, regional or central levels who confirm that system intentions will, in fact, be addressed. The second approach is the formation of teams of staff at the district, regional or central levels who systematically collect information from schools about the extent to which centrally determined priorities have been addressed. In many respects these teams operate in the style of inspectorial teams of the past, but their roles are more clearly and narrowly defined and they do not involve the inspection of teachers in the classroom setting. The names of such units vary, with 'review' and 'audit' frequently included.

The issues for consideration here are the extent to which the centre should specify matters on which schools should provide information; the manner in which different individuals and groups shall collect, analyse and interpret this information; and the forms of redress which may be deployed in the event that a school does not meet expectations for the achievement of centrally determined priorities.

Appraisal of staff

Issues related to the appraisal of staff have come into sharper focus with developments of the kind outlined in Chapter 1. In accounting for megatrends in education, we referred to growing concern for quality and equity and emergence of the service ethic. Schools and school systems are coming under increasing pressure to ensure that the needs of all students are addressed. There will be no place for teachers who cannot play their part. The trend to self-management and the collapse of bureaucracies in education means that responsibility for ensuring the highest standards of teaching is shifting to the school level, with particular attention given to procedures for the selection, placement, promotion, appraisal and ongoing professional development of teachers, including, of course, the principal and other leaders. That the context differs from that which exists in the past is evident from developments in Britain and New Zealand, where the intention is to have teachers contracted to individual schools through their boards or councils rather than with a central authority.

The issues here include the roles to be adopted by different individuals in appraisal of teachers, including the principal and other leaders, and the extent to which appraisal is linked to the achievement of outcomes.

Feasibility of approach

Issues of feasibility are also evident in planning for accountability. The gathering and reporting of valid information related to the achievements of students, especially that which enables conclusions to be drawn about the contribution made by the school, are both complex and costly. On the one hand, concerns are raised if indicators of performance are too narrow, addressing only a few goals of education, or if relatively cost-effective paper and pencil tests are utilised. On the other hand, there is resistance to the employment of large numbers of non-school personnel to carry out inspectorial or review and audit functions, or if apparently excessive amounts of time are spent by teachers on repeated testing over the full range of learning objectives.

Issues related to feasibility of approach are especially evident in the early 1990s as the demand for accountability is mounting. At the same time, making the issue comprehensively problematic, are pressures for greater efficiency and effectiveness, if not cost-cutting, under conditions of recession and, in some instances, financial crisis. Experience in New Zealand and plans in Britain furnish evidence of the difficulties in planning for accountability.

In New Zealand an Education Review Office was established following government implementation of the major recommendations in the Picot Report of 1989. These recommendations were directed at the creation of a national system of self-managing schools. Within a short time the government called for 'a wide ranging review of the process and outcomes of the reform of education administration to date and to recommend any improvements in the process or the structure.' The report of this further review, entitled *Today's Schools* (the title contrasts with *Tomorrow's Schools*, the statement of government intentions following broad acceptance of Picot), included recommendations to reduce the Education Review Office staff to approximately half its initial level and to 'redirect a significant proportion of the present funding for the Education Review Office to schools.'[2]

While all of the intentions and rationale for plans in Britain were not known to us at the time of writing, it appears that the government is unwilling to expand or possibly even sustain at current levels the body of people who constitute Her Majesty's Inspectors. In *The Parent's Charter* of 1991, the government signalled its wish to see an increase in the frequency of inspection of schools, with summary reports being made available to all parents by right.[3] To accomplish this, it plans to pass legislation which will allow the accreditation of independent inspectors, with schools free to hire their own inspectors under the provisions of local management. Information to hand suggests that the number of Her Majesty's Inspectors employed by government may decline from 480 to 175, with only forty-three remaining to carry out inspections of schools.[4]

It is clear that the demand for accountability is increasing at a time when governments are unable or unwilling to sustain current levels of staff who can be directly involved in the inspection or review of schools. At the heart of the resolution of this issue is the extent to which valid information can be furnished for accountability purposes under these conditions. We suggest some ways in which this can be done in another section of this chapter.

Evaluation and Review in the Self-Managing School

The refined model for self-management, as described in Chapter 2, is reproduced here for convenience in Figure 7.1. Evaluation and review is one of the key phases of the annual management cycle. Half of the circle is shaded in black, the other is not, indicating that the policy group and program teams have separate, important but related tasks in program evaluation. The policy group has responsibility for ensuring that the charter of the school is the starting point and focus for evaluation efforts and, more specifically, for the collection of information and making of judgments in respect to the extent to which policies, priorities and plans have been addressed. Program teams, will, of course, contribute to this effort but have the special responsibility for the gathering of information and the making of judgments on the extent to which plans for teaching and learning have been addressed. Included here will be information gleaned from the school's testing program. Consistent with all that we have encouraged, there are high levels of participation in these activities: teachers in program teams and representatives of the school community in working parties of the policy group.

Figure 7.1. The Refined Model for Self-Management

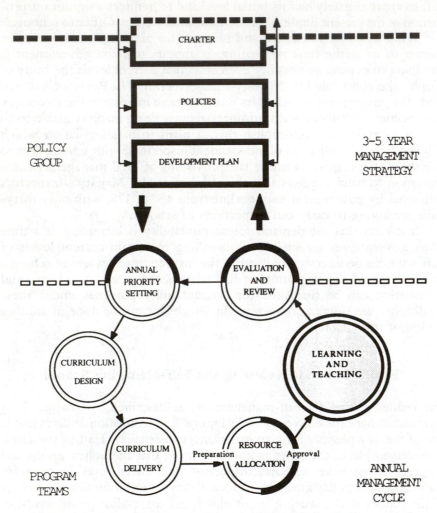

We stressed that this aspect of the model highlighted the major features of a key phase of an ongoing cycle, acknowledging that program evaluation occurs formally and informally all the time. We were also conscious of the time-consuming and burdensome approaches to whole-school evaluation in the past. Accordingly, we devised a set of guidelines which might make the process of program evaluation relatively straightforward, integrated with ongoing management processes, maintaining a focus on learning and teaching, with outcomes which can be easily taken up in the next cycle of self-management. The following are the major features of the approach we recommended.

- Distinguish between minor evaluations and major evaluations; for each program, the former is carried out informally by members of the program team once each year, while the latter is carried out in relatively comprehensive fashion on a cyclical basis (say, once every three, four or five years) by a working party or evaluation team appointed by the policy group.
- The minor evaluation may rely on informed opinion among members of the program team, the aim being to identify matters for fine tuning in the next year (although evidence of major problems should result in a major evaluation in anticipation of significant change); the major evaluation calls for more extensive and objective gathering of data from sources outside the membership of the program evaluation team, the aim being to appraise policies and programs in searching fashion.
- Reports of evaluations should be relatively brief, with one and two pages being the maximum length recommended, respectively, for minor and major evaluations of a particular program.
- Reports of all evaluations should be gathered together and published in simple, jargon free, easy-to-read form. Copies should be made available to each member of all program teams, to the policy group and to others upon request.
- Minor evaluations can be carried out in an hour or so toward the end of each school year; major evaluations are more time-consuming but can generally be carried out in the second half of a school year.
- Program evaluation reports are utilised immediately in the next phase of the model for self-management. With all evaluations completed by the end of the preceding school year, the published collection of evaluation reports can be on the table at the first meetings of policy group and program teams at the commencement of the next school year. The policy group may immediately review each report in turn and may ask questions such as the following: 'Are new needs identified?' 'Is there a need to review policy in areas related to this program?' 'Should the development plan be modified in the light of this report?' 'Should priorities be changed?' 'What are the implications in respect to the allocation of resources to this program?' Program teams may address similar questions. Policy groups will seek the comment of program teams.

Performance indicators

An indicator is an attribute of a program or school, a measure of which is utilised in making judgments about the program or school. Such attributes may be related to inputs, such as resources allocated to a program or the number of years of teaching experience among staff; processes, including aspects of teaching and learning such as time allocated to particular tasks or the extent to which certain technologies are used; or outcomes, such as results on tests of achievement. The measures may be relatively subjective, such as opinions of teachers or perceptions of parents, or they may be relatively objective, such as frequency of use of a service or scores on tests. Performance indicators are concerned with outcomes, but the term is often used to encompass all that we have included here. Many performance indicators such as rates of retention, attendance, suspension or graduation describe the general 'health' of the school.

Indicators may be utilised in making judgments about aspects of a program, a program as a whole or the school as a whole, including the extent to which matters of fundamental importance in the school charter have been addressed, policies have been implemented or the development plan has progressed. The policy group should ensure that appropriate indicators have been specified in plans, budgets and documents of strategic importance to the school. The group should be satisfied that the indicators will meet requirements for accountability to the community and to the centre.

Consistent with all the guidelines for self-management, indicators should be easy to understand, to the extent that their validity will be easily accepted by all with an interest, and that information associated with each can be readily and inexpensively acquired and communicated. This is especially important, given that a range of indicators will usually be required in order to make sound judgments. For example, scores on tests do not tell all about the worth of a program or a school.

Satisfying requirements for accountability

The broad arrow above the circle labelled 'evaluation and review' in Figure 7.1 is intended to indicate the utilisation of information in the review of charter, policies and development plan. It is also intended to indicate a relationship to requirements for accountability. Those at the centre of the school system will seek information on the extent to which centrally determined goals, policies and priorities have been addressed. Appropriate indicators should have been identified to ensure ease of reporting. Similar considerations are required in reporting to the community of the school. In the refined model for self-management, all the matters for report should be contained in the school charter which should thus be a helpful document in planning what might be formally titled the School Report.

Consistent with all guidelines for self-management, the School Report should be a relatively brief document of no more than, say, five pages. It should be free of jargon, with tabular or point form presentation of information based on agreed indicators related to goals, policies, priorities and other matters of importance as set out in the charter of the school.

We described earlier the issue of feasibility of approach, referring in particular to the potentially high costs to a system of employing large numbers of inspectors and other officers engaged in review and audit. We suggest that with the approach to accountability described here, with accountability expectations including the specification of indicators incorporated in the school charter, there will be no need for large cadres of external reviewers. Indeed, we envisage information being provided annually to the centre and the community in routine fashion with only one system officer normally involved. Even for major reviews conducted on a cyclical basis, there will rarely be need for a heavy commitment of external staff.

A final matter in connection with indicators and accountability is concerned with national or system-wide testing programs and the manner in which they may be incorporated in the approach we outline here. We see no difficulty unless, of course, test scores constitute the sole set of indicators, but this should never be the case; they become one of many indicators which, taken together, provide information which representatively samples the goals, policies and priorities of the system and school.

Accountability in Action in a System of Self-Managing Schools

The Edmonton experience

We selected the Edmonton Public School District in Alberta, Canada, to illustrate the approach to accountability we have described thus far. This city school district introduced school-based management to all of its more than two hundred schools in the early 1980s, following a three-year trial in seven schools. Known originally as school-based budgeting, the practice has broadened to encompass most of the characteristics we have described for a system of self-managing schools. Absent is a policy group for each school which includes parents and others from the school community. The elected school board is the policy group for the system as a whole; there are no school councils or school boards at the local level. A detailed account of the Edmonton experience is provided by Brown.[5]

Framework for accountability

The following kinds of information are gathered for purposes of accountability. A description of key processes follows this listing.

- All students at grades 3, 6 and 9 levels take district tests in language arts, mathematics, science and social science; students in grade 12 take the Alberta Education Examinations.

- Each year a panel of experts defines a 'benchmark' (standard) for each of the district tests, this being a level of achievement which is considered an attainable target for all students in all schools. Performance on these tests is gathered for each school, area (region) and for the system as a whole. Results are reported according to the numbers of students at each grade level, who wrote and achieved the benchmark, who wrote and did not achieve the benchmark, who were declared exempt, who were absent, and who attained a standard of excellence (a score of 80 per cent or higher).

- All students, teachers, principals, district staff and a representative sample of parents complete an opinion survey each year. Students at the primary level rate their satisfaction with 23 factors in the categories of courses and programs, organisation, staff, and services and facilities. The category of communications is added to provide a total of 35 and 37 factors for junior and senior high school students respectively. Teachers, principals and district staff rate their satisfaction with 28 factors in the categories of confidence with senior personnel, support from senior personnel, communications, goals, working conditions and recognition for their contributions. Parents rate their satisfaction with 29 factors in the categories of courses and programs, organisation, staff, services and facilities and communication. Responses are gathered for each school, area (region) and the district as a whole for each sector of the school system (primary, junior high and senior high). Reports include percentages of respondents who were satisfied or dissatisfied, with an indication of lowest, mean and highest percentages of satisfied respondents among the schools in each sector.

- Comparative data are reported for each year since 1987 for district tests and since 1981 for opinion surveys.

- Results of tests and surveys which are made public are aggregated by sector for the district as a whole so that the public at large is not able to make school-by-school comparisons. Schools receive detailed analyses of their own tests and surveys, and are able to compare their outcomes with the range of results for other schools in their area and in the district. Analyses for a particular school are available to parents and others upon request.

- Other information reported for each school are retention rates for enrolment in grade 12 subjects; student attendance rates; percentages of students achieving acceptable and excellence standards in Alberta Education Examinations at the grade 12 level; percentages of students receiving the Alberta Education High School Diploma; percentages of students receiving Edmonton Public Schools Honour Awards; numbers of staff attending in-service and external professional development activities; number of bookings for community use, considered an indicator of community attitudes toward schools; costs of repair and maintenance borne by the district on the one hand and by the school on the other; costs of capital projects; budget allocations and actual expenditure on utilities (gas, electricity, water); total budget allocation and actual expenditure, specifying surplus or deficit to be carried forward.

The processes for accountability

The processes for accountability are consistent with the approach described in this chapter. The key person in the link between school and centre is the Associate Superintendent responsible for the management of schools in a particular area of the city. For example, Bob Smilanich is Associate Superintendent for Area 6 which in 1990–91 had 9618 students enrolled in twenty-eight schools spread throughout the district (areas in this context are not defined by geographic boundaries). Smilanich has responsibility for ensuring that district goals, policies and priorities are known to principals who then work with their staff and others in planning for the forthcoming year. Schools set their own priorities in a manner which reflects the central framework as well as local considerations. Program plans and budgets are prepared and performance indicators are specified. Among these performance indicators are those drawn from the central framework for accountability as listed above.

In preparing plans for the forthcoming year, schools are guided by the results from tests and surveys in the previous year. The Associate Superintendent meets with principals to review these results, explore factors underlying areas of concern related, for example, to performance which falls short of school expectations or at the lower end of the range in the area and district. The Associate Superintendent also sets priorities for the area, taking account of these results for all schools as well as the goals, policies and priorities for the district as a whole.

The Associate Superintendent is also the key person in the accountability framework in terms of reporting to the district's elected Board of Trustees. For example, Associate Superintendent Bob Smilanich met with the Board on 5 October 1991 to review the results for the previous academic year in 1990–91. His sixty-page report was prepared by a Review Committee of four which included a school principal. In addition to a tabulation of test scores and survey responses for all schools in the area, along the lines listed earlier in this section, an overview highlighted aspects where gains and losses were made in a comparison with results for 1989–90. He was able to report, for example, that:

> The 1990–91 results at the elementary level are most encouraging. With fewer exemptions, there were gains in the numbers of students meeting the benchmark in all four subject areas at both the grade

3 and 6 levels. Collectively, the results of the grade 9 level failed to show comparable gains and will become the focus of attention for the current year.[6]

Smilanich reported that 'the performance of students on the district's achievement exams was a key component in the performance review of all principals.'[7] Another feature of Smilanich's report was a section which summarised priorities for attention in each of the schools in the area for the preceding year.

Three observations are made in relation to the resources required to sustain the approach to accountability in the Edmonton Public School District. The first is that it is evident that the system has established a sophisticated array of survey processes over the last decade in addition to the testing program. Survey instruments are typically brief and 'respondent friendly' such that high rates of return are received. Item responses have been selected so that computerised scoring is possible. Once established, the survey process has become routine at a relatively low cost to budget. Subject area specialists are required, of course, to design the tests and to set the benchmarks. The second observation is that the approach to accountability in Edmonton does not call for large numbers of external review personnel. Indeed, the Associate Superintendent is virtually the only person involved in the district-school link. The third observation is that the district has been able to highlight steady gains in most areas over the course of a decade given its now substantial database and the setting of benchmarks from year to year by teams of experts in the different subject areas. This is a commendable achievement considering the general concern in Western nations at the quality of education throughout the 1980s. Indeed, there has been remarkable stability in the district as evidenced by the fact that Michael Strembitsky has been Superintendent of Schools since the early 1970s, bringing his vision to realisation throughout the intervening years.

Accountability and outcomes of education

Questions are often raised as to whether this relatively sophisticated approach to accountability in Edmonton has provided information which reveals that the system has done better than if it had not moved to self-management, or if it has done better than comparable districts over the period of adoption and institutionalisation. Before and after data on student achievement were not collected, and there is no evidence to suggest that Edmonton students are achieving at higher levels than their counterparts in comparable systems. However, Brown's study of school-based management in Edmonton and other systems led him to the following conclusion in respect to the links between school-based management and outcomes in education:

The Edmonton surveys reveal an increase in outcomes in the form of satisfactions registered by large numbers of parents, students, and personnel working in schools and the district office. These results appear to be stable, significant, and superior to those observed from general surveys conducted in the rest of Canada and the United States.[8]

We suggest that this is a considerable achievement for Edmonton Public Schools, but the most significant aspect of Brown's finding is that the district had the means of demonstrating these effects during a period of widespread concern about education in Canada and the United States. Indeed, most school systems around the world would be unable to do so because they lack a framework for accountability which might furnish the information.

It is also worth noting that the levels of satisfaction about which Brown reports are not just marginally positive. For example, for 1990–91 the percentage of parents reporting their satisfaction exceeded 80 for each category in the survey (courses and programs, organisation, staff, services and facilities, and communications).[9] The percentage of teachers across all levels K-12 reporting their satisfaction exceeded 70 over all categories in the teachers' survey and exceeded 80 in the category concerned with working conditions (the items in this category dealt with the fairness of assigned responsibilities, whether the district and the school were good places in which to work, involvement in the budget process, opportunities for professional development, support received from central services, the extent to which workloads were distributed equitably, the appropriateness of class size, parental involvement, and non-parental involvement).

Transitions in Leadership for Accountability

Reference has already been made to changes in the role of the inspectorate in Britain which were foreshadowed in *The Parent's Charter*. In summary, a reduction in the numbers of HMIs from 480 to 175 has been intimated, but, with an increase in frequency of inspections of schools being an expectation, it means that the workload will shift to inspectors employed by local education authorities (LEAs) and, most significantly, to individuals, organisations and agencies who gain accreditation to carry out inspectorial work in schools.

Given the issue of feasibility of approach raised earlier in the chapter, and the associated pressure to reduce costs at the level of the LEA, we question whether the proposed course of action can be sustained. Far better, we believe, for authorities to build approaches to accountability of the kind now well established in Edmonton, embedding evaluation and accountability in the culture of the authority and its schools, to the extent that only one officer of the authority need be involved in the authority-school accountability link.

All other expectations for reporting to parents set out in *The Parent's Charter* can still be achieved. Schools would, of course, be entitled if not encouraged to contract additional external support, utilising, where appropriate, one or more accredited inspectors.

Similar possibilities can be explored for Australia and New Zealand. For the latter, we reported reduction in the number of staff in the Education Review Office following the review of reforms in the wake of the Picot Report. The course of action we suggested for the British scene might be considered here. For Australia, one of the most comprehensive and sophisticated systems of educational review has been established in South Australia under the direction of Dr Peter Cuttance, who has a world-wide reputation for his expertise in matters related to evaluation and school effectiveness. The inspectorate has been abolished in Queensland, with plans and appointments in train at the time of writing for a similar scheme. The questions we raise here are similar to those implied in our commentary on the British scene. Essentially, these question the long-term desirability of sustaining a large and potentially costly central arrangement for evaluation and review when alternatives such as that in Edmonton are available.

Perhaps it is best to see what is occurring in Australia, Britain and New Zealand as transitions to the approach which fully develops an evaluation and review capability at the school level and minimises, even to one, the number of system officers who are directly involved in the system-school accountability chain.

Nothing in these comments should be construed as detracting from the achievements and value of the work of inspectors in the past or suggesting that the kind of expertise they have acquired is no longer required. We are contending that different working arrangements are possible and desirable for a system of self-managing schools which maximise the capabilities of schools in respect to resources and skills in evaluation and review.

Some Implications for Appraisal of Principals and Schools

It was not our intention to describe and illustrate approaches to the appraisal of staff in the self-managing school. However, some implications are readily apparent in the foregoing accounts and some general principles are offered here as a guide to practice. Addressed here is the appraisal of principals. Included are some cautions in respect to the validity of school-by-school comparisons on the basis of test scores.

1   Appraisal will remain problematic as long as there is ambiguity or uncertainty in the relationship between the school and the system

on the one hand and the school and its community on the other. The concept of the school charter has the potential to resolve the matter, for such a document will set out system and community expectations in a form which has been negotiated and agreed. The charter will be an important starting point in all matters related to accountability of the school and the appraisal of people such as the principal.

2 Government has a legitimate interest in how well the school addresses centrally determined expectations. The charter should specify the kind of information to be gathered from time to time to monitor the progress of the school. In similar fashion, the local community through the policy group has a legitimate interest in how well the school addresses locally determined expectations, with appropriate specification in the school charter.

3 Information on how well the school is meeting expectations is appropriately the focus of discussion between officers of the system and the principal on the one hand and the policy group and the principal on the other. These discussions should occur in the context of the charter, policies and development plan.

4 There is no need for large review and audit agencies at central or other levels to carry out the task of monitoring school progress in addressing system expectations in the school charter.

5 Momentum is gathering for national student testing programs in Australia and other countries. Such tests already exist in Britain. Without pursuing here the many issues related to the content of such tests, the argument in favour of appropriate tests is strong, given growing acceptance of the need to monitor the educational health of a nation. Within a system the results of such tests for particular schools may be helpful in discussions on school effectiveness and school improvement, providing due recognition is given to situational factors. However, we know enough about the limitations of such tests to declare that school-by-school comparisons without appropriate account of situational factors are invalid if we wish to find out if one school is 'better' than another. There will be great pressure to release the raw data of school-by-school comparisons in a manner which will distort the accountability process described thus far. In our view the strongest possible stand should be taken against the release of such data when accompanied by claims or implications of relative effectiveness.

6 Subject to the considerations set out above, the major characteristics of an approach to appraisal of principals may be described. The starting point is, of course, the school charter, which should specify the principal's role as leader and manager in addressing the expectations of the system and local community. Formative and summative appraisal can thus be referenced to the manner in which

this role is specified. Those involved in the appraisal would likely include a person representing the system (in relation to system expectations), the local community (in relation to local expectations), teachers (in relation to the role of the principal as the leader of the school), the principal and, preferably, the principal's mentor (reflecting here a preference for mentoring in the principalship).

7   Assuming that principals are appointed for fixed terms, it is suggested that a formative appraisal is appropriate at the end of the first year and a summative appraisal is appropriate in the final year.

8   While both kinds of appraisal may suggest areas for professional development, it is suggested that the latter may more appropriately emerge from ongoing consideration of progress in school development in the context of the school charter.

9   Clearly, the foregoing are general considerations which require detailed specification of a host of matters. For the appraisal of principals, these will include procedures which ensure natural justice.

The Responsive Leader

We conclude with consideration of the attributes of a responsive leader who works successfully within the approach to accountability we have offered in this chapter.

Responsive leaders are committed to the notion that the public school is an institution which has been established to serve the interests of society as a whole and the community in which it is situated, as well as, of course (and most fundamentally) its students. Reflecting this commitment, the responsive leader is at ease with the notion that all whose interests are served are entitled to have information to enable judgments to be made about the extent to which the school is addressing and achieving expectations, as these are set out in the school charter.

Demonstrating also the attributes of cultural leaders, responsive leaders are able to work with others to nurture a culture which values critical reflection on their work.

Demonstrating also the attributes of educational leaders, responsive leaders are knowledgeable about learning and teaching, and the support of learning and teaching, to the extent that they are able to identify valid and reliable indicators for use in accountability. They are mindful of the limitations of indicators and of the importance of identifying a range of indicators which samples in comprehensive fashion the goals, policies and priorities of the school as well as key strategies in the school development plan. They can select those which optimise the allocation of resources for collection and analysis.

Demonstrating also the attributes of strategic leadership, responsive leaders are able to analyse information derived from evaluation and review and are able to work with others to draw implications for refinements to overall management strategy as well as for decision-making in the annual management cycle.

Responsive leaders are mindful of the dangers of inappropriate or unethical or fraudulent claims based on information which arises from evaluation, especially in respect to results in system-wide testing programs.

Responsive leaders are knowledgeable about different purposes and approaches to evaluation, including distinctions between program evaluation and personnel appraisal. On the other hand, responsive leaders ensure that appropriate connections are made between program evaluation and practices such as peer coaching and mentoring arrangements. Essentially, they ensure that the driving force in these and related activities is a burning desire for improving the quality of learning and teaching.

Responsive leaders ensure that the force which should drive activities in a systematic approach to accountability is a desire for improvement. Indeed, responsive leadership itself may well be viewed as an underpinning of each of the dimensions of leadership we have considered in Chapters 4 to 7, and the driving force behind the efforts of the whole school community to enhance the quality of education.

Part C

Transforming Our Schools

8   Transforming the System: Avoiding the Perils of Restructuring

Self-managing schools are emerging in times of dramatic restructuring in education around the world. While changes to roles and responsibilities at the school level are challenge enough in themselves, there are concomitant changes at the central and other levels of the system which are even more far-reaching in terms of their impact on people. This chapter is concerned with the manner in which school systems may be transformed to achieve self-management, minimising the frequently cited perils of restructuring.

The Perils of Restructuring

These experiences are not unique to education; they have their counterpart in most fields of public and private endeavour. In the private sector, for example, Rosabeth Moss Kanter catalogued the possible harms from restructuring, referring to the cost of confusion, misinformation, emotional leakage, loss of energy, loss of key resources, breakdown of initiative, weakened faith in leaders' ability to deliver and the need for scapegoats.[1] She referred also to 'the backlash, the resistance, the cynicism, and the sheer fatigue of taking on so much change', and to a 'crisis of commitment' which may be found among members of the organisation.[2]

This 'downside' of restructuring is the fear, if not the recent reality, in education. It has been documented most graphically in the Australian setting by Harman, Beare and Berkeley when they reviewed case studies of change in the 1980s in each of the six states and two territories. They observed that 'while restructuring has had various obvious adverse effects, especially on morale, career structures and stability of school systems, the positive effects appear to be limited.'[3]

On a more positive note, Kanter outlined three key strategies which she asserts lie at 'the core of the post-entrepreneurial management revolution':

> restructuring to find synergies among pieces of the business, both
> old and acquired ones; opening their boundaries to form strategic

alliances with suppliers, customers and venture partners; and developing explicit programs of investment and coaching to stimulate and guide the creation of new ventures from within.[4]

One senses that a parallel statement could be written for education. We believe that systems of self-managing schools along the lines described and illustrated offer a real possibility for developing these organisational attributes. In their review of developments in Australia, Harman, Beare and Berkeley concluded that 'the emerging new model for the delivery of public education is likely to be through self-managed schools', but declare that 'one major challenge is to explore and to specify what particular conditions are necessary in order to make the self-managing school work really well.'[5] We address this challenge in this chapter.

Five areas are addressed. The first outlines ways in which a system must change in respect to *the manner in which resources are allocated to schools*. This is crucial to the success of self-management, given the often expressed concern that there will be adverse effects on equity. We take a contrary view, believing that equity may be enhanced through a transition to school self-management. In the second section we examine *the role of the teacher union* in a system of self-managing schools. Drawing on the example of Dade County Public Schools in Florida, we offer recommendations for a new role for teacher unions which fosters a higher level of professionalism among teachers yet provides the safeguards which are normally expected in collective agreements negotiated at the system level. We then return to the concept of culture, introduced in the school context in Chapter 4, and outline *ways in which the system must nurture a culture of service in support of self-managing schools*. In the fourth section we acknowledge the painful effects of system restructuring, much of which has occurred at the same time as initiatives in school self-management have been undertaken. We address here the harmful effects noted by Kanter in the business sector and by Harman, Beare and Berkeley in their account of restructuring in Australian education. We provide guidelines in *'caring and cushioning' for people affected by restructuring at the centre* as the system is transformed to support school self-management. In the final section we summarise *the attributes of system leadership* observed in different places in the transition to school self-management.

We do not provide a step-by-step account of how systems are transformed for self-management. A detailed account of change in selected school systems in Canada and the United States is provided by Brown and, in a single system in the United States, by Wissler and Ortiz.[6] Nor do we deal with a system requirement for professional development. We addressed this in Chapter 6 in the context of educational leadership. Our primary purpose in Chapter 8 is to address selected strategic issues at the system level that have proved problematic over time across all nations.

Achieving Equity through Self-Management

Harman, Beare and Berkeley identified equality of provision and opportunity (equity) as a critical consideration in addressing the challenge of self-managing schools:

> It should be remembered that, in the late nineteenth century, the highly centralised 'state'-wide bureaucratic system we knew for a hundred years was developed largely in order to ensure equality of educational provision and opportunity, across vast geographic areas. Unless the new systems of publicly self-managed schools can ensure a large measure of equal provision across states, they will soon come under considerable political pressures, perhaps leading even to a new movement for recentralisation.[7]

It is disappointing that much of the literature on restructuring has not presented the evidence that has accumulated over the last decade which reveals that allocation of resources in a system of self-managing schools is likely to be more equitable than approaches that have been utilised for decades under more centralised arrangements. Given the frequency with which concerns such as those expressed above have been raised, we set out in this section of the chapter some of the ways in which fears about this facet of restructuring can be alleviated. What follows is an account of how a system may be transformed by allocating resources to self-managing schools in a manner which more adequately reflects the values which are held about education and schooling than the uniform or equal, allegedly fair, approaches in the past.

The case for equity through self-management

The case for achieving equity through self-management was expressed best in an influential text in the 1970s by Garms, Guthrie and Pierce.[8] They addressed the apparent paradox that school-site budgeting is more equitable than relatively uniform, centralised allocations of resources to schools. They argued that centralised budgeting along these lines, with minimal opportunity for schools to budget to address local priorities, impaired the achievement of equality (equity), efficiency and choice. Equity is impaired because a centralised budget makes it difficult for schools to match services to student needs. Efficiency is impaired because incentives for its achievement are not provided. Diversity within and among schools is difficult, thus constraining choice. All these limitations can be addressed through school-site budgeting or, in the broader view we have taken, through school self-management.

The challenge for school systems, then, is to determine a means of allocating resources to schools in an equitable manner, taking account of the various factors which make schools differ, one from another, thus providing what is called in some places a 'global budget' within which schools can address their own priorities within the framework offered by the school charter.

We have had the opportunity to observe at first hand the efforts of different school systems to determine an equitable way of allocating resources to schools for school-site or global budgeting. These efforts have invariably been successful, despite some errors in the early stages in some instances. Such errors reflect more than anything else the fact that the actual cost of operating a school has rarely been known with any degree of accuracy under centralised arrangements, thus raising serious doubts about claims of equity under such conditions.

Making the transition: the perils of 'getting the formulae right'

The derivation of formulae to allocate equitably resources to schools has been the occasion of much anguish. It is helpful to understand how this has come about. Invariably the process begins with an attempt to unravel historical costs, that is, the actual costs of running schools in the past in each of the various categories of resource usage. Evidence of past inequity usually emerges, with some schools consistently receiving more resources than others which are comparable in all other respects. These inequities came about because of the way in which some allocations were determined under centralised arrangements: a combination of special case decisions or favours granted by supervisors in subject areas or others charged with decision-making, successful attempts to exert influence ('the squeaky wheel gets the grease') or the maintenance of favoured status that accrues to some schools that are deemed exceptional.

Many school systems have commenced the transition to self-management by devising formulae based on historical costs, but the inequities are soon revealed because the process is open and data not previously known or available soon come to light. Any attempt immediately to redress the situation will, understandably, bring cries of concern from schools which were specially favoured in the past, for they will lose resources while others will gain. Some instances of initial opposition to self-management can be traced to this factor alone.

Alternatives are usually explored, such as allocations on the basis of inputs, that is, on mean costs of providing schooling to students at different levels of the school system. Another approach is to allocate resources on the basis of needs, that is, on mean costs of meeting learning needs in particular programs across the curriculum. Similar concerns are raised in each instance because, as with approaches based on historical costs, there will appear to be winners and losers in the transition, especially in times of financial constraint.

Some Guidelines and Illustrations for Achieving Equity in Resource Allocation

We offer the following guidelines with a view to easing the pain in moving from a centralised approach to allocating resources, which frequently results in institutionalised inequity, to a decentralised approach, in which the search for equity is ongoing, open and invariably successful, judging from the satisfaction of participants in the process. These guidelines are based on observations of and experience in teams charged with the task of deriving formulae in Australia, Britain, Canada and New Zealand.

1   There should be **a clear understanding at the outset that formulae for allocating resources to schools will be continually refined and improved** as more information is acquired about the actual costs of meeting the educational needs of the full range of students in a particular school system. It should also be understood that changes will occur with shifts in values, priorities and other circumstances in the school system.

2   Assurance should be given that **'safety nets' will be provided in the years of transition or whenever there are rapid changes in system priorities or local circumstances** so that no school experiences a sudden decline in the resources allocated to it. By confining changes to, say, less than 2 per cent, if staffing costs are included, or 5 per cent, if staffing costs are not included, then a measure of stability and continuity in planning will be assured. Interestingly, there was evidence in England that schools experiencing large increases in resources had greater difficulty coping than schools experiencing a sudden decline, at least in the early stages of transition.

3   There should be **an expectation that formulae for allocating resources to schools will reflect a concern for meeting the learning needs of all students** and that factors which do not have this central concern will be progressively phased out. There will be an unrelenting search for valid indicators of the contribution of resources to learning. In the early stages of transition it is usual to see many factors specified in the various staff and non-staff components of a budget allocation: so much for electricity, so much for telephones, so much for equipment, so much for maintenance and so on. To some extent this stage is necessary, because it provides reassurance of a relationship between the placement of funds in school-based budgets and the areas of visible expenditure in the school. In the early stages, however, there may be little discretion for schools to budget across these areas. Even with these restrictions removed, it is usually difficult to establish a relationship between the total of funds allocated and the learning needs of students. Moreover, disparities among schools are soon made evident to a greater extent than in the past when salaries of teachers are taken into account. Some schools have a preponderance of teachers at the upper end of the salary scale, other schools have the opposite pattern. Disparities calculated on a per student basis may be as high as

25 per cent, a range difficult to justify if it is students and their learning needs which should drive the search for approaches to ensure equity in the allocation of resources to schools.

4 The potential for conflict is high when approaches are demonstrably inequitable or when sudden changes to patterns of resource allocation are made. Such **conflict has been managed when the transition has involved a series of stages which have steadily sharpened the focus on the learning needs of students**. These stages may be described as follows.

STAGE 1   *The GOK formula*. The somewhat irreverently titled 'God only knows' approach predates the systematic developments of recent years. It is typified by the historical disparities described earlier. Significant inequities have been institutionalised.

STAGE 2   *The AWPU formula*. The Age Weighted Pupil Unit is evident in the early stages of the transition to self-management. Essentially, it provides a direct relationship between age of student and the amount of the per student allocation. To a large extent it perpetuates inequities embedded in historic practice, since school systems have often provided students at the senior secondary level, for example, with the best buildings and equipment and the most highly paid and best qualified teachers.

STAGE 3   *The NWPU formula*. The Need Weighted Pupil Unit is predominantly a reflection of degrees of learning need, with allocations varying according to costs for particular kinds of educational program. A range of other factors may be utilised in supplementing the NWPU; examples include allocations related to student transiency rate or 'start-up' costs for the introduction of a program or a residual factor based on age of student. School systems develop a capacity to determine the amount of NWPUs when sources of data become more extensive and some experience in refinement of formulae from year to year has been gained. An interim arrangement has been observed in which two allocations are made, one based on age and one based on need.

STAGE 4   *The KIAK formula*. The 'Kid Is a Kid' approach involves a search for a single, uniform per student allocation for all students in the system derived from aggregated costs. We have not observed the KIAK approach in practice but have sensed the pressure to move toward it. Supporters contend that the full range of learning needs of students is distributed throughout the population of a school system, and devising complex formulae to identify costs of differential degrees of need is unnecessary. We disagree and suggest that successive refinements of the NWPU approach will achieve optimal levels of equity.

Figure 8.1. Needs-based Allocation of Resources to Schools in the Edmonton Public School District, Alberta, Canada

Level	Ratio	Per student allocation 1992 ($C)	Illustrations of learning needs to be satisfied at this level of resourcing
1	1.00	3077	Students in regular kindergarten, primary, junior high or senior high programs
2	1.27	3922	Students enrolled in primary or junior high who require differentiated programs of instruction; senior high other than learning needs at Level 1; English as a Second Language
3	1.55	4776	Students in trades and services programs
4	1.80	5550	Students with serious difficulties in academic learning who require special assistance
5	2.61	8019	Students enrolled in specialist facilities for the learning disabled
6	2.88	8861	Students of primary, junior high and senior high age who are moderately mentally or physically handicapped
7	4.40	13523	Students who are behaviour disordered, dependent handicapped, hearing impaired, multi-handicapped, physically handicapped, or visually impaired
8	6.41	19713	Students who are hearing impaired, visually impaired, autistic, deaf and blind, or physically handicapped requiring resourcing at levels higher than Level 7
9	7.89	24268	Students who are hearing impaired and visually impaired requiring resourcing at levels higher than Level 8

Figure 8.1 summarises the approach to resource allocation in the Edmonton Public School District in Alberta, Canada which extended self-management to all its schools in the early 1980s. A feature has been the steady evolution and successive refinements along the lines reflected thus far in these guidelines. The structure and amounts in Figure 8.1 are those in effect in January 1992. We believe it is an excellent illustration of the needs-based approach. Nine levels of per student allocation are defined, with the total of all such allocations to a particular school forming the major part of the school budget. Other factors, consistent with the description we have provided of the NWPU, are related to such factors as transiency rate, level of community disadvantage, extent of community use of school, and cost of 'start-up' for new programs. The total allocation constitutes a global budget for the school which can then plan its expenditure according to system and school priorities. It should be noted

that salary costs in a particular classification of staff are charged to schools at the average rate for the system as a whole.

5 A working party, supported by high-level technical expertise, should be established to devise formulae for equitable resource allocation. It is apparent in some systems moving toward school self-management that there is a surprising lack of information about what it actually costs to operate a school or a particular educational program within a school or across a system. To devise an equitable approach to allocating resources to schools can, therefore, become a time-consuming and difficult task in the early stages. At least two kinds of expertise are required, one a capacity for financial analysis, the other a capacity to relate educational philosophies, policies and programs to resources. Working parties preparing options for resource allocation should contain both kinds of expertise, with one or more members being school-based staff. In the early stages, in particular, the working party will be preparing a series of options, each of which should be subjected to trial on a simulation basis to confirm validity for a representative sample of schools prior to the selection and implementation of a preferred option. The working party should be reconstituted annually, given experience in school systems such as Edmonton which indicates the need for ongoing monitoring, development and refinement of formulae for resource allocation.

6 The manner in which budget allocations for staff are addressed is complex and must be handled with great care if the transition to school self-management is not to be jeopardised. It is understandable, in the early stages, that formulae for the allocation of staff to schools (expressed as the number of staff) will be separated from formulae for allocations in the non-staff components of the total allocation to schools (expressed as an amount in dollars, or whatever the currency). Over time the issue will arise as to whether these two broad kinds of allocation should be amalgamated to produce a single global resource formula along the lines illustrated in Figure 8.1. The issue will then arise as to whether schools should be charged for staff according to actual costs of salaries on a school-by-school basis, or whether a notional mean salary for the system shall be the basis of costing. We note that England and Wales have opted for the former, Edmonton for the latter. This issue is highly contentious as the process invariably unmasks major inequities in traditional and current per student costs of staff. Hypothetically, three different per student costs of staff may be $2000, $3000 and $4000 in three different schools in a system, reflecting, respectively, unit costs of staff in an urban school in a disadvantaged community staffed by mostly beginning teachers; in a school in an upper-class community staffed by experienced highly paid teachers; and a remote small rural school of beginning teachers where smallness drives up unit costs. This type of disparity exists now, but is largely hidden. School self-management with a global budget component brings it into the open. The lack of equity implied in the first of these per student costs should lead to vigorous debate. In general, we recommend that those with responsibility for leading a system of self-managing schools become acquainted with these issues and with practices in the different places we have mentioned.

The Role of the Teacher Union in School Self-Management

An important aspect of system transformation in the transition to school self-management is the role of the teacher union. Our observations in the different countries of which we have knowledge is that teacher unions have, in the main, been opposed to school self-management, at least at the time at which policy decisions on its adoption were made or early in the period of transition. There are usually signs of acceptance after the institutionalisation of the reform, for reasons which probably include the view of most principals and teachers that they prefer school self-management to the more centralised arrangements which preceded the change. Most, if not all, the initial fears were not justified or, if they were, they were successfully addressed once experience was gained, as in the instance of ensuring equitable allocation of resources to schools.

There are exceptions to this pattern of opposition, notably in the United States, where the President of the American Federation of Teachers, Albert Shanker, adopted a generally supportive stance toward school-site management which has proved highly influential in the restructuring movement in that country. Leaders of many professional associations have since taken the same position as restructuring gathers momentum. This is not to say that all officials and all members have shared this view.

The stance of the United Teachers of Dade, affiliated with the American Federation of Teachers, was crucial to the success of the School-Based Management/Shared Decision-Making Project in Dade County Public Schools in Florida, where union officials were involved in key decisions from the outset in 1987. Further information about their role is given later in this section, but it is noteworthy that Dade County was, at least until 1989, the only system in the United States where state, district and union authorities were working in concert in the implementation of school-based management.[9]

The traditional conservative stance of the teacher union

The traditional stance of the teacher union is explained, indeed justified, by system structures which prevailed until the advent of the phenomena we are considering in this book. Since decision-making was centralised, and relatively uniform arrangements prevailed across the system, it made sense for teacher unions to match the centre in structures and processes of decision-making. In Australia, for example, teacher unions negotiated with state governments or state agencies on matters affecting teachers across the state. In the United States and Canada teacher unions connected with authorities at the school district level in the negotiation of collective agreements. In England and Wales, and in New Zealand, these connections were invariably at the national level.

The situation became more complex for unions over the last twenty years as trends to school self-management were in their infancy and then gathered momentum. In Victoria, Australia, for example, school councils were given policy-making powers in 1983, leaving unions with the problem of coping with increasing diversity among schools as tensions developed with state-wide union-negotiated working conditions. The matter was resolved through a requirement that each principal consult with a committee of teachers (Local Administrative Committee) in decisions related to the implementation of government guidelines and school council policies.

Unions were generally opposed to proposals for more comprehensive approaches to school self-management. The argument was usually based on fears of (i) inequitable allocation of resources to schools, with teachers affected by these allocations; (ii) teachers being at the mercy of arbitrary decision-making by school council and school board, or school principals if the approach became principal-based decision-making rather than school-based decision-making; (iii) smaller schools or schools in remote areas being closed, given an apparent connection between the trend to school self-management and concern for efficiency; and (iv) progressive weakening of hard fought centrally negotiated working conditions. Unions were often quick to point to the lack of research demonstrating before-and-after effects on learning outcomes. A further argument against school self-management was presented when change was made at the same time that a system was in financial crisis. A recent example is in Tasmania, Australia. An often heard view, though not formally expressed as a teacher union stance, was that the government was decentralising to schools decisions which were too hard to make at the centre. Self-management became associated with self-funding. Finally, critics of the teacher union stance have referred to the perceived fear of union leaders that their power base is eroded or fragmented by a shift to school self-management, in much the same way as the power of senior officers in school systems is apparently threatened.

At the same time, however, there is a tension in the union position between opposition to self-management and commitment to the empowerment of the teacher. In the latter professional dimension of the role of the teacher union, a shift of decision-making to the school level, if implemented in the manner intended, should provide teachers with an increased opportunity to participate in decision-making.

It is fair to say that teacher unions have generally taken a conservative stance in school self-management and that major thrusts to self-management have only occurred where there have been the active involvement and support of the union, as in the United States in the case of Dade County, or when the government or school board or chief executive officer has been in a very strong position in a political sense, as in England and Wales, with the Thatcher and Major governments; in New Zealand, with the Lange and Bolger governments; or in the Edmonton Public School District in Canada, with the strong long-term leadership of Superintendent Michael Strembitsky and a supportive board.

The union response to self-management

As best we can determine, most of the fears of teacher unions have proved groundless as events unfolded. We refer, in particular, to concerns about the equitable allocation of resources to schools (see the account earlier in this chapter on the resolution of this issue) and the involvement of teachers in decision-making (see satisfaction of teachers reported in Chapter 7 in the Edmonton Public School District), although unions have maintained a cautious, if not sceptical, stance. It would seem appropriate for them to remain vigilant.

In our view the model response by a union has been in Dade County, Florida. While this system must be regarded as unique in virtually every aspect of its demography, making comparisons with most other systems inappropriate, the general approach of the union appears transferable. In relation to this account, it should be stressed that the major thrust for self-management in this thirty-three-school pilot was explicitly in relation to the professionalisation of teachers and the encouragement among schools of a capacity for 'self-evaluation'. There were no formal expectations for achieving improvement in learning outcomes of students, although some indicators in relation to these were utilised in the summative report of the project.[10]

As noted earlier, the union in Dade County was involved in decision and planning from the outset. Collective agreements were negotiated with the school board in the normal way, but with one very important exception: provision was made for school-by-school variation through a system of waivers. Swanson and King describe the approach in the following terms:

> School board rules, teacher contract provisions, and State Department of Education regulations may be waived. The school board has suspended requirements regarding maximum class size, length of school day, number of minutes per subject, and distribution of report cards. The union has allowed teachers to give up planning

periods, work longer hours for no additional pay, and engage in peer evaluation programs.[11]

Jim Spinks visited a number of schools in Dade County in 1988 and had the opportunity to observe at first hand these variations from negotiated system-wide arrangements. He reports an interview with one teacher who indicated that she was prepared to work longer and work harder but only if she was party to making such decisions. In most schools in any system it is likely that most teachers work longer hours than specified in job specifications or collective agreements, and they do so by their own choice. What Dade County has done is formalise the arrangement through the waiver system, on the condition that teachers at the system and school levels are participants in the decision.

It is worth noting the findings of a summative evaluation of the project in Dade County, recalling that its primary purpose was the professionalisation of teachers. Hanson and Collins, Principal Evaluators of the SBM/SDM Project, report the following:

> In terms of the major thrust of the project, the involvement of teachers in decision-making toward the end of making the profession more attractive, there is substantial evidence to say that the project has succeeded. Teachers are involved in decision-making experiences in school cadres; 'teacher status' has improved; and there is evidence that school environment is perceived as being more collegial and less autocratic.[12]

Collins and Hanson report that ratings on key items related to the above are not as high as in the early years of the pilot and note the need for continuing in-service:

> All this is not to say that there is no room for improvement in the project. There is evidence that SBM is losing its 'unique visibility' within schools, as a myriad of other innovations are superimposed over SBM school programming. Principals report that there is substantial need for inservice in the area of converting ideas into workable products or processes and that the role of the principal in SBM schools is increasingly 'difficult'.[13]

The increasing load of innovations and the increasing difficulty experienced by principals described by Collins and Hanson match the conditions emerging in most school systems. It is under these conditions that we have refined the model for self-management (Chapter 2) and have highlighted the importance of strategic leadership (Chapter 5) so that schools can, to a greater extent than initially appeared possible, 'take charge of their own agenda'.

Recommended stance for the teacher union

In general, we urge the strong support of self-management by teacher unions who seek to enhance the professionalisation of their members. The levels of involvement and satisfaction of teachers, as reported in Edmonton (Chapter 7) and in Dade County (Chapter 8), are illustrations of favourable outcomes. We believe that the concerns of teacher unions on matters such as resource allocation have been addressed, although vigilance is urged in respect to implementation.

In summary, we would support a continuing and powerful role for teacher unions at the national, state or district levels, depending on the context, on matters related to frameworks for salaries and working conditions, including advocacy for the highest possible levels of resourcing for schools. But none of these frameworks, we urge, should impair the capacity for a system or a school to waive certain requirements, providing teachers participate in the decision-making process. At the school level the policies and procedures for allowing this diversity within centrally determined frameworks may be incorporated in the school charter. Subject to these arrangements, we see no reason why there may not be diversity in respect to the structure of the school year, the size of classes, the days of the week on which classes are scheduled and the work load of teachers. In one sense what we are advocating is a form of school-based enterprise bargaining, to use the language in vogue in Australia. All of this reflects a vision of an empowered profession, a vision we extend to the next century in our concluding chapter.

Nurturing a Culture of Service

At the heart of the transformation is a change of culture at all levels. At the system (central, regional, district) levels this is captured by the notion of a culture of service. The concept of culture and the need for change were captured well by Dr Brian Scott, who conducted the review of the administration of education in New South Wales. He concluded that 'the inflexibility of the Department's structures and procedures has made it unresponsive to the real educative needs of students and teachers' and proposed that senior officers 'will be agents of change during a fundamental redefinition of corporate culture. Such a role will not come easily to those who have been part of a different culture, in some cases for more than 30 years.'[14]

Recalling that a simple way of viewing organisational culture is 'the way we do things around here', we define a culture of service at the system level as one in which all day-to-day activities are driven by the value of providing support to schools in a manner which meets needs in a precise and timely manner, negotiated within the limitations of resources which are known and understood by all parties.

We acknowledge that many aspects of the centralised operations of a system of education are more concerned with direction than support, given the importance of centrally determined goals, policies, priorities, standards and other elements in a framework for accountability. Even for these functions, however, a culture of service should prevail. For example, there is a host of matters related to the framework where communications are received from schools and timely and helpful responses are required. Many organisations in the private sector now pride themselves in speed of turnaround; as citizens we demand it of agencies in the public sector. The following account by Jeremy Sutcliffe of changes in the Department of Education and Science (DES) in Britain suggests that this shift in culture has occurred at the centre as the nation moves toward school self-management within a tight central framework: 'DES officials are eager to point out that things have changed. There have been changes at the top. Papers that used to lie around on civil servants' desks for a fortnight, are now turned around in 24 hours, they say.'[15] It should be pointed out, however, that Sutcliffe offers a negative prognosis, suggesting that 'the changes may have come too late. Ministers show no signs that the leopard has changed its spots. . . . The DES in its present form looks unlikely to survive another Conservative victory.'[16]

We believe that a transformation to achieve a culture of service is imperative for those involved in the direction and support of schools. The massive restructuring at the centre reported in nation after nation is likely to continue unabated unless this occurs. What follows are illustrations and guidelines for those involved in one important function, namely, the provision of consultancy services to schools.

Changing the culture for consultancy services

A helpful example of changing the culture is offered by experience in the Edmonton Public School District in Alberta, Canada. We drew on experience in this school system in Chapter 7 when describing a comprehensive framework for accountability for self-managing schools.[17]

Of particular interest in Edmonton is the decision in 1986 to include district consultancy services in the framework for school self-management. A representative sample of fourteen schools was selected from eighty-four which volunteered for participation in the project, the purposes of which were to improve the effectiveness and efficiency of the service, to improve the capability of school personnel to determine the nature and level of services required, and to improve the way in which consultancy services were accessed and delivered. Schools in the project had their lump-sum or global budget allocations increased by amounts which reflected the historical use of consultancy services, according to type of school and level of student need. Standard costs for various types of service were then determined, on a per hour or per incident basis, with costs charged to schools as services were provided. Schools could choose services outside those provided by the district. It is noteworthy that the level of utilisation of central services declined in the first year of the trial, with many schools choosing to acquire other resources or utilise alternative approaches to solving their problems. For example, additional teachers were deployed or private sector resources (for example, social workers) were used, or schools turned to neighbouring schools in their search for expertise. The extent to which central services were utilised returned to a more traditional pattern in succeeding years.

It seems that the purposes of the trial were largely achieved after three years, with evidence of a strengthening of a culture of service. Outcomes included (i) a 'mission' which included the support of schools and central services as well as the opportunity to influence the setting of district policies and priorities; (ii) a clarification of the division of responsibility between central support and schools; (iii) approaches to needs assessment which encouraged schools to plan and then allocate resources in their budgets for the provision of appropriate services; (iv) service agreements with schools; (v) enhancement of client autonomy; (vi) integrated delivery of services to schools; (vii) flexible modes of service delivery; (viii) flexible staffing patterns for those employed in central support services; (ix) development of generic knowledge, skills and attitudes as well as skills in consultation and areas of specialisation; (x) an enhanced capacity for networking; and (xi) an enhanced capacity for monitoring the quantity and quality of service, including the identification and utilisation of centrally determined outcomes, standards and indicators.

The initial set of fourteen participating schools in Edmonton had been expanded to thirty-six by 1991. Approval has been given to extend the scheme to all schools on a progressive basis. Even though the number of schools wishing to participate has always exceeded the number of places available, the move has been gradual to provide a more orderly transition for those providing the service. There is evidence that the culture of service engendered in the trial has extended to consultancy services in general, since the results of system-wide opinion surveys (see Chapter 7 for an account of these) reveal a steadily increasing improvement in ratings by school staff. Consultants now have a wider range of generic skills and visit schools several times each year to plan the manner in which services can be matched to school needs. It seems that initial fears by many consultants that their jobs might be in jeopardy proved groundless. The trial would appear to have had an impact by fostering a stronger culture of service which was increasingly valued by schools.[18]

Nurturing a culture of service

We have gleaned from these experiences a number of guidelines for nurturing a culture of service in the support of schools. The starting point is our view that a continuing role for consultancy services is both pre-ferred and probable. The concern of many who provide such support that their services will be neither valued nor necessary should be laid to rest. However, the viability of service centres or similar units will be dependent on the extent to which a strong culture of service can be nurtured. We do not address in detail how consultancy services are carried out, just as we do not address the way in which teachers carry out their work in the classroom.

1   In terms of attitudes to change, **there is little to be gained from blaming 'the system' for the apparent lack of stability or certainty which characterises the provision of consultancy services**. There is much to be gained from acquiring an understanding of the forces which are shaping the provision of services in the public and private sectors. Leaders at the senior level should thus do all they can to ensure that staff who provide services to schools understand the reasons for changes which are occurring in education. Consistent with the view expressed in Chapter 5, this is an important aspect of strategic leadership.

2   Leaders in the service sector of a school system should **exercise the same four dimensions of transformational leadership in relation to their own work that we have advocated for leaders at the school level**, namely, cultural leadership, strategic leadership, educational leader-ship and responsive leadership. They should also have an understanding of these aspects of the roles of school leaders since they must support these people in their work. In some instances, of course, consultants will be directly involved in professional development for principals and other school leaders to assist in the acquisition of knowledge and skill which are required in these roles.

3   Leaders and others who provide consultancy services to schools should **help principals and other school leaders by providing infor-mation** to help the latter set priorities as they work 'to take charge of their own agenda'. This is support in the exercise of strategic leadership. In similar fashion information should be provided to support the other dimensions of leadership at the school level.

4   **A capacity to negotiate service agreements with schools is critical.**

5   **Marketing and entrepreneurship, in the best senses of these concepts, will enhance the capacity of consultants to provide services to schools**. In Chapter 4 we provided a checklist for leaders at the school level for approaches to marketing and entrepreneurship which had educa-tional integrity. In Figure 8.2 we have provided a similar list for appraising a culture for marketing in a consultancy service centre at the system level. We again draw attention to the fact that this is a different view of market-ing and entrepreneurship from that which educationists have traditionally and properly rejected, namely, one limited to 'selling' a service, regardless of whether it is needed.

6   It should be accepted that there will be competition from the private sector for the provision of support to schools. Indeed, many consultants may leave the system to enter private practice. However, if experience around the world is a guide, a service centre along the lines we have described will remain viable, if not indispensable.

7   Notwithstanding the continuing need for their services, **it is likely that service centres, as with their counterparts in the public and private sectors, will become even leaner and more adaptable** than is now the case. Increasingly, most if not all appointments will be temporary. In reality, as well as in rhetoric, it should be accepted that the school and the classroom will be the most important units in a system of education, and the premier leadership positions in a system of education will lie at the school level.

Caring and Cushioning

It is unfortunate that school self-management has been introduced in many systems at the same time that the 'downsizing' of the centre has occurred, and that both have taken place in a time of financial crisis for many governments. The context for self-management in the early 1990s contrasts with that of the mid- to late 1970s when many early initiatives in the United States and Canada were not associated with massive system restructuring and financial crisis. Similarly in Australia the foundations of self-management were laid through programs of the Commonwealth Schools Commission which encouraged choice and diversity within and among schools, and established expectations for participation in decision-making by teachers and members of the community. In each of these countries and others these were the days of the special purpose grants which, in many instances, were decentralised to schools as far as decisions on allocation were concerned. These were the conditions in Tasmania which allowed the model for school self-management, based on practice at Rosebery District High School, to emerge.

While many at the centre have always been sceptical about the concept of school self-management, it is clear that conditions which prevail in the 1990s are not always conducive to support of and commitment to the concept. Restructuring at the centre is, understandably, traumatic enough in itself. We cited at the beginning of the chapter the description by Kanter of the harmful effects of restructuring in the private sector, referring to the cost of confusion, misinformation, emotional leakage, loss of energy, loss of key resources, breakdown of initiative, weakened faith in leaders' ability to deliver and the need for scapegoats.[19] She referred also to 'the backlash, the resistance, the cynicism, and the sheer fatigue of taking on so much change' and to a 'crisis of commitment' which may be found among members of the organisation.[20] We also noted the frequency and scale of

177

Figure 8.2. Appraising the Marketing Culture of a Consultancy Service Centre

APPRAISING THE MARKETING CULTURE OF A CONSULTANCY SERVICE CENTRE

SCALE

Provide a rating for each of the ten sets of questions according to the following ten-point rating scale:

1– 2 A strongly negative response to all questions
3– 4 A mixed but mostly negative response
5– 6 A mixed but mostly positive response, with matters for major improvement readily apparent
7– 8 A positive response to all or most questions, with matters for minor improvement readily apparent
9–10 A strongly positive response to all questions

While the total of ratings may be of interest, it is the item-by-item analysis which may be of value as a starting point in planning the manner in which the marketing capacity in the service may be enhanced.

1 *EXPECTATIONS OF SCHOOLS*

Are expectations of schools known to consultants? Are there clearly defined processes for monitoring these?

[RATING =]

2 *MISSION AND PROGRAM*

Does the service centre have a statement of mission (or equivalent), setting out the primary purpose for its existence? Is this statement clearly understood and accepted by consultants? Is it consistent with the expectations of schools? Is the program of support consistent with the statement of mission and the expectations of schools? Are there clearly defined processes for ensuring alignment of these?

[RATING =]

3 *COMMUNICATION*

Are details of mission and program communicated to schools in an effective manner which makes clear how these are consistent with expectations? Are printed materials and other means of communication of the highest quality or at least consistent with the standard set by competitors?

[RATING =]

4 *SPECIAL AND ORDINARY ACTIVITIES*

Is attention paid to the marketing potential of special events and, especially, ordinary day-to-day activities, including the manner in which school personnel are welcomed to the service centre; key events such as visits to schools and negotiations in respect to the provision of services are conducted; mail and telephone calls are initiated and answered?

[RATING =]

5 *UNIQUENESS*

Has the uniqueness of the service centre been identified and addressed in marketing efforts? Have efforts been made to align interests and expertise of particular consultants with particular needs and expectations of schools? Where the opportunity arises for the development of service traditions, have appropriate priorities been set as far as attracting staff is concerned?

[RATING =]

Figure 8.2.   (Cont.)

6   *WIDER COMMUNITY*

Have the needs of schools in other systems or independent schools been taken into account in the marketing effort? Are there needs in the public and private non-educational sector which can be satisfied? Have possibilities been explored for corporate involvement or corporate support in the design and delivery of services to schools and others? Are appropriate means utilised to keep the wider community informed of the services provided?

[RATING =]

7   *STRATEGIC LEADERSHIP*

Is there a capacity for strategic leadership among staff in the service centre? Are priorities set and re-set according to a continuing appraisal of opportunities and threats, strengths and weaknesses? Does the marketing effort reflect the outcomes of these analyses? Is there ongoing appraisal of services and of the marketing effort?

[RATING =]

8   *HUMAN RESOURCE MANAGEMENT*

Is the development of a capacity for marketing a priority in human resource management? Have those with particular flair and expertise been identified and appropriately involved? Do all members of staff appreciate that they have a role to play in the effort? Are marketing implications considered as a matter of course in planning processes? In these and other respects, is marketing seen as a continuous, ongoing activity rather than a discrete event of short duration for a particular purpose such as fending off threatened cuts in staff or close down of services?

[RATING =]

9   *ENTREPRENEURSHIP*

Does the culture of the service centre foster 'a passionate commitment to use all available resources to create new ideas and actions that will enrich the quality of service'? Is this entrepreneurial spirit encouraged in the marketing effort? Is there a budget allocation for marketing? Is there a sharing of resources among different units in the service centre and others who may be viewed as collaborators in a combined marketing effort?

[RATING =]

10   *INTEGRITY*

Is there integrity in the marketing effort? Is there consistency between the values evident in marketing and those underpinning the culture of the service centre? Is this consistency clearly evident?

[RATING =]

[TOTAL RATING =]

system restructuring in education in Australia, citing the recent study by Harman, Beare and Berkeley.[21] George Berkeley, a former Director-General in Queensland, described the impact in graphic terms. He offered the following observations in reference to the case for recruiting new people with commitment and energy:

> One cannot really argue with this as a principle, but it would seem to me, particularly as education is meant to belong to the caring professions, that, in a number, if not most Australian restructures, there has been little regard, if not a callous disregard, for people caught up in changes. There would seem to be a belief that for the exercise to succeed, the sacrifice of professional lives of public servants many of whom have served well and long across the vast and unpopular areas of their State must be made. The consequences of such sacrifices for the morale of the administrative staff of departments are well known and predictable.[22]

Berkeley then considered the investment of resources in making new appointments, asserting that the 'human resource waste and costs are well known' and, in the case of the 1991 restructure in Queensland, that 'one cannot help but wonder what productive work is occurring in that Department at this time.'[23]

Changes in New Zealand may be described in similar terms. The same may be foreshadowed in England and Wales, with a substantial reduction in the number of Her Majesty's Inspectors, a scaling down if not phasing out of LEAs, and an extensive restructure of the Department of Education and Science all on the cards.

The problem in the context of leadership in a system of self-managing schools may be expressed in a series of questions. Given that organisational structures should match organisational ends ('form should follow function'), how can a system restructure itself, when there is a need for restructure, and at the same time minimise the painful personal effects noted in the above accounts? How can a caring profession reorder its own affairs in a caring manner? What 'cushioning' can be provided when major change to career paths is indicated? Above all, how can direction and support be provided for schools during times of system transformation?

At the heart of it all

Before turning to approaches for addressing the problem, it is worthwhile to look more closely at some of the reasons why governments believe that large-scale restructuring is necessary. At the heart of it, we suggest, is the loss of faith by governments that a system of education can restructure or renew itself. Governments were, until recently, content to leave the running to powerful permanent heads. The global and national perspectives which are now demanded were not yet formed; curriculum was stable; public expectations were clear and consistent; and a bureaucratic organisational form was more or less appropriate. For a host of reasons, some of which were recounted in Chapter 1, a need for change on a large scale was perceived, commencing in the 1970s, gathering momentum in the 1980s and sweeping around the world in the 1990s. Large centralised bureaucracies were considered to be ill-equipped to cope with calls for greater efficiency in times of competing public priorities, financial crises, the need for education to be more responsive to national economic needs, the associated rapid change in curriculum, the social and economic demand for equity, and the achievement of full retention to the end of secondary schooling, and a better educated and more affluent community expecting higher standards from, and choice in, the selection of schools.

Another way of explaining what has occurred is to reflect on the tensions which have been evident for some time in countries which are governed and administered in the Westminster tradition. On the one hand, there has been pride that senior officers, especially the permanent head, could successfully serve governments of differing political persuasion in a politically neutral and professional manner. On the other hand, these officers had become used to being the dominant influence in policy-making and policy implementation. In the final analysis, when rapid change was called for, governments perceived an inability on the part of senior officers to respond, for whatever reason, and certainly not in a way which required a change in organisational form and function, with 'downsizing' after several decades of steady growth. The outcome, especially in Australia, has been an unprecedented number of commissioned reports, invariably by consultants outside the education system, who have all made similar recommendations in terms of leaner, flatter central structures and a system of self-managing schools. In every instance in Australia governments have chosen to advertise all positions at the senior level, requiring incumbents to reapply for positions at or near their current levels of appointment. Again there is the implication that the system lacks the capacity or the commitment to carry through the reforms. The only cushioning has been in the form of redundancy packages or encouragement to take early retirement.

In general, in education as in other fields of public and private endeavour, it seems that the prevailing organisational culture was unable to adapt in a way which would satisfy those who held power.

A better way

What kind of organisational culture would have enabled organisational adaptation without the trauma experienced by so many leaders who, as

Berkeley correctly noted, had served with distinction in earlier years? Now that changes have been made, how can the perils of restructuring be avoided in the future? Kanter is optimistic in the manner suggested by the title of her book, *When Giants Learn to Dance*, conjuring the same image as Scott who, in writing of the future of the Department of School Education in New South Wales, opined that 'it *is* possible to teach the elephant to dance', but added a cryptic warning that 'backsliding is the one dance step which the elephant must not be permitted to learn.'[24]

In suggesting answers to these questions, it is important to note that a change in culture, in addition to ongoing change in the operational domain, will entail experience of loss on the part of those affected by change. As Terrence Deal, an influential writer on the theme of organisational culture, has argued: 'cultural change typically creates significant individual and collective loss',[25] with individuals so affected responding in ways that may not be dissimilar to those experiencing loss through death: denial, anger, depression, bargaining, acceptance. The organisational response, according to Deal, is to use the culture to support those affected, especially through transition rituals: 'A vital leadership task is consciously to plan rituals and to encourage ritualistic activities that arise from the spontaneous actions of individuals or groups as they struggle to come to grips with the ambiguity and loss that change produces.'[26]

This task of leadership will be difficult in the case of large-scale restructuring, where the culture has been fragmented if not destroyed. The leader will be attempting to utilise that enduring aspect of a culture that befits a caring profession at the same time as an attempt is made to build a new culture. A host of possibilities emerges as far as transition rituals are concerned. Wakes may be held to mark the demise of a particular organisation or unit; celebrations may be held to mark the arrival of the new.

Above all, as far as possible, there should be no imputation of past failure, even where the organisation has apparently been unable to renew itself. The achievements of large centralised bureaucratic organisations in education have been monumental, and those who have led them have been heroes and heroines who should be accorded a status of great esteem. Stories will be told of their achievements, and these will become the myths which bind and drive the organisation in the future. In a restructured organisation a new story must be told, and that is a story of a new type of organisation and organisational response in a new era of public education.

Deal notes the limitations of rational approaches in making the transition: setting objectives, formulating plans, allocating resources, implementing and monitoring outcomes may be necessary but they are insufficient. Symbolic approaches are also required: 'Leaders need to think about how they can convene, encourage and become active participants in rituals, social dramas and healing dances as a means of transforming modern organisations.'[27]

The following are offered as a framework for accomplishing this task of creating new organisational forms which will be self-renewing and service-oriented as well as caring in the manner in which people are supported through transition.

1 **The dominant value in the organisational culture at the centre of a school system is service**, service to the government or system authority, and service to schools.

2 Given the organisational context for education in the 1990s, **there will be few aspects of the organisation structure that need to be organised along bureaucratic lines**, only those which are relatively stable and routine. All other aspects of the structure should be flexible in nature, with patterns of authority, responsibility and communication expected to change relatively frequently.

3 Accordingly, **most if not all appointments to the centre will be on a short-term contract basis**, although there may be tenure of appointment within the system.

4 Since service to schools is a dominant feature of the system, and since most leadership positions lie at the school level, **most appointments to the centre should not be viewed or valued as promotions or as elevations in status**: they are opportunities for service. For those whose appointments at the centre are of a more permanent nature, the culture should not encourage a view that a particular person 'owns' a particular position. While specialist skills are valued, generalist capability should prevail in the longer term.

5 **Organisational symbols should reflect the values embodied in the foregoing**. For example, *organisational charts* are of little value if they represent the organisation in strictly bureaucratic and hierarchical terms. It is to be expected that *job titles* for particular positions and particular tasks will change frequently. *Salary differentials* between principals of schools and most leaders at the centre should be minimal, if they exist at all.

6 **The dimensions of transformational leadership defined for principals and other school leaders apply also to leaders at the centre.** *Cultural leadership* at the centre calls for a capacity to build an organisation with the values implied in this framework, with service at the core. *Strategic leadership* calls for unprecedented awareness of 'the larger picture' for education in the 1990s on the part of all who work at the centre. *Educational leadership* calls for a capacity to work on behalf of government or employing authority, and with schools, to design and deliver educational programs to meet the needs of all students and to ensure that schools are resourced in appropriate fashion, with resources ranging from the knowledge, skills and attitudes of staff to the provision of an adequate global budget. *Responsive leadership* calls for a capacity to gather information, not only about the manner in which schools are achieving expectations in their charters, but also about the quality of service provided by the centre,

with systematic approaches along the lines described and illustrated in Chapter 7.

7 Nothing in these guidelines should be construed as advocacy of anything other than strong leadership. While the characteristics of strong transformational leaders at the system level are highlighted in the final section of the chapter, it is noted here that the senior officers of the system must have a vision of service in a system of self-managing schools and a powerful capacity to articulate that vision and manage the system so that it is brought to realisation. This will mean a high level of strength and commitment.

8 Continuing professional development on the part of staff at the centre is as important as it is for those at the school level. Included here will be intensive programs with other senior officers in the public and private sector which focus on strategic capability.

9 The notion of change as a process rather than an event has become almost a cliché in the lexicon of education. Its parallel in broader organisational terms might well be that **restructuring is a process rather than an event**; it is continuous and ongoing because that is what is required in the context of the 1990s. The notion of a capacity for organisational self-renewal may be more helpful than that of continuous organisational restructuring.

10 The organisational culture must include components that will enable staff at the centre to cope with the sense of loss which invariably accompanies change, even if change is managed along the lines suggested in this framework. The encouragement of appropriate rituals and ceremonies of transition is important. While arrangements such as redundancy packages and early retirements were the main means of cushioning at the height of the restructuring phenomenon, and will continue to be appropriate in some instances, every effort should be made to maintain the accumulated wisdom and commitment of those who have given long service and who can work within a framework such as that outlined here.

Transformational Leadership

To conclude the chapter, we address the issue of leadership at the most senior levels of a school system. For a superintendent (in the context of Canada or the United States) or a director-general or director or chief executive officer (in the context of Australia or New Zealand), we address questions such as 'What are the attributes of leadership required to transform the system?' 'How can the culture of the system be changed so that all who work in it are committed to the core values of school self-management (such as subsidiarity, empowerment, trust, synergy, responsibility, accountability and, particularly at the system level, service)?' We draw on two instances we have had the opportunity to observe at first hand in Canada and New Zealand but, in the main, offer responses to these questions through a synthesis of the guidelines presented at various points throughout this chapter.

The vision of the pioneers

The driving forces behind self-management in the relatively small number of districts in the United States which pioneered the practice in the late 1960s and the early 1970s were mainly school superintendents. For example, Seward reviewed the trend to school-based management in a consortium of school systems outside the major urban areas in California and noted that:

> Typically, the pressure for decentralisation in these districts has come from superintendents primarily interested in participative management, and not from the communities which, unlike their urban neighbours, have been generally trusting and supportive of the leadership in this area. Often community participation is seen as the next step and ultimate goal after principals and school staff have accepted and practised their new role. . . .[28]

In contrast to these initiatives in school self-management, the decentralisation of large urban school districts into subdistrict or regional administrative units was largely an outcome of pressure from external interests, including interest groups within the community.[29]

The focus of these early initiatives in school-based management was largely on finance and the introduction of school-site budgeting. The involvement of the community in decision-making at the school level occurred in a few systems in the United States, but in the late 1970s and early to mid-1980s the momentum for school-based management appeared to be lost. In general, it is fair to say that there was no system transformation; the driving forces were not strong enough or sustained sufficiently to achieve institutionalisation.

We contrast this dissipation of the movement with what occurred in the Edmonton Public School District in Canada where the first steps were taken in the mid-1970s. A seven-school pilot in the late 1970s led to system-wide adoption of a comprehensive approach to self-management in 1980–81 which is now institutionalised. The driving force in the mid- to late 1970s, like that in California, was the superintendent who at the time of writing still held that office. In 1977 Brian Caldwell studied the seven-school pilot in Edmonton and identified the factors leading to its adoption. While external factors were noted, mainly in the form of a general interest in decentralisation, the internal factors were dominant:

The most frequently cited factor was the management strategies of the Superintendent based on his philosophy and perception of the problems with existing practice . . . a relatively centralised budgeting system, which had proved satisfactory in former times, was now attempting to meet the needs of over 150 different schools in a much larger system with little organised input from persons at the school level.[30]

Some people interviewed by Caldwell referred to Strembitsky's desire to 'deliver the system to the schools'.[31]

Brown brought the story of Strembitsky's leadership up-to-date in 1990. Noting a reputation which now 'is something of a legend in western Canada and beyond', he reported that:

Many interviewees described Strembitsky as visionary, a person with firmly-held convictions who is able to translate those beliefs into action by working with people. Perhaps most apparent are some of his beliefs about individuals. He says that they want to be creative at their work . . . that they would like to participate in a cause greater than themselves.[32]

This appraisal of Strembitsky by Brown is expressed in words which are similar to the classical definition of a transformational leader, with its reference to vision and the capacity to engage people in 'a cause greater than themselves'. A reading of Brown's account reveals a leader who, for nearly twenty years, has largely satisfied his desire 'to deliver the system to the schools', albeit within a framework of centrally determined goals, priorities and standards. Scepticism or opposition from a variety of interests has been evident from time to time, but we are left with an image of an enduring vision and strong leadership, highlighted by a capacity to articulate that vision and harness all the available leadership forces (technical, human, educational, symbolic and cultural) to mobilise and institutionalise.

Wissler and Ortiz provide an extended study of the superintendency of E. Raymond Berry in Riverside Unified School District in California,[33] who led the introduction of school self-management from the time of his appointment in 1968, although a number of initiatives can be traced to his service as associate superintendent in the early 1960s. While the process of change is more evolutionary than that in Edmonton, the following account highlights the transformational nature of Berry's leadership:

The intentional acts of the superintendent were to change the central office from a command to a service structure, flatten the organisation, give the principals site budgetary and programmatic autonomy, and allow participation in organisational decision-making. Consistent with Burns' . . . definitions of real change, 'as a transformation to a marked degree in the attitudes, norms, institutions, and behaviours that structure our daily lives', the Riverside Unified School District was transformed in significant ways.[34]

Realising the vision of others

We contrast pioneers with vision like Michael Strembitsky with change agents who have frequently filled positions of leadership in the late 1980s and early 1990s. A characteristic of these times has been the dramatic restructuring of school systems, which has invariably involved the replacement of many senior officers, including the chief executive. As we have noted elsewhere, and as described most recently in the Australian context by Harman, Beare and Berkeley,[35] the driving forces for these changes have come from outside the system. With a shift to school self-management usually a key component of the new structure, governments and other authorities have then been placed in a position of appointing a new chief executive officer to oversee the change. In the Australian context it is now rare for appointees to be people who have come through the ranks of the teaching profession. Those with backgrounds in education have usually worked for extended periods in other settings. The notion of a 'permanent head' has disappeared; appointments on contract are the order of the day.

The appointment which captures most starkly the characteristics of leadership under these conditions is that of Dr Russell Ballard in New Zealand. Ballard is not an educationist and, prior to his appointment in education, headed the forestry department. The brief for his eighteen-month contract appointment was to implement the reforms of government following its acceptance of the major recommendations of the Picot Report, a major feature of which was a further thrust toward school self-management in a system which was already highly decentralised. For those in New Zealand, the speed of these changes was still more akin to that of revolution; to observers from other nations they appeared of earthquake proportion.

Ballard's brief was, in essence, to bring the vision of others to realisation. This clearly contrasts with that of Strembitsky in Edmonton where the vision was his own. We had the opportunity to work in New Zealand at around the mid-point of Ballard's appointment. Our task was to conduct seminars and workshops for principals and parents, relating the model for self-management set out in *The Self-Managing School* to expectations for schools under the new arrangements in New Zealand.

Three characteristics of Ballard's leadership were evident to us during this time. The first was his capacity to articulate clearly what was expected of schools and their communities. An engaging and energetic speaker, his presentations made clear his conviction that the complex changes could be accomplished in the limited time frame that had been specified by government.

The second was his capacity to mobilise the human resources of the system, acquiring expertise from outside as necessary. There were always flow charts and schedules, setting out the sequence and timing of key events, all leading to system-wide implementation on 1 October 1989. Refinements were made from time to time but the endpoint was always the same. High levels of public awareness and commitment were also required in the months leading up to the election across the nation of the new school boards. These elections were on the same scale as those for the national parliament. Funds were committed and expertise acquired for a sophisticated media campaign which secured large numbers of candidates and voters in most parts of the country. Aside from the election of school boards, this campaign was a symbol of the government's commitment to the process of reform and to education in the life of the nation. There were also many task forces or working parties addressing different aspects of the reforms, including matters related to school charters and the determining of formulae to allocate equitably resources to schools. Each of these groups was representative of different interests and expertise. Each required a commitment and recommitment of effort in the apparently headlong rush to 1 October 1989. Ballard was a visible leader in each instance, with his aforementioned drive, energy and commitment helping to sustain the energy of all.

The third characteristic, implied in the foregoing, was a personal strength and confidence that all could be accomplished. The nature of the reforms made them highly contentious, with different interest groups within the system and outside it expressing major concerns about various aspects of the proposed changes. In public statements as well as private meetings Ballard was prepared to face these concerns directly, alleviating them wherever possible, but always expressing unwavering commitment and confidence in the intended outcomes. He concluded his work on the date specified in his contract, to be succeeded by Dr Maris O'Rourke, a distinguished educationist who has worked in succeeding years to institutionalise the reforms across the nation.

An affirming view of leadership

While this section of the chapter is not intended as a comprehensive study of leadership at the senior levels of a system of self-managing schools, we have found in the examples of Michael Strembitsky and Russell Ballard an affirmation of the contemporary view of transformational leadership. Transforming the system calls for a change in culture, whether it be in approaches to allocating resources to schools or in the unrelenting focus on service on the part of system personnel who are not employed in schools. To achieve these changes in 'the way we do things around here' calls for a clear vision, powerfully, attractively and consistently articulated, and a capacity to mobilise all the resources of the system in an imaginative manner. These same qualities are required in leaders of teacher unions, as suggested in the account we have offered of the leadership of Albert Shanker in the American Federation of Teachers. Stability of leadership is clearly an advantage, as in the cases of Strembitsky and Shanker in their respective settings, but not necessarily so, as demonstrated in the case of Ballard.

We have offered guidelines for all who serve as leaders at the system level. With attention to the human factor, as suggested in our view of 'caring and cushioning', there seems no reason why the oft-cited perils of restructuring need be experienced in the transformation of a system to school self-management.

9   Schools in Transition:
A Vision for the 1990s

Despite the almost continuous restructuring which has occurred in many nations over the last decade and the associated emergence of systems of self-managing schools, we believe that education is not yet approaching a period of stability as far as governance or management are concerned. Expressed simply, we are still in a period of transition in education, as in other fields of public and private service.

The purpose of this chapter is to offer a vision for leadership and management in schools in the 1990s. This vision has four major elements. The first deals with the concept of self-management: our vision is for inexorable transition to self-government. The second deals with restructuring of school systems: our vision is for new forms of organisation in which there is continuous adaptation of roles, relationships and responsibilities as a culture of service emerges in reality as well as in rhetoric. The third deals with the nature of teaching as a profession: our vision is for a level of professionalism unprecedented in public education, closing the gap between education and the other professions such as medicine and the law. The fourth, and a common thread through the first three, is strong and widely dispersed leadership.

Toward the Market Model and the Self-Governing School

If developments around the world are taken into account, one may discern four models which contain what may be the key characteristics among scenarios for the management of education. None exists as a pure or ideal type, with practices now evident or emerging being variations or combinations.

These models vary according to the governance framework within which schools are managed, looseness or tightness in the coupling between centre and school, the extent to which schools are assisted through system support services, and the degree to which market conditions apply to student enrolments.

Four scenarios

The Market Model. School self-management within a central framework will become school self-government in a nation of free standing schools, with public schools receiving their core funding directly from treasury. There will be a national curriculum framework and national testing but little else in terms of central direction and support. The capacity of schools to enrol students will be the chief determinant of their survival. Schools will purchase support services in a largely private market. Staff will be employed by their schools. Elements of this scenario are clearly evident in England and Wales, with the demise of local education authorities foreshadowed.

The Charter Model. Systems of self-managing schools will continue to evolve, with a charter the key mechanism for resourcing and accountability. The charter is a formal agreement between government and school council or board on arrangements at the school level for addressing national and state policies and priorities on the one hand and local policies and priorities on the other. Due account is taken of local situational factors. Agreement provides a guarantee of resourcing and a focus for accountability. Minimal support is provided. Staff are employed by their schools within a national framework of salaries and working conditions. The major features of this scenario are evident in New Zealand.

The Local Support Model. The centre is a strategic core; regions or local education authorities will be phased out. The trend to establish school clusters (geographically adjacent schools) and school districts gains momentum, with these arrangements being the means of providing schools with support services more efficiently and more effectively than if schools were to seek such services independently. Schools are largely self-managing within a centrally determined framework. Elements of this model are emerging in most states in Australia. Canada and the United States have always had school districts.

The Recentralisation Model. This scenario describes a response to widespread concern that schools do not serve the national need. Despite expectations, large numbers of students do not complete their secondary schooling; new knowledge, skills and attitudes do not create 'the clever country' (the words of former Australian Prime Minister Bob Hawke in the national election campaign of 1990). The outcome is a national system, tightly monitored and extensively supported through a network of

Figure 9.1. Opinions of Educational Leaders on Alternative Scenarios for the Management of Education

Model		Distribution of rankings (percentages)				Mean	Order
		1	2	3	4		
Market	PROB	23	20	31	26	2.59	3
	PREF	13	13	50	24	2.85	3
Charter	PROB	21	36	31	12	2.33	2
	PREF	44	39	15	2	1.75	1
Local support	PROB	34	30	21	14	2.16	1
	PREF	39	42	15	4	1.83	2
Recentralisation	PROB	21	18	18	44	2.68	4
	PREF	3	5	23	70	3.59	4

Note: Respondents were 242 participants at the 1991 Annual Conference of the Australian Council for Educational Administration who provided rankings (1 is top ranking, 4 is bottom ranking) of probability (PROB) and preference (PREF) for scenarios implied in four models for the management of education.

arrangements at all levels, with a rebuilding of structures at the state or regional levels which were steadily dismantled in the late 1980s and early 1990s. This model has not emerged, although it is probably the wish of many who are nostalgic or who fear the outcomes of recent attempts to restructure education.

Acceptance among educationists of Charter and Local Support Models

We believe there is growing acceptance among educationists of the Charter and Local Support Models as well as a rejection of the Recentralisation Model. An indication of this pattern was provided in a survey of participants at the 1991 Annual Conference of the Australian Council for Educational Administration (ACEA). Participants numbered 242, drawn from every state and territory as well as from all levels and sectors of education, with most from government or public schools. Participants in the survey were invited to rank in two ways the four models described above: probability ('the probability that this scenario will unfold') and preferability ('my preference for this scenario'). A summary of rankings is contained in Figure 9.1.

If mean rankings are considered, participants believed that the Charter and Local Support Models, in that order, were the most probable, with 64 and 57 per cent, respectively, ranking these first or second. In contrast, the Market and Recentralisation Models were ranked first or second by 43 and 39 per cent, respectively.

The contrast in rankings between the Charter and Local Support Models on the one hand and the Market and Recentralisation Models on the other hand was much greater when rankings for preferability were provided. The Charter and Local Support Models were ranked first or second by 83 and 81 per cent, respectively. The Market and Recentralisation Models were ranked first or second by small minorities, just 26 and 8 per cent respectively.

We believe these reflect the opinions of an experienced and informed cross-section of leaders in Australian education. As such, they indicate a broad acceptance of the concept of self-management. While comparable data are not available for, say, five or ten years ago, we believe there has been a significant shift in opinion and degree of acceptance.

Moving to the market model

With this shift in a relatively short time, we believe further movement to embrace the market model is both probable and preferable, subject to the qualifications we set out below. A number of reasons may be advanced. The first takes account of the fact that the survey reported here involved only educationists. The pressure for the market model will come from parents, the public at large and others who influence policy-making in education, including representatives of business and industry.

The initiative of the British government in the production of *The Parent's Charter*, as described in Chapters 1 and 7, illustrates our contention.[1] The government in our view realises it has a vote-winner by encouraging a market model for education. Given the parity of support for government and opposition at the time of its release, it is clearly not anticipating an adverse reaction from a disapproving electorate. The following features illustrate its market orientation:

- five key documents which every parent has the right to have: pupil progress report, reports from independent inspectors, performance tables of schools, a school prospectus, and an annual report from school governors;
- accreditation of independent inspectors; and
- a right to a place in a school of choice unless it is full to capacity with students who have a stronger claim.

Our second reason for believing movement to a market model is both probable and preferable relates to a change in the views of educationists. While first and second rankings of probability and preferability were 43 and 26 per cent, respectively, in the Australian survey, we believe that many of the barriers to educationist acceptance will be removed in the years ahead. We have in mind here such matters as scepticism that formulae can be developed for the equitable allocation of resources. In virtually all systems of which we have knowledge, educationists were initially concerned that a movement away from centralised allocations would result in inequity, with significant disadvantage to schools in areas where there are market imperfections, for example, in remote areas where there is only one school. There has now been enough experience with resource allocation for school self-management to know that these fears are soon alleviated, with greater equity than with uniform centralised approaches.

We further believe that educationists will soon embrace the view of marketing described in Chapters 4 and 8. This view, we contend, has educational integrity. In similar fashion, we believe that fear of a lack of support services under the market model will be alleviated as skilful consultants currently employed by school systems at the central, regional or district levels gain confidence and experience success as they move into private practice.

Concern at excessively tight and centralised frameworks at the national level will dissipate as educationists realise that these are no more than what is implied in the concept of a framework. The major locus of decision-making in learning, teaching and the allocation of resources is, in fact, at the school level.

Finally, we believe that the concern on the part of many in government that they must keep tight rein on schools will also lessen with time and experience. Essentially, this development will parallel that for educationists as governments also develop confidence in approaches to resource allocation and that information available to the public, such as that proposed in *The Parent's Charter* in Britain, will ensure responsiveness on the part of schools. In other words, expectations for the market model will be realised; anxieties will be dissipated.

The conditions for moving to the market model

Reference was made in Chapter 1 to the Chubb and Moe study in the United States that has shaped much public discussion on a market model for public education in that country.[2] We cited the Glass and Matthews critique which, quite properly, pointed to the limited evidence in the study that the deregulation of public schools would lead to major improvement in student performance.[3] Glass and Matthews defended the current centralised arrangements, asserting that these helped ensure equity in the provision of educational services. Harman, Beare and Berkeley expressed the same concern at the prospect of a further shift to self-management in Australia, a shift which they expected over the course of the decade.[4]

We expressed our belief in Chapter 8 that these concerns about a threat to equity, especially in respect to the manner in which resources (defined broadly) are allocated to schools, can be laid to rest if practice in systems with long experience in school self-management is taken as a guide. We do not believe that the equity issue is any longer a valid argument against self-management, although all with an interest in the issue must remain vigilant.

We offer the following conditions for now moving toward the market model in a system of self-managing schools.

1 The very best expertise should be deployed in all systems moving to self-management to ensure that resources are allocated to schools in the most equitable fashion, accepting that 'getting the formula right' is a complex and ongoing process, but that the effort is worthwhile, given the inequities of even the best of centralised approaches.

2 For a time, schools should have an opportunity to 'opt in' to self-management under conditions which approximate the market model, that is, a comprehensive school-based budget is provided which includes staffing as well as an amount reflecting the fact that the cost of many of the services formerly provided and paid for by the centre will now be planned and resourced at the school level.

3 The centre should become a strategic core, formulating goals and priorities; determining the manner in which resources are allocated to schools; and furnishing a framework for accountability. Support services should be provided during the period in which schools may 'opt in', but thereafter at a minimal level. Schools should establish cooperative arrangements in clusters or districts, with many consultants working under contract in ongoing arrangements, and others on a fee-for-service basis which approximates that in the medical profession.

4 Governments and leaders of school systems should articulate a vision of self-management under these conditions and be prepared to display the commitment and will to see it to realisation.

We believe that these conditions can be satisfied so that a vision of self-management in the market mode can be realised by 2001 in the countries to which we have given special attention in this book, namely, Australia, Britain (England and Wales), Canada, New Zealand and the United States. Some nations, states and authorities will achieve the vision well before this date. This will certainly be the case in England and Wales as well as New Zealand. In the Australian setting the targets recommended by the Industry Education Forum seem reasonable:

• By the Year 2000, to have all school systems within Australia operating with decentralised management structures with maximum responsibility for operational decisions at the school level but within a rigorous system of accountability for performance and a clear set of educational objectives for systems and for the nation.

- By the Year 1995, to have in place the management plans, industrial relations reforms and the management development programs necessary to achieve the above.[5]

A Positive Image for Continuous Restructuring

In their recent co-edited book on the restructuring of school education in Australia, Harman, Beare and Berkeley drew on studies in the different states and territories to highlight some of the adverse effects:

> . . . the loss of talent and experience at senior levels in education systems, the changes for career structures in education, the loss of stability and continuity in organisations, and the tremendous disruption caused by recurring waves of major reorganisation.[6]

We concur in this account and offered guidelines in Chapter 8 for avoiding these perils in restructuring. In the longer term, however, in our vision for the 1990s we do not advocate that restructuring necessarily cease. We see restructuring as a process rather than an event (picking up what has become, virtually, a cliché in referring to change in organisations). Restructuring or reorganisation are inappropriate words to describe a continuous process in which the key principle is subsidiarity and the dominant value is service.

The principle of subsidiarity, as described in Chapter 4, suggests that those at the centre should only do what those in schools are unable to do for themselves, and then only in a manner which reflects a commitment to excellence in service to schools. Core educational values will prevail, of course, and these will be set out in centrally determined frameworks and embodied in school charters. This principle surely offers a vision of a centre which is not only lean but also flexible, since the particular configuration of needs for system-wide service will change from one year to the next.

Changing career expectations

It will be important for leaders at the system level to have for themselves, and to set for others, more realistic expectations for career paths than have existed in recent decades. Until now the career path for the educationist led through the classroom into the principal's office then into central office and up through the hierarchy to the top. Outstanding teachers sometimes missed the principal's office to move to central office as a consultant or an inspector. Those at the top had, until recently, followed one of these paths without interruption. Once having reached the top, they stayed at the top in a style captured by the notion of a 'permanent head'. Such careers are now rare, especially in Australia, as recounted in such graphic fashion in the Harman, Beare and Berkeley study.[7] Some of the disruption and loss of morale as systems have reorganised is surely a consequence of changed or unfulfilled expectations in the new structure.

Our vision for the next decade thus includes a major change in career expectations so that the principalship is seen as the premier leadership position in school education, with most at the central, regional or district levels serving out of their schools for fixed terms. In addition, of course, there must be high status accorded to leaders in schools who do not become or wish to become principals. A variety of schemes is emerging to ensure that this occurs.

To achieve these outcomes will require governments and leaders of school systems to articulate a vision of self-management and, as noted in the previous section of the chapter, be prepared to display the commitment and will to see it to realisation. There must be no doubt in the minds of those planning their careers that 'the way we do things around here' has been changed, dramatically and irrevocably.

Schools at the centre

An illustration of the kind of culture which might be nurtured is contained in the experience of the system of International Schools in Papua New Guinea. At first sight, such an illustration may appear remote from the interests of readers and, in most respects, of course, it is. International Schools were originally established to serve expatriate students whose parents were working in Papua New Guinea, with most from Australia. They were funded by fees. Enrolment patterns have changed since independence to the extent that the majority of students are now Papua New Guinea nationals. At their peak there were more than fifty such schools, but the number has now been reduced by closure and consolidation to a little over twenty.

The particular feature we select for comment is the manner in which the framework for central direction and support is determined. Expressed simply, the framework is determined by the schools. The board of the system is composed mainly of representatives of schools and, in an arrangement which has as much symbolic as substantive value, holds meetings as part of the annual principals' conference. Among decisions made on these occasions are those related to curriculum and the kinds of support services which will be needed in the year ahead. The costs of maintaining the centre are met by schools which draw their income mainly from student fees. The senior officer of the system is appointed on a contract basis, as are others in the lean central arrangement which changes its form from year to year.

The counterpart to the Papua New Guinea experience in our vision for self-management is a system of self-managing schools which receive funds directly from treasury. Schools in a particular geographic location would then determine the kinds of support which might be most effectively and efficiently deployed on their behalf, including administrative support, and they would meet the costs of such services on an equitable basis, with provision as appropriate for 'fee for service'. For other parts of the central framework, including those associated with accountability, the small strategic core would also be funded directly from treasury.

The Maturing of the Profession

The rationale for self-management usually includes reference to the contribution it will make to teaching as a profession, including an increased opportunity for teachers to be involved in decision-making. Indeed, in Dade County Public Schools in Florida this was the primary reason for the pilot project in school-based management. The strong support of the teachers' union in Dade County is derived from this intention. This objective was also evident from the outset in the pioneering practice in the Edmonton Public School District in Alberta, Canada. In Chapter 7 we described the high levels of satisfaction with working conditions in that system in 1990–91, with more than 80 per cent of teachers reporting their satisfaction with the fairness of assigned responsibilities, involvement in the budget process, opportunities for professional development and whether the district and the school were good places in which to work.

We include in our vision for the 1990s an image of teaching as a maturing profession, with school self-management being, arguably, a necessary although not sufficient condition for this to occur. It is helpful to explore the nature of a profession before explaining why we believe self-management will make this contribution and before sketching some features of the maturing profession.

Optimising the conditions for professionalism

Hedley Beare provides a useful listing of the characteristics of a profession: an esoteric service, calling for expert knowledge, intellectual insights and specialist skills; pre-service education; registration and regulation by the profession itself; peer appraisal and review; professional code of conduct; earned status; an ideal of public service; and client concern.[8] For the last of these, Beare asserted that: 'The final, pre-eminent, and absolute criterion of the professional is that he or she puts the concern for the client's best interests above every other consideration.'[9]

It is our contention that self-management along the lines we have proposed in this book, especially in respect to meeting the needs of parents and students ('client concern'), will do more than just lay the foundations for a high level of professionalism. Providing that schools are equitably resourced, self-management optimises the matching of resources, programs and needs of students; structures for decision-making provide opportunity for client involvement in the setting of priorities and formulation of policies; approaches to marketing are focused on matching the quality of programs for learning and teaching to the needs of clients; and clients have access to understandable, up-to-date and relevant information about the school, and are consulted in the process of obtaining it. To accomplish these things, teachers will need to engage in ongoing professional development, and there is provision for this in the refined model, as we made clear in Chapter 6 in our examination of educational leadership. For those who serve schools, such as consultants based at the centre, self-management may result in conditions similar to those enjoyed by their counterparts in private practice, including a fair fee for service based on clear understandings on the part of client and consultant, often with a contract which specifies needs and services.

These conditions do not necessarily follow from a decision to develop a system of self-managing schools. After all, self-management may stop 'at the principal's desk', providing little or no opportunity for the empowerment of parents, students and teachers, or there may be a narrow focus on finance. If a culture of service is not nurtured at the centre, then the professionalism we have described above for consultants may not eventuate.

We have concentrated here on just one of Beare's characteristics of a profession, namely, client concern, although our reference to ongoing professional development underscored the esoteric nature of the knowledge base. To achieve the full potential for professionalism, other characteristics in the Beare list should also be addressed, hence our image of self-management in the decade ahead includes further progress in matters such as matching pre-service education more closely to the needs of teachers who will serve in systems of self-managing schools; a higher level of registration and regulation by the profession than is currently the case, frameworks for public accountability notwithstanding; and further development of programs for peer appraisal and review.

Constraints on professionalism

A powerful constraint on achievement of a high level of professionalism is the welter of rules and regulations which have accreted in many systems over the years. These obstacles were highlighted in a 1990 conference of educationists from Australia and the United States. Dr Max Angus, Executive Director (Corporate Services) in the Ministry of Education in

Western Australia, where significant efforts to shift toward school self-management have been made, referred to the view of schools that 'bureaucratic controls and the controls thrown up by the agreements reached between Ministry and the teachers' union are a thicket which block schools which want to *do* something.' He described a dependency culture in schools and a 'pathological attachment to rules and regulations'.[10]

These comments are an echo of the findings in the Chubb and Moe study in the United States, reported in Chapter 1, which found that: '. . . all things being equal, schools with greater control over school policies and personnel — or schools subject to less control over these matters — are more effectively organised than schools that have less organisational autonomy.'[11] We addressed in Chapters 1 and 8 the different points of view on the need for rules and regulations, and concluded that there can be significant reduction in many places without doing harm to the achievement of equity. The introduction of the concept of 'waivers' from existing rules and regulations, as in Dade County Public Schools in Florida and other places in the United States, is a promising start, but is best viewed as a transition to a more deregulated arrangement which is a feature of our vision.

A vision for a maturing profession

In summary, our vision for the profession of teaching in the decade ahead includes the following:

1 schools are able optimally to match programs for learning and teaching to the educational needs of their students;
2 there is equitable allocation of resources among schools, including a capacity on the part of schools through their principals to select teachers and other staff to ensure the optimal match described in 1 above;
3 there is full empowerment of teachers to participate in these processes, secured through appropriate pre-service education, ongoing professional development, and opportunities in the structures and processes of schools for them to participate in decisions related to their work;
4 central, regional and district levels of an education system are resourced only to the extent necessary to serve schools in arrangements for support determined by schools, thus maximising public resources that are allocated to schools as opposed to other levels of the system;
5 conditions of work for consultants employed by the system or by a consortium of schools enable them to practise as professionals in the same manner as their counterparts in the private sector;
6 there is progress in the achievement of practitioner control over

registration and regulation of the profession, and in the implementation of schemes for peer appraisal and review;

7   a change in culture at the school level is achieved to remove dependency on 'the system' and 'pathological attachment to rules and regulations';

8   concomitant changes at the government and system levels succeed in removing the mass of rules and regulations which constrain schools, so that the few that remain are largely concerned with the achievement of equity across the system; and

9   there is a re-imaging of the teacher union so that it maintains an interest in maximising resources for education and ensuring natural justice for all dealings between employing authorities and individual teachers, but is otherwise and largely concerned with empowerment of the individual teacher in all the senses we have described.

Leading the Self-Managing School

We provided guidelines in Chapters 4 to 8 for leadership in and for self-managing schools. There were too many to attempt a summary or synthesis here. In general, we find that all the contemporary perspectives on transformational leadership, as set out in Chapter 3, have been demonstrated in leaders at the school and system levels where the transition to self-management has been successfully accomplished. The major dimensions were described as cultural leadership, strategic leadership, educational leadership and responsive leadership. Leaders at *all* levels need these capabilities. The scope of the restructuring effort around the world has resulted in a traumatic experience for many, but we suggested in Chapter 8 that the oft-cited perils of restructuring can be avoided, and we provided guidelines for action in key areas of change. The two notions we highlight in conclusion are those of 'strong leadership' and 'widely dispersed leadership'.

A vision for the decade ahead calls for strong leadership. We do not use the term in its traditional sense where an autocratic style within a hierarchical structure is often implied. Instead, we refer at the system level to leaders having a commitment to and a capacity to articulate a vision for self-management where schools are, quite literally, at the centre of the system, with a culture of service pervading every aspect of arrangements for direction and support. They have the strength of will to see the complex and demanding processes of change to realisation. We refer at the school level to these same areas of strength, with an even sharper focus on meeting the educational needs of every student. For all leaders, there is also strength in a moral sense, not only through the concept of service but also in the manner of working with people and a commitment to and capacity for what we described in Chapter 8 as 'caring and cushioning' through very challenging and potentially painful periods of transition. This is an aspect of ennoblement in Sergiovanni's view of value-added leadership.[12]

One reaction to the capacities we describe is that we call for a superperson as leader in a self-managing school. This will only be the case if one conceives of leadership residing with one or a few people. Consistent with the value of empowerment, which pervades the original and refined model for school self-management, we cannot stress too highly the need for widely dispersed leadership in the school. This also implies a capacity and commitment on the part of the principal to establish and utilise structures and processes for empowerment.

We are optimistic that the transition to systems of self-managing schools, and then to self-governing schools, will be successful in the years ahead, offering promise of a richly fulfilling career for those who have the privilege of serving as leaders in our schools.

Notes and References

Chapter 1

1   Department of Education and Science (1991) *The Parent's Charter*, London, DES.
2   Drucker, P. (1981) *Managing in Turbulent Times*, London, Pan.
3   Drucker, P. (1989) *The New Realities*, Oxford, Heinemann Professional Publishing.
4   Caldwell, B. and Spinks, J. (1988) *The Self-Managing School*, Lewes, Falmer Press.
5   Drucker, P. (1981) *op. cit.*, p. 10.
6   *Ibid.*
7   Naisbitt, J. (1982) *Megatrends*, London, Futura Press.
8   Naisbitt, J. and Aburdene, P. (1990) *Megatrends 2000*, New York, William Morrow.
9   *Ibid.*, p. 13.
10 Beare, H. (1990) 'Educational administration in the 1990s', Monograph No. 7, Australian Council for Educational Administration, p. 19.
11 Macpherson, R. (1990) 'The context, process and recommendations of *Schools Renewal*: The restructuring of New South Wales School Education as genetic engineering', Paper presented at the Annual Meeting of the American Educational Research Association, Boston, March.
12 Macpherson, R. (1990) 'The reconstruction of New Zealand education: A case of "high politics" reform', Paper presented at the International Intervisitation Program of the Commonwealth Council for Educational Administration, Manchester, April 20–29.
13 Boyd, W. (1990) 'The national level: Reagan and the bully pulpit', in Bacharach, S. (Ed.), *Education Reform: Making Sense of It All*, Boston, Allyn and Bacon, p. 42.
14 Boyd, *loc. cit.*, suggested that the term 'bully pulpit' was appropriate

to describe the stance taken by President Reagan and his Secretary for Education, William Bennett, during the first wave of reform in the United States in the early to mid-1980s.

15 OECD (1987) *Quality of Schooling: A Clarifying Report*, Restricted Secretariat Paper ED (87)13, p. 123.

16 *Ibid.*, p. 125.

17 *Ibid.*, p. 127.

18 Guthrie, J.W. (1991) 'The world's new political economy is politicising educational evaluation', *Educational Evaluation and Policy Analysis*, 13, 3, p. 311.

19 Dr Hywel Thomas, University of Birmingham, has suggested that the student is, in effect, 'the voucher', since government grants follow the student to the school of the students'/parents' choice in the Local Management of Schools (LMS) scheme in England and Wales. See Thomas, H. (1988) 'Pupils as vouchers', *The Times Educational Supplement*, 2 December 1988, p. 23 for a development of this view and an overview of the potentially far-reaching nature of LMS.

20 D'Arcy, E. (1989) 'What is an excellent school?', A presentation to a breakfast seminar for leaders in education sponsored by the University of Tasmania and the Department of Education and the Arts, September. D'Arcy is the Roman Catholic Archbishop of Hobart.

21 Beare, H. (1990) 'An educator speaks to his grandchildren: Some aspects of schooling in the new world context', ACEA Monograph No. 8, Australian Council for Educational Administration, p. 18.

22 Scott, B. (1990) *School-Centred Education*, Report of the Management Review, New South Wales Education Portfolio, xiii.

23 Caldwell, B. and Spinks, J. (1988) *The Self-Managing School*, Lewes, Falmer Press, pp. 6–7.

24 Burns, J. (1978) *Leadership*, New York, Harper and Row.

25 Chubb, J.E. and Moe, T.E. (1990) *Politics, Markets and America's Schools*, Washington, D.C., The Brookings Institution.

26 Miles, M. (1987) 'Practical guidelines for school administrators: How to get there', Presented at a symposium on Effective Schools Programs and the Urban High School, at the Annual Meeting of the American Educational Research Association, Washington, D.C., 23 April.

27 Chubb and Moe, *op. cit.*; Goodlad, J.I. (1984) *A Place Called School*, New York, McGraw-Hill; Johnson, S.M. (1990) *Teachers' Work: Achieving Success in Our Schools*, New York, Basic Books; Sizer, T. (1984) *Horace's Compromise*, Boston, Houghton Mifflin.

28 Malen, B., Ogawa, R.T. and Kranz, J. (1990) 'What do we know about school-based management? A case study of the literature — A call for research' in Clune, W.H. and Witte, J.F. (Eds), *Choice and Control in American Education Volume 2: The Practice of Choice, Decentralisation and School Restructuring*, Lewes, Falmer Press, pp. 289–342.

29 Chubb, J. (1990) 'Political institutions and school organisation' in Clune and Witte, *op. cit.*, p. 233.
30 Glass, G.V. and Matthews, D.A. (1991) 'Are data enough?' *Educational Researcher*, 20, 3, April, pp. 24–27; quote from p. 26.
31 *Ibid.*

Chapter 2

1 Caldwell, B. and Spinks, J. (1988) *The Self-Managing School*, Lewes, Falmer Press; Caldwell, B. (1986) 'Effective Resource Allocation in Schools Project: A summary of studies in Tasmania and South Australia', Centre for Education, University of Tasmania; Misko, J. (1986) 'Effective Resource Allocation in Schools in Tasmania and South Australia', Part 1 of the Report of the Effective Resource Allocation in Schools Project, Centre for Education, University of Tasmania; Smith, C. (1986) 'Effective Resource Allocation in Non-Government Schools in Tasmania and South Australia', Part 5 of the Report of the Effective Resource Allocation in Schools Project, Centre for Education, University of Tasmania.
2 Tasmanian Parliament (1981) *White Paper on Tasmanian Schools and Colleges in the 1980s*, Education Department of Tasmania.
3 Peters, T. and Waterman, R. (1982) *In Search of Excellence: Lessons from America's Best-Run Companies*, New York, Harper and Row.
4 Misko, *op. cit.*
5 A detailed report of participant evaluations is contained in Caldwell, *op. cit.*
6 Ministry of Education, Victoria (1987) *Implementation of School-level Program Budgeting*, Progress Report, Policy and Planning Unit.
7 Caldwell, B. and Spinks, J. (1986) *Policy-Making and Planning for School Effectiveness: A Guide to Collaborative School Management*, Hobart, Education Department of Tasmania.
8 Bryson, J. (1988) *Strategic Planning for Public and Nonprofit Organisations*, San Francisco, Jossey-Bass.
9 Accounts and analyses of recent reforms in the United States may be found in Bacharach, S. (Ed.) (1990) *Education Reform: Making Sense of It All*, Boston, Allyn and Bacon; and Elmore, R., *et al.* (1990) *Restructuring Schools: The Next Generation of Educational Reform*, San Francisco, Jossey-Bass.
10 Deal, T. (1985) 'The symbolism of effective schools', *The Elementary School Journal*, 85, 5, p. 605.
11 The notion of 'mutual adaptation' emerged from the Rand Change Agent studies from 1973 to 1978 and was confirmed in a recent review. Implementation does not proceed in a uniform manner as proposed in policies and centrally determined plans and models; local

factors dominate project outcomes. See McLaughlin, M. (1990) 'The Rand Change Agent study revisited: Macro perspectives and micro realities', *Educational Researcher*, 19, 9, December, pp. 11–16.

12 Swanson, A.D. and King, R.A. (1991) *School Finance: Its Economics and Politics*, New York, Longman, p. 326.

13 Marsh, C. (1988) *Spotlight on School Improvement*, Sydney, Allen and Unwin.

14 *Ibid.*, p. 193.

15 Brown, D. (1990) *Decentralisation and School-Based Management*, Lewes, Falmer Press.

16 Glatter's review was contained in *Journal of Educational Administration and History*, January 1990.

17 Corson, D. (1990) 'Applying the stages of a social epistemology to school policy making', *British Journal of Educational Studies*, 28, 3, August, pp. 259–276.

18 Dye, T. (1975) *Understanding Public Policy*, Englewood Cliffs, N.J., Prentice-Hall, p. 21.

19 Sergiovanni, T. and Starratt, R. (1988) *Supervision: Human Perspectives*, 4th ed., New York, McGraw-Hill Book Company, pp. 40–41.

20 *Ibid.*

Chapter 3

1 Duke, D.L. (1986) 'The aesthetics of leadership', *Educational Administration Quarterly*, 22, 1, p. 10.

2 Dubin, R. (1968) *Human Relations in Administration*. 2nd ed., Englewood Cliffs, N.J., Prentice-Hall, p. 385.

3 Fiedler, F.E. (1967) *A Theory of Leadership Effectiveness*, New York, McGraw-Hill, p. 8.

4 Stogdill, R.M. (1950) 'Leadership membership and organisation', *Psychological Bulletin*, 47, p. 4.

5 Pondy, L.R. (1978) 'Leadership is a language game' in McCall, M.W. Jr. and Lombardo, M.M. (Eds), *Leadership: Where Else Can We Go?* Durham, N.C., Duke University Press, p. 94.

6 Burns, J.M. (1978) *Leadership*, New York, Harper and Row.

7 Beare, H., Caldwell, B.J. and Millikan, R.H. (1989) *Creating an Excellent School*, London, Routledge, pp. 106–118.

8 Sergiovanni, T.J. and Starratt, R.J. (1983) *Supervision: Human Perspectives*. 3rd ed., New York, McGraw-Hill, p. 227.

9 Coleman, J.S. and Hoffer, T. (1987) *Public and Private High Schools: The Impact of Communities*, New York, Basic Books.

10 Sergiovanni, T.J. (1984) 'Leadership and excellence in schooling', *Educational Leadership*, 41, 3.

11 *Ibid.*

12 See 'Decision-Making' in Hoy, W.K. and Miskel, C.G. (1987) *Educational Administration: Theory, Research and Practice*. 3rd ed., New York, Random House.

13 Holly, P. and Southworth, G. (1989) *The Developing School*, Lewes, Falmer Press.

14 Miles, M. (1987) 'Practical guidelines for school administrators: How to get there', Presented at a symposium on Effective Schools Programs and the Urban High School, at the Annual Meeting of the American Educational Research Association, Washington, D.C., 23 April.

15 Lightfoot, S.L. (1983) *The Good High School*, New York, Basic Books, p. 333.

16 Naisbitt, J. and Aburdene, P. (1990) *Megatrends 2000*, New York, William Morrow, p. 218.

17 *Ibid.*, p. 217.

18 *Ibid.*

19 Sergiovanni, T.J. (1990) *Value-Added Leadership*, San Diego, Harcourt, Brace, Jovanovich.

20 *Ibid.*, p. 104.

21 Murphy, J. (1990) 'Principal Instructional Leadership', Thurston, P. and Lotto, L. (Eds), *Advances in Educational Administration*, Greenwich, Conn., JAI Press, Volume 1, Part B: Changing Perspectives on the School', pp. 163–200.

22 *Ibid.*, pp. 165–166.

23 Fullan, M.G. (1991) *What's Worth Fighting For in the Principalship?*, Melbourne, Australian Council for Educational Administration. A valuable companion monograph is Fullan, M.G. and Hargreaves, A. (1991) *What's Worth Fighting For: Working Together for Your School*, Melbourne, Australian Council for Educational Administration. Both were originally published by the Ontario Public School Teachers' Federation in Toronto, Ontario, Canada.

24 Fullan, *op. cit.*, p. 10.

25 *Ibid.*

26 Patterson, J., Purkey, S. and Parker, J. (1986) *Productive School Systems for a Non-Rational World*, Alexandria, Virginia, Association for Supervision and Curriculum Development; Block, P. (1987) *The Empowered Manager*, San Francisco, Jossey-Bass.

27 Fullan, *op. cit.*, pp. 24–40.

28 Block, *op. cit.*, pp. 17–18 cited in Fullan, *op. cit.*, p. 40.

29 Fullan, *ibid.*

Chapter 4

1 Deal, T.E. (1985) 'The symbolism of effective schools', *The Elementary School Journal*, 85, 5, p. 605.

2 Beare, H., Caldwell, B.J. and Millikan, R.H. (1989) *Creating an Excellent School*, London, Routledge, p. 176.

3 D'Arcy, E. (1989) 'What is an excellent school', A presentation to a breakfast seminar for leaders in education sponsored by the University of Tasmania and the Department of Education and the Arts, September.

4 Fantini, M.D. (1986) *Regaining Excellence in Education*, Columbus, Merrill Publishing.

5 We have not been able to locate the origin of this statement on subsidiarity. The *Oxford English Dictionary* traces the word 'subsidiarity' to a statement by Pope Pius X1, with subsequent use largely in the church setting. The statement we have used here was cited without source in Saskatchewan School Trustees Association (1976) *A Handbook for School Trustees*, Regina, Saskatchewan, p. ii.

6 Michael Strembitsky used the term in setting out his views on the roles of central office in a paper published in 1973, nearly five years before he initiated the pilot project in school-based budgeting in the Edmonton Public School District in Alberta, Canada. See Strembitsky, M.A. (1973) 'The central office in a new era: Roles and relationships', in McIntosh, R.G. and Bryce, R.C. (Eds), *School Administration in a Humanistic Era*, Edmonton, Council on School Administration, Alberta Teachers Association, pp. 68–77.

7 Kotler, P., Shaw, R., FitzRoy, P. and Chandler, P. (1983) *Marketing in Australia*, Sydney, Prentice-Hall.

8 *Ibid.*, pp. 18–19.

9 *Ibid.*, p. 20.

10 Campbell, D. and Crowther, F. (1991) 'What is an entrepreneurial school?' in Crowther, F. and Caldwell, B. (Eds) (1991) *The Entrepreneurial School*, Sydney, Ashton Scholastic, p. 13.

11 Scott, B. (1989) *Schools Renewal*, Report of the Management Review, New South Wales Education Portfolio, p. 6.

12 Scott, Brian (1990) *School-Centred Education*. Report of the Management Review: NSW Education Portfolio, p. 69.

13 *Ibid.*, p. xii.

14 Naisbitt, J. and Aburdene, P. (1990) *Megatrends 2000*, New York, William Morrow.

15 Scott (1990) *op. cit.*, p. xii.

16 Starratt, R.J. (1990) *The Drama of Schooling/The Schooling of Drama*, Lewes, Falmer Press, pp. 4–5.

17 Nadebaum, M. (1990) 'Noah or butterfly: The changing role for school principals in the 1990s', Paper presented to the National Conference of the Australian Council for Educational Administration, Australian Primary Principals Association and Australian Secondary Principals Association, Hobart, 1 October.

Chapter 5

1   Miles, M. (1987) 'Practical guidelines for school administrators: How to get there', Presented at a symposium on Effective Schools Programs and the Urban High School, at the Annual Meeting of the American Educational Research Association, Washington, D.C., 23 April.
2   Fullan, M.G. (1991) *What's Worth Fighting For in the Principalship?*', Melbourne, Australian Council for Educational Administration. A valuable companion monograph is Fullan, M.G. and Hargreaves, A. (1991) *What's Worth Fighting For: Working Together for Your School*, Melbourne, Australian Council for Educational Administration. Both were originally published by the Ontario Public School Teachers' Federation in Toronto, Ontario, Canada.
3   Bryson, J. (1988) *Strategic Planning for Public and Nonprofit Organisations*, San Francisco, Jossey Bass, Ch. 3, 'An Effective Planning Approach for Public and Nonprofit Organisations'.
4   Holly, P. and Southworth, G. (1989) *The Developing School*, Lewes, Falmer Press.
5   Coleman, J.S. and Hoffer, T. (1987) *Public and Private High Schools: The Impact of Communities*, New York, Basic Books.
6   Slaughter, R.A. (1990) 'The foresight principle', *Futures*, October, p. 801.
7   Cited in Slaughter, R.A. (1990) 'Assessing the *QUEST* for knowledge: Significance of the quick environmental scanning technique for futures', *Futures*, March, p. 155.

Chapter 6

1   We acknowledge the writing of Holly and Southworth in respect to this concept; see Holly, P. and Southworth, G. (1989) *The Developing School*, Lewes, Falmer Press, especially Chapter 1, 'The Learning School'.
2   This three-fold classification is the basis of Wendy Cahill's exploration of the concept of entrepreneurial leadership; see Cahill, W. (1991) 'Entrepreneurship and leadership' in Crowther, F. and Caldwell, B. (Eds), *The Entrepreneurial School*, Sydney, Ashton Scholastic. Colin Marsh extends the notion of community in his study of school improvement. He describes teachers, principals, parents, students and consultants as the 'protagonists' in efforts to bring about school improvement; see Marsh, C. (1988) *Spotlight on School Improvement*, Sydney, Allen and Unwin.
3   Picot, B. (1988) *Administering for Excellence*, Report of the Task Force

to Review Education Administration, Wellington, New Zealand, Government Printer; Scott, B. (1990) *School-Centred Education*, Report of the Management Review, New South Wales Education Portfolio.

4   Miles, M. (1987) 'Practical guidelines for school administrators: How to get there', Paper read at a symposium on Effective Schools Programs and the Urban High School, Washington, D.C., Annual Meeting of the American Educational Research Association, April.

5   Sizer, T. (1984) *Horace's Compromise*, Boston, Houghton Mifflin; Goodlad, J.I. (1984) *A Place Called School*, New York, McGraw-Hill; Johnson, S.M. (1990) *Teachers' Work: Achieving Success in Our Schools*, New York, Basic Books.

6   Sizer, *op. cit.*, p. 214.

7   Goodlad, *op. cit.*, p. 275.

8   Johnson, *op. cit.*

9   *Ibid.*, xvii.

10 *Ibid.*

11 *Ibid.*

12 *Ibid.*, xxiv.

13 Malen, B., Ogawa, R.T. and Kranz, J. (1990) 'What do we know about school-based management? A case study of the literature — A call for research' in Clune, W.H. and Witte, J.F. (Eds), *Choice and Control in American Education Volume 2: The Practice of Choice, Decentralisation and School Restructuring*, Lewes, Falmer Press, pp. 289–342.

14 Miles, *op. cit.*

15 David, J. (1990) 'Restructuring in progress: Lessons from pioneering districts' in Elmore, R., *et al.*, *Restructuring Schools*, San Francisco, Jossey-Bass.

16 *Ibid.*, pp. 222–224.

17 An increasing number of these consortium arrangements are being established in the United States. John Goodlad at the University of Washington has taken the lead here, following the publication of *A Place Called School*; see Goodlad, *op. cit.*

18 Schön, D. (1983) *The Reflective Practitioner*, New York, Basic Books.

19 The three concepts of reflective practice, dramatic consciousness and double looping learning are developed by Starratt, R. (1990) *The Drama of Schooling/The Schooling of Drama*, Lewes, Falmer Press, pp. 82–96.

20 *Ibid.*, p. 338.

21 Healy, C. and Welchert, A. (1990) 'Mentoring relations: A definition to advance research and practice', *Educational Researcher*, 19, 9, December, p. 17.

22 This statement is attributed to Joyce in Davis, L. (1985) 'Coaching: The many dimensions', *PRISM Manual*, The Board of Education, Pittsburgh, Pennsylvania.

23 Gray, W. and Gray, M. (1985) 'Synthesis of research on mentoring beginning teachers', *Educational Leadership*, 43, 3, November, p. 40.

24 Healy and Welchert, *loc. cit.*

25 See Gray, W. and Gray, M. (1986) *Mentoring: A Comprehensive Annotated Biography of Important References*, Vancouver, B.C., International Association of Mentoring; Caldwell, B.J. and Carter, E.M.A. (forthcoming) (Eds) *The Return of the Mentor*, Lewes, Falmer Press.

26 Watts, A. (1990) 'School improvement through staff development', Unpublished report of research for the degree of Bachelor of Education, University of Tasmania, p. 80.

27 Report of this program may be obtained from the Staff Development Branch, Division of Technical and Further Education, Department of Employment Industrial Relations and Training, Hobart, Tasmania. A summary is provided in Caldwell and Carter, *op. cit.*

28 Gray, W. and Gray, M. 'Synthesis of research on mentoring beginning teachers', *op. cit.*

29 Colin Marsh anticipated this situation in his review of school improvement in Australia. In describing the effect on professional development programs, he reported that 'The downturn of the cycle now appears to be reached for professional development activities, in that all federal funding has recently been terminated and it is unlikely that state systems, in a period of financial restraint, will be able to give this aspect a high priority'; see Marsh, *op. cit.*, p. 140.

30 *Ibid.*, p. 82.

31 Marsh, *op. cit.*

32 Coleman, J. and Hoffer, T. (1987) *Public and Private High Schools: The Impact of Communities*, New York, Basic Books.

33 Chrispeels, J. and Pollack, S. (1990) 'Factors that contribute to achieving and sustaining school effectiveness', Paper presented at the Third International Congress for School Effectiveness, Jerusalem, Israel, January.

34 Marsh, *op. cit.*, Ch. 5.

35 *Ibid.*, Ch. 6.

36 Johnson, *op. cit.*, xxiv.

37 We are indebted to Professor Jotham Ombisi Olembo, former Chair, Department of Educational Administration, Planning and Curriculum Development at Kenyatta University, Nairobi, for his explanation of 'harambee'. He reports that 'There is no aspect of life in Kenya that has not been touched by the movement. Hospitals, bridges, roads and schools have been constructed with voluntary funds and labour which in essence is the meaning of harambee'; see Olembo, J. (n.d.) 'Educational trends in East Africa', Occasional Paper No. 3050, Bureau of Educational Research, Kenyatta University College [now Kenyatta University], Nairobi, pp. 24–25.

Chapter 7

1 Department of Education and Science (1991) *The Parent's Charter*, London, DES.
2 Lough, N.V. (Chair) (1990) *Today's Schools*, A Review of the Education Reform Implementation Process prepared for the Minister of Education, New Zealand, p. 8.
3 Department of Education and Science, *op. cit.*
4 This information comes from working papers allegedly prepared by senior HMIs and leaked to Jack Straw, Labour's education spokesman, as reported in *The Times Educational Supplement*, 25 October 1991, p. 8.
5 Brown, D.J. (1990) *Decentralisation and School-Based Management*, Lewes, Falmer Press.
6 Smilanich, B. (1991) '1990–91 Results Review', Report for Area 6 to the Board of Trustees, Edmonton Public Schools, October 5, p. 3.
7 *Ibid.*
8 Brown, *op. cit.*, p. 247.
9 The data reported here for 1990–91 are contained in Smilanich, *op. cit.*

Chapter 8

1 Kanter, R.M. (1990) *When Giants Learn to Dance: Mastering the Challenges of Strategy, Management and Careers in the 1990s*, London, Unwin, pp. 62–64.
2 *Ibid.*, p. 21.
3 Harman, G., Beare, H. and Berkeley, G.F. (1991) *Restructuring School Management: Administrative Reorganisation of Public School Governance in Australia*, Canberra, Australian College of Education, p. 309.
4 Kanter, *op. cit.*, pp. 52–53.
5 Harman, Beare and Berkeley, *op. cit.*, pp. 308 and 313.
6 Brown, D.J. (1990) *Decentralisation and School-Based Management*, Lewes, Falmer Press; Wissler, D.F. and Ortiz, F.I. (1988) *The Superintendent's Leadership in School Reform*, New York, Falmer Press.
7 Harman, Beare and Berkeley, *op. cit.*, p. 313.
8 Garms, W.I., Guthrie, J.W. and Pierce, L.C. (1978) *School Finance: The Economics and Politics of Public Education*, Englewood Cliffs, N.J., Prentice-Hall.
9 As reported in Timar, T. (1989) 'The politics of school restructuring', *Phi Delta Kappan*, 71, 4, pp. 265–275.
10 The purposes of the School-Based Management/Shared Decision-Making Project in the Dade County Public Schools are noted in Collins, R.A. and Hanson, M.K. (1991) *Summative Evaluation Report School-Based Management/Shared Decision-Making Project 1987–88 through 1989–90*, Miami, Florida, Dade County Public Schools.

11 Swanson, A.D. and King, R.A. (1991) *School Finance: Its Economics and Politics*, New York, Longman, p. 322.

12 *Ibid.*, p. iv.

13 *Ibid.*

14 Scott, B. (1990) *School-Centred Education*, Report of the Management Review: New South Wales Education Portfolio, p. xii.

15 Sutcliffe, J. (1991) 'Every day is market day', *The Times Educational Supplement*, 25 October, p. 11.

16 *Ibid.*

17 This account is drawn from Caldwell, B., Smilanich, R. and Spinks, J. (1988) 'The self-managing school', *The Canadian Administrator*, 27, 8, p. 4.

18 Information on recent developments in the utilisation of consultancy services in the Edmonton Public School District was provided by Lloyda Jones, a senior officer in Consulting Services.

19 Kanter, *op. cit.*, pp. 62–64.

20 *Ibid.*, p. 21.

21 Harman, Beare and Berkeley, *op. cit.*

22 Berkeley, G.F. (1991) 'Restructuring education in Australia' in Harman, Beare and Berkeley, *op. cit.*, p. 71.

23 *Ibid.*, pp. 71–72.

24 Scott, *op. cit.*, p. xii.

25 Deal, T.E. (1990) 'Healing our schools: Restoring the heart', in Lieberman, A. (Ed.), *Schools as Collaborative Cultures: Creating the Future Now*, New York, Falmer Press, Ch. 7, p. 128.

26 *Ibid.*, p. 142.

27 *Ibid.*, p. 146.

28 Seward, N.J. (1975) 'Centralised and decentralised school budgeting', Unpublished doctoral dissertation, University of California, Berkeley, p. 8.

29 This conclusion was drawn by Wissler and Ortiz, *op. cit.*, p. 137, who draw from a range of studies of administrative decentralisation in the 1960s and 1970s. They contrast administrative decentralisation into regions within a district and school-based management where the school is empowered.

30 Caldwell, B.J. (1977) 'Decentralised school budgeting in Alberta: An analysis of objectives, adoption, operation and perceived outcomes in selected school systems', Unpublished doctoral dissertation, University of Alberta, p. 413.

31 *Ibid.*, p. 415.

32 Brown, D.J. (1990) *Decentralisation and School-Based Management*, Lewes, Falmer Press, p. 202.

33 Wissler and Ortiz, *op. cit.*

34 *Ibid.*, p. 78.

35 Harman, Beare and Berkeley, *op. cit.*

Chapter 9

1 Department of Education and Science (1991) *The Parent's Charter*, London, DES.
2 Chubb, J.E. and Moe, T.E. (1990) *Politics, Markets and America's Schools*, Washington, D.C., The Brookings Institution.
3 Glass, G.V. and Matthews, D.A. (1991) 'Are data enough?' *Educational Researcher*, 20, 3, April, pp. 24–27.
4 Harman, G., Beare, H. and Berkeley, G. (Eds) (1991) *Restructuring School Management*, Canberra, Australian College of Education, p. 313.
5 Industry Education Forum (1991) 'Declaration of goals for Australia's schools'. [The Industry Education Forum is a national body established by the business community to coordinate the activities of business and industry in relation to education. Chair at the time of writing was Ian Fletcher, Chief Executive of the Australian Chamber of Commerce, at PO Box E139, Queen Victoria Terrace, ACT 2600.]
6 Harman, G., Beare, H. and Berkeley, G., *op. cit.*, p. 309.
7 Harman, G., Beare, H. and Berkeley, G., *op. cit.*
8 Beare, H. (1990) 'What does it mean to be professional: A commentary about teacher professionalism', Paper prepared for the Annual Conference of the New South Wales Secondary Principals Council, Coffs Harbour, 13 June, pp. 3–6.
9 *Ibid.*, p. 6.
10 Cited in Ashenden, D. (1991) 'Professionalism of teaching in the next decade', Report of discussions by US and Australian educators held at the University of Wollongong, NSW, as part of the USA/Australia Education Policy Project, October, p. 8. [This document is available from the Vice-Chancellor's Office at the University of Wollongong.]
11 Chubb, J. (1990) 'Political institutions and school organisation' in Clune, W.H. and Witte, J.F. (Eds), *Choice and Control in American Education Volume 2: The Practice of Choice, Decentralisation and School Restructuring*, Lewes, Falmer Press, p. 233.
12 Sergiovanni, T.J. (1990) *Value-Added Leadership*, San Diego, Harcourt, Brace, Jovanovich.

Index